University Foundation Study

Transferable Academic Skills Kit

Course Book

Amanda Fava-Verdé, Prue Griffiths,
Anthony Manning, Clare Nukui,
Andrew O'Cain, Frances Russell,
Elisabeth Wilding

Published by
Garnet Publishing Ltd
8 Southern Court
South Street
Reading RG1 4QS, UK

This edition first published 2009.

ISBN 978 1 85964 536 9

A catalogue record for this book is available from
The Library of Congress.

With special thanks to the sub authors:
Jennifer Book, Jane Brooks, Paul Harvey, Fiona McGarry,
Lucy Norris, Ray de Witt

Production

Project managers:	Maggie MacIntyre, Richard Peacock
Project consultants:	Dan Carpenter, Rod Webb
Editorial team:	Emily Clarke, Fiona McGarry
American English adaptation:	Jennifer Allen
Design:	Mike Hinks
Layout:	Nick Asher
Illustration:	Doug Nash
Photography:	Clipart.com, Digital Vision, Image Source, Photodisc

Garnet Publishing and the authors of TASK would like to thank
the staff and students of the International Foundation Programme
at the University of Reading for their respective roles in the
development of these teaching materials.

Every effort has been made to trace the copyright holders and
we apologize in advance for any unintentional omissions. We will
be happy to insert the appropriate acknowledgements in any
subsequent editions.

All website URLs provided in this publication were correct at the
time of printing. If any URL does not work, please contact your
instructor, who will help you find similar resources.

Printed and bound
in Lebanon by International Press

Contents

Module 1: Key Foundation Skills

Introduction

Do you know what your strengths and weaknesses are? How could you improve your efficiency? Are you disorganized? Have you ever forgotten a deadline or an assignment? Are you often late for classes?

Coping with the requirements of higher education is very different from what you have already experienced in other educational environments. Making the best use of resources available to you and knowing where you need to make a special effort are major challenges both in education and the world of work.

This module provides you with a framework of strategies that will enhance organization and efficiency in academic situations. Through applying the strategies in this module, you will be able to maximize your effectiveness and manage your independent learning skills more successfully.

Unit 1 will help you identify skills that are needed to study successfully in higher education. Unit 2 will help you identify your own strengths and weaknesses and will also focus on how the skills you already possess can be used in an academic environment. Unit 3 will look at ways to improve your organizational skills and systems, and Unit 4 will focus on time management to help you use your available time more efficiently.

After completing this module, you will have a clearer idea of the skills and strategies you need to function in an academic environment. You will also be able to distinguish between skills you already possess and those you need to develop by working through the other modules in the series.

Skills Map

What are transferable academic skills?
Identify key transferable skills and understand an overview of the modules in the TASK series.

Skills self-assessment
Familiarize yourself with your existing skills and determine the strengths and weaknesses of your current approach.

How organized are you?
Improve your organizational systems to improve your efficiency.

Time management
Target your time management skills in order to maximize the time you have available and to meet deadlines.

Destination: Key Foundation Skills

1 What are transferable academic skills?

At the end of this unit you will:
- be able to identify key transferable skills;
- be familiar with the key skills covered in the 12 modules of the TASK series.

Task 1 Identifying skills

An education at college or university level provides more than just an understanding of the subject matter. The skills you will develop throughout your studies are often referred to as transferable skills.

1.1　The skills below are examples of transferable skills in the TASK series. Think about their meaning and discuss your ideas with another student.

> communication skills　　working in teams　　critical thinking skills
>
> research skills　　IT skills　　problem solving skills

1.2　Look at photographs a–f. Which of the skills in Exercise 1.1 are needed for each occupation/profession? Discuss with another student, giving the reasons for your choice.

a

b

c

d

e

f

Task 2 Examining micro-skills

It is important to identify what skills are required in a particular situation, but it is even more important to know what the skills involve. This task will help you understand more about the twelve key skills in the TASK series.

2.1 Think about the six module titles below and what each one might include.

   a) Teamwork

   b) Academic Culture

   c) Exam Technique

   d) Research and Referencing

   e) Introduction to IT Skills

   f) Key Foundation Skills

2.2 Check your ideas by reading the module descriptions below and matching each one to one of the six module titles a–f above.

Teamwork

Research and referencing

IT skills

Module 1

Provides a framework of strategies to help improve organization and efficiency in an academic environment. Application of these strategies will help development of independent learning skills and maximize their effectiveness.

Module 2

Shows how to adapt to life in American higher education; it provides insights into the expectations of fellow students and professor.

Module 4

Demonstrates how to maximize the efficiency of group work to achieve collaborative goals. This module encourages reflection on the different roles played by individuals within a group and provides support strategies for personal contributions.

Module 7

Covers the use of common word processing and database packages. This module provides a clear framework for the appropriate presentation of a broad range of academic assignments.

Module 10

Helps develop the essential skills of identifying appropriate supporting statements and acknowledging expert opinion. This module covers the key features of direct and indirect quotation, in addition to conventions for preparing a bibliography.

Module 12

Provides a toolkit of techniques to help prepare for a wide range of timed assessments within all fields of academic study.

2.3 Choose two modules and study the explanations. Then with books closed, explain what they involve in your own words.

2.4 Think about the other six module titles in the TASK series and what each of these might include.

a) Critical Thinking

b) Participating in Seminars

c) Scientific Writing

d) Presentations

e) Problem solving

f) Essay Writing

2.5 Check your ideas by reading the module descriptions below and matching each one to one of the six module titles a–f above.

Module 3

Helps prepare for smaller group activities by providing strategies to optimize personal contributions and enhance interaction with both the professor and fellow students.

Module 5

Highlights the different stages of problem solving, and provides a structure to help identify appropriate solutions according to context. This module encourages objectivity and offers insights into critical thinking and reasoning skills.

Module 6

Shows how to structure an argument in a balanced, well-researched and unbiased manner. This module provides the tools for identifying fact from opinion, and gives training in how to evaluate knowledge claims and detect bias in others' work.

Module 8

Gives an introduction to the process of academic writing. The focus on title analysis, arrangement of key information, and the creation of effective introductions and conclusions will improve the structure and organization of essays and ensure that they comply with academic conventions.

Module 9

Teaches the skills for writing scientific reports according to accepted academic conventions. It focuses on organization, procedures for presentation (including the descriptions of tables and graphs) and guidance on editing and revision.

Module 11

Introduces the process of researching, structuring, and delivering a short talk using appropriate software. This will help develop confidence through the refining of existing communication skills.

2.6　Choose two more modules and study the explanations. Then with books closed, explain what they involve in your own words.

Reflect

A complex task is more manageable if it is broken down into manageable micro-tasks using transferable skills. For example, the work involved in writing an essay may seem a daunting task. However, if this is broken into a series of smaller tasks, the overall task will not seem so overwhelming.

Think about the assignment tasks you have at the moment. How could you break these into smaller micro-tasks? What skills would you need to use to do this?

Student notes for Unit 1

2 Skills self-assessment

At the end of this unit you will be able to:
- **identify your personality type;**
- **recognize your own learning strengths and weaknesses.**

Task 1 Classifying personality types

Different students have different personality types, which can affect the way they deal with a task or activity. A clear understanding of your own learning style is therefore a good place to start when looking for ways to improve your approach to work and study.

Although the personality of each student contains a unique range of features, we can gain a lot of useful information by first identifying our basic personality type. One classification divides personalities into four types: action taker, practical realist, cautious thinker, and methodical reasoner.

1.1   Match these people with the best description of their personality types.

a) Jens

*" I really don't like disorganization. "
In fact, I'd describe myself as a perfectionist. I always try to use a logical approach to my work, and I often notice the flaws in other people's arguments.*

b) Khalud

*" I don't like to waste time. "
I usually come straight to the point when I express my views. I don't think there's any point pursuing an idea unless it's viable and realistic.*

I'm usually careful not to make rash decisions. I enjoy listening to other people's views before I give my opinion. I don't like rushing things, and I probably listen more than I talk.

c) Hadi

In class I often come up with a lot of ideas on the spot. That means I end up talking a lot! To be honest, I find specific plans and methods a little restrictive sometimes.

d) Yuka

1 action taker
I enjoy new experiences, and I really get a buzz out of doing new and different things.

2 practical realist
When someone gives me a new idea, right away, I think about how it will work in practice.

3 cautious thinker
I get a sense of pride out of doing a job thoroughly and properly.

4 methodical reasoner
More often than not, I find solutions using a systematic approach.

1.2 Compare your answers with another student, giving reasons to justify your choices.

1.3 Think about yourself. What personality type are you? Do you think you are mainly one type or a mixture of types? Use the following questions to help you decide.

- Do you like listening to others?

- Are you good at planning ahead?

- Do you adapt well to new environments?

- Do you like working within a clear framework?

Task 2 Identifying your own personality and learning style

We can understand someone's individual personality by thinking about the different proportions of the basic personality type he or she has.

2.1 Look at the example bar chart for Theo, a student from Greece. What does this say about his learning style?

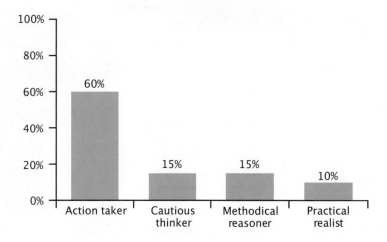

2.2 Talk to another student and find out which elements of the personality descriptions from Task 1 best describe his/her learning style. Draw a bar chart to show this. Then compare and discuss each other's charts.

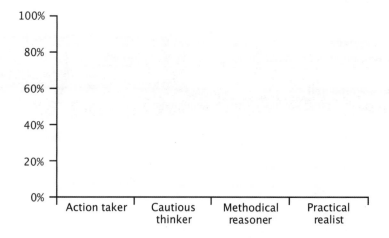

2.3 Present to the class what you have found out about your own personality. Let the student you worked with in Exercise 2.2 engage in the presentation.

Task 3 Understanding your strengths and weaknesses

Each learning style has both positive and negative aspects. A clear understanding of how these interact with each other will provide guidance on improving your approach to work and studies.

3.1 Study the characteristics of different learning styles below and decide which might be an advantage (A), a disadvantage (D) or both (B). Think of examples to back up your opinion. Make notes below.

> adventurous   pragmatic   not easily able to compromise   blunt and to the point
> disorganized   hesitant   safe   unadventurous   dynamic   poor planner   imaginative
> poor listener   logical   bossy   objective   careful   good listener   obsessive   thorough

3.2 Look back at the assessment that Jens, Khalud, Hadi and Yuka gave of their personality types in Exercise 1.1. Use the information to complete the table with the characteristics from Exercise 3.1.

Learning style	Strengths	Weaknesses
Action taker		
Practical realist		
Cautious thinker		
Methodical reasoner		

3.3 Discuss your answers with another student and add any further characteristics you can think of.

You will have another opportunity to explore your learning style if you complete *Module 12: Exam Technique*.

Task 4 Skills audit

4.1 Before you continue with TASK, it would be helpful to complete a skills audit.

Think about your strengths and weaknesses within an academic environment. This will provide you with insights into which areas you need to focus on and which other modules to complete.

4.2   Complete the skills audit. Mark an X in the correct place for you.

SKILLS							
Organization skills	weak					strong	not sure?
	0	1	2	3	4	5	
Understanding of academic culture/conventions	weak					strong	not sure?
	0	1	2	3	4	5	
Seminar skills	weak					strong	not sure?
	0	1	2	3	4	5	
Teamwork	weak					strong	not sure?
	0	1	2	3	4	5	
Problem solving	weak					strong	not sure?
	0	1	2	3	4	5	
Critical thinking	weak					strong	not sure?
	0	1	2	3	4	5	
IT skills	weak					strong	not sure?
	0	1	2	3	4	5	
Essay writing skills	weak					strong	not sure?
	0	1	2	3	4	5	
Scientific writing skills	weak					strong	not sure?
	0	1	2	3	4	5	
Research and referencing skills	weak					strong	not sure?
	0	1	2	3	4	5	
Presentation skills	weak					strong	not sure?
	0	1	2	3	4	5	
Exam skills	weak					strong	not sure?
	0	1	2	3	4	5	

4.3   In which areas do you feel you need to improve?

Task 5 Addressing your needs

Now that you have completed the skills audit, you can identify the modules in the TASK series that you feel will address your particular needs. Write the titles of the modules that you would find useful below.

Reflect

To develop a better understanding of your learning style and the skills that you need to develop, think about and reread any feedback that you have received recently from your professors. What sort of comments do they give you? What weaknesses can you identify?

It is not always easy to identify your own weaknesses. Try to discuss your feelings with other students, friends or family.

Student notes for Unit 2

Unit 3 How organized are you?

At the end of this unit you will be able to:
- identify factors involved in good organization;
- analyze your organizational weaknesses and learn how to improve them.

Task 1 Organization quiz

If you want to succeed academically, it helps to be organized. There is a huge amount of advice available on how to improve your organizational skills, but to benefit you must first be convinced of its value. The place to begin is with an assessment of how organized you are at the present time.

1.1   Find out how organized you are by answering these questions.

Are you ORGANIZED?

		often	sometimes	rarely
1	Do you lose things?	☐	☐	☐
2	Do you waste time looking for things?	☐	☐	☐
3	Do you waste time in other ways?	☐	☐	☐
4	Are you late for classes or tutoring sessions?	☐	☐	☐
5	Do you forget or miss appointments?	☐	☐	☐
6	Do you find it difficult to meet deadlines?	☐	☐	☐
7	Do you forget to do assignments?	☐	☐	☐
8	Do you forget to do background reading for class?	☐	☐	☐
9	Do you forget to bring what you need to class?	☐	☐	☐
10	Do you rely on other people to organize you?	☐	☐	☐
11	Do you lose your notes?	☐	☐	☐

Check your answers on page 27.

1.2   Work with another student. How similar/different are you? Try to learn from each other's strengths and weaknesses.

Task 2 Targeting your weaknesses

You have made the first step to improving your organization by identifying your weaknesses. Now you need to find strategies for avoiding problems caused by these weaknesses.

2.1 Look back at the organizational weaknesses you have identified. Discuss possible reasons for your weaknesses and ways to avoid them in the future. Make notes in the table, including more than one strategy for each.

2.2 Which areas of weakness do you need to target first? Rate the weaknesses you have written in column one from 1 to 5 (1 = most important, 5 = least important). Find another student with similar priorities; discuss the strategies you have each chosen and how you feel your work and studies will improve when you apply them.

Weakness	Reason(s) why	Strategies to avoid future problems
forgetting homework deadlines	poor planning	take notes in a planner or add to your to do list

2.3 What have you learned about organizational skills from this task? Report your conclusions to the class.

Task 3 Useful aids

There are a variety of systems and support mechanisms designed to help you to be more organized, as well as to make student life easier. They range from simple, low-tech solutions to expensive, high-tech solutions.

3.1 Work in pairs or small groups. Decide which items are vital (V), or useful but not vital (U). Add any additional items to the table that you think would be useful. Give reasons for your decisions in column three.

Item?	V or U?	Why/Why not?
alarm clock	U	cell phone—same function
planner		
watch		
binder for each subject		
notebook paper		
schedule		
electronic organizer		
computer		
calendar		
radio		
digital voice recorder		
cell phone		
dictionary		
stapler		
folders		
dividers		
notebook		
correction fluid		
sticky notes		
hole punch		
reading lamp		
highlighters		
?		

3.2 Compare your list of vital items with another student and agree on a definitive list. Present your ideas to the whole class, justifying your choices.

Reflect

It is usually difficult to change our habits. The ones that lead to disorganized behavior may have been in place for years and could therefore be particularly difficult to modify. You need to work out a clear strategy that will lead to a successful transition.

Focus on one area of your life where disorganization has caused you difficulty. Then identify any patterns of behavior that might have led to this disorganization. Once you have done this, try to solve this problem using strategies you have learned in this unit.

When you have succeeded in changing one area of your life, it should be easier to try the same strategies in other areas.

Student notes for Unit 3

Unit 4 Time management

At the end of this unit you will be able to:
- identify factors involved in good time management;
- analyze your own time management skills and learn how to improve them.

Task 1 What is time management?

The first step towards using your time in higher education constructively is to clarify what is meant by good time management. It is then possible to decide what sort of activities contribute to your own effective management of time.

1.1 Work in pairs. Discuss which of the statements a–g best summarizes what time management is and explain your reasons.

Time management is ...

a) completing and submitting assignments as quickly as possible.

b) knowing how to write an assignment the night before its deadline and still manage to attend classes the next day.

c) developing a reliable system to organize and allocate time to tasks or situations so as to use the time effectively and achieve objectives.

d) foregoing social activities in favor of study for up to one month before and during the exam period.

e) learning how to use your time more effectively to accomplish your goals.

f) maximizing time available to you by studying until late in the evening.

g) getting a friend or family member to remind you of deadlines and appointments.

1.2 Decide which of the other statements give useful ideas for managing time and which statements need changing. Discuss your ideas with other students.

Task 2 Importance of time management

It is useful to identify the ways in which time management affects your life and the consequences of good and bad time management.

2.1 Think about which areas of your life as a student could be affected by good or bad time management, and what the consequences of this could be. Complete the diagram on the next page with possible consequences and add any other ideas you can think of.

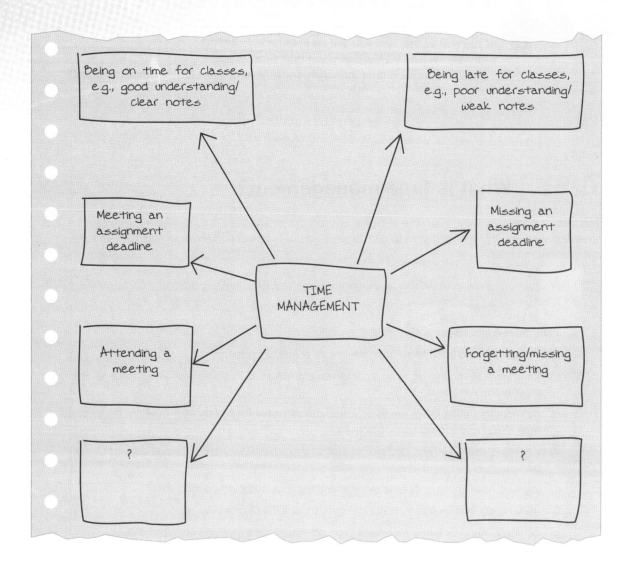

2.2 Compare your diagram with another student and discuss similarities and differences. Add any more ideas you have to your diagram.

Task 3 Improve your time management

Now that you have identified potential problem areas, you need to work on maximizing effective time use. One strategy is to keep a record of how you organize your time. This raises your awareness of how long you spend on different activities and allows you to adjust and improve your time management.

3.1 Use the schedule on the next page to indicate when you are busy. Mark your class times and when you usually eat meals, sleep, do leisure activities, etc. Use a colored circle to show any deadlines you have. All the times that remain blank can be used to organize your study times outside class time.

Monday	Tuesday	Wednesday	Thursday	Friday
06:00	06:00	06:00	06:00	06:00
07:00	07:00	07:00	07:00	07:00
08:00	08:00	08:00	08:00	08:00
09:00	09:00	09:00	09:00	09:00
10:00	10:00	10:00	10:00	10:00
11:00	11:00	11:00	11:00	11:00
12:00	12:00	12:00	12:00	12:00
1:00	1:00	1:00	1:00	1:00
2:00	2:00	2:00	2:00	2:00
3:00	3:00	3:00	3:00	3:00
4:00	4:00	4:00	4:00	4:00
5:00	5:00	5:00	5:00	5:00
6:00	6:00	6:00	6:00	6:00
7:00	7:00	7:00	7:00	7:00
8:00	8:00	8:00	8:00	8:00
9:00	9:00	9:00	9:00	9:00
10:00	10:00	10:00	10:00	10:00
11:00	11:00	11:00	11:00	11:00
12:00	12:00	12:00	12:00	12:00

3.2   Compare your schedule with another student. Discuss the differences and comment on how realistic the schedule is. Suggest any improvements you can think of. Copy the improved schedule for each week in the term, semester, or quarter to help you keep track of what you have to do.

Reflect

When you have used your schedule for a week, think about these questions:

How well are you making use of the free time on your schedule during the day? Can you think of a way to use the time between lectures and seminars more constructively? How could you do this?

Can you move some private study time into the daytime to free some evening hours for leisure activity? How could you do this?

Student notes for Unit 4

Module 1

Web work

Website 1 — Free learning styles inventory

You can analyze your own learning style in more depth on this website. This site provides an analysis of your approach to learning and will generate results in graphic form, so you can compare these.

http://www.learning-styles-online.com/inventory/default.asp?ref=ga&data=gbp

The questionnaire on this website can be completed online or downloaded for use on paper. Full instructions are provided on the test.

Website 2 — Are you a good time manager?

You can test your time management skills on this website. It is part of a health- and welfare-oriented website that considers poor time management as a contributor to stress-related ailments. The feedback from this quiz will give you a further indication of the extent to which you need to improve your approach to time management.

http://www.betterhealth.vic.gov.au/bhcv2/bhcarticles.nsf/pages/quiz_time_management?OpenDocument

Complete the questions on the website and click the button to calculate your score.

Extension activities

Activity 1 — Peer review

The impression that we have of our own strengths and weaknesses is frequently different from the impression that others have of us. After you have completed the learning styles assessment and the skills audit, ask a close friend or family member to repeat the exercise on your behalf, but this time, from their perspective. You might be surprised at some of the observations that they make about you. You could find that you have overlooked some important strengths, or that you have disregarded some weaknesses that may need attention.

Activity 2 — Study buddies

An organized approach to work both inside and outside the classroom can have an important impact on the extent of your success. However, motivation can sometimes be difficult to maintain, as private study is often a solitary practice. Team up with someone from your group or class and arrange to study together at the same time. Having a study buddy can keep you both on track and relieve some of the loneliness or boredom you may find when you study independently. Having someone to share or challenge your ideas can help confirm understanding of a subject. By arranging to meet at specific times, you might also be more likely to follow your study schedule.

Glossary

Academic conventions (n) Widely used and accepted practices that are agreed on at academic institutions. For example, standard practices in research, academic writing, attendance regulations, etc.

Academic culture (n) The values and beliefs that exist in academic institutions, particularly those that inform and influence *academic conventions*.

Academic writing (n) Writing that students and academics produce. It normally involves research, demonstrates learning or knowledge, and follows clear conventions in its style and organization. For example, essays and assignments, reports, dissertations, theses.

Analyze (v) To break an issue down into parts in order to study, identify and discuss their meaning and/or relevance.

Assignment (n) A piece of work, generally written, that is set as part of an academic course and is normally completed out of class and submitted by a set date to be assessed.

Bias (n) An attitude you have, or a judgment you have made, based on subjective opinion instead of objective fact. It can make you treat someone or something in an unfair way.

Collaborate (v) To work together with another person (or other people) on a piece of work or an assignment.

Communication skills (n) Skills that enable you to listen, talk, and write to other people effectively. Good communication skills allow you to make a positive impression, participate well in discussions, and convey ideas clearly.

Critical thinking (n) The academic skill of being able to look at ideas and problems in a considered, critical way in order to evaluate them. It also involves the ability to see links between concepts and develop one's own ideas.

Database (n) A file of electronic information (such as documents, articles, records, statistics, and pictures) that is regularly updated. It is usually related to a specific subject and is organized so that a computer can search and find it quickly (on the Internet or on a CD).

Deadline (n) The date or time that something needs to be completed by. In academic situations, deadlines are normally given for handing in essays and assignments.

Evaluate (v) To assess information in terms of quality, relevance, objectivity, and accuracy.

Feedback (n) A response to an activity, process or product that gives information about how successful it was, and deals with any problems that arose. (v = **feed back**)

Framework (n) A basic structure that is an outline of something more detailed.

Goal (n) An aim or end purpose that someone tries to achieve or reach.

Higher education (n) Education that comes after secondary education and is usually for students aged over 18. It may involve a university course or another higher or continuing education course.

IT skills (n) Skills connected with using and working with information technology. For example, computer systems and applications.

Key information (n) The most important information given, such as the main points in a lecture, essay, or set of instructions.

Knowledge claim (n) Something that is stated as true by a person or people, but is not universally accepted as a fact.

Learning style (n) A style of thinking about, processing and remembering information that you have to learn. Different styles can be classified in a variety of ways. For example, you may be an action taker or a cautious thinker.

Micro-skill (n) A sub-skill that contributes to your ability to master macro-skills, such as reading, listening, writing, or speaking. It is useful to isolate micro-skills and work on them individually. For example, to improve your academic writing (macro-skill) you may work on developing the micro-skill of researching.

Objective (adj) (n) 1 (adj) Not influenced by personal feelings or emotions. 2 (n) The aim, or what you want to achieve from an activity.

Organizational skills (n) Skills that enable you to manage the way your study, domestic life, and/or social interaction is organized. For example, your ability to keep track of and manage time, activities, and objects.

Personality type (n) A classification of someone's temperament and personality traits. These can be classified in different ways. For example, you may be an extrovert personality type or a risk taker.

Pie chart (n) A graphic representation of amounts or percentages that are shown as segments of a circle (like a pie that has been divided up). It can be used instead of a table in the results section of a scientific writing report.

Presentation (n) A short lecture, talk or demonstration given in front of an audience. The speaker prepares his or her presentation in advance and will often use visual aids or realia to illustrate it.

Reference (n) (v) 1 (n) Acknowledgment of the sources of ideas and information that you use in written work and oral presentations. 2 (v) To acknowledge or mention the sources of information.

Research (v) (n) 1 (v) To gather information from a variety of sources and analyze and compare it. 2 (n) Information collected from a variety of sources about a specific topic.

Self-assessment (n) The process of gathering and evaluating information about yourself in order to decide which areas you need to work on, and/or select for future study or employment.

Seminar (n) A small group discussion led by a professor, graduate assistant or guest speaker. Students are expected to take an active part in the seminar.

Skills audit (n) A type of *self-assessment* where someone measures and evaluates which skills he/she has already developed and which ones he/she needs to work on.

Strategy (n) A plan of action that you follow when you want to achieve a particular *goal*. For example, it is possible to have a clear strategy for passing an exam.

Structure (n) (v) 1 (n) A framework or arrangement of several parts, put together in a particular way. 2 (v) In academic terms, to put together ideas or arguments in a logical way for an essay or presentation.

Study aid (n) A device, system or support mechanism that makes study easier or helps you organize your study. For example, electronic organizer, study handbook, highlighter.

Team-working (v) Working supportively and co-operatively in a group to achieve a common goal.

Technique (n) A method or way of doing something that involves skill and/or efficiency. For example, it is possible to learn useful techniques for answering exam questions.

Time management (n) The ability to organize your time so that you use it more effectively and efficiently.

Toolkit (n) In academic life, this is a collection of resources, *techniques,* or aids that help you to do something. For example, prepare for an exam.

Transferable skills (n) Skills that may be learned in one situation but transferred to others. For example, you may learn *critical thinking* skills at university or college, but also be able to use them in the workplace or in social situations.

Unit 3 Quiz results

- Did you answer *often* or *sometimes* to 5 or more? You need to get organized. However, first you must recognize that you are not the most organized person, and you must want to improve your organizational skills.

- Did you answer *often* or *sometimes* to only 2 or 3? You are generally well-organized though you have the occasional lapse. You will still benefit from focusing on your weaker areas in order to become more organized.

- Did you answer *rarely* to all of the above? You are either extremely well-organized or you are deluding yourself! Check your self-assessment with another student. If the result is still positive, be ready to share your successful strategies with others.

Module 2: Academic Culture

Introduction

The transition between secondary and higher education can be a time of upheaval. It is necessary to learn about and understand the customs, requirements and expectations of your college or university, or in other words to familiarize yourself with its academic culture. As you will encounter other students and academics from a wide range of backgrounds, a certain amount of cross-cultural understanding will also be necessary.

This module examines the academic culture that exists in higher education and the conventions and concepts that you will need to acquaint yourself with when you study in an English-speaking institution.

Unit 1 defines academic culture and checks understanding of key concepts. Unit 2 encourages discussion of common problems that are associated with the transition between secondary and higher education. In Unit 3 you will look at assumptions you have about higher education, in order to identify and challenge unrealistic expectations. This will help you plan for potentially problematic situations more realistically. In Unit 4 you will look at some of these situations and discuss appropriate responses. Unit 5 examines common communication problems and will help you to avoid cross-cultural misunderstandings in an academic environment. Finally, Unit 6 asks you to examine and reflect on your expectations of teaching and learning and encourages you to take an active part in your learning.

This module seeks to raise awareness of the conventions of academic culture and to help avoid breakdown in communication due to erroneous expectations and cross-cultural misunderstandings. It also aims to provoke thought and discussion that will enhance communication with other students and make you more aware of their attitudes and beliefs.

Skills Map

Understanding academic culture

Familiarize yourself with key terminology related to academic life.

The transition to higher education

Identify and discuss important issues in this transition.

Expectations of higher education institutions

Examine both your own expectations of the teaching staff and the institution as well as the expectations placed on you as a student.

Critical incident analysis

Discuss issues relating to potential misunderstandings and miscommunication in academic life.

Cross-cultural communication

Evaluate and participate in effective and appropriate communication techniques for academic situations.

Philosophy of teaching and learning

Examine your attitudes to and beliefs about what both teaching and learning involve.

Destination: Academic Culture

Understanding academic culture

At the end of this unit you will be able to:
- understand key terminology and concepts relating to academic culture.

Task 1 Defining academic culture

When people go overseas to live and work, it is necessary for them to get used to a culture that they may not be familiar with. It is the same when you go abroad to study.

1.1 Discuss the words in the box with another student. Decide what they mean to you, which ones have a similar meaning, and how they relate to the topic of academic culture.

attitudes	beliefs	culture	regulations	research	rules
philosophy	study	thinking	values		

1.2 Read and complete this definition of academic culture using some of the words you have discussed. Compare your completed definition with another student.

Academic culture refers to the ① _____ , values, and ② _____ that exist in higher education institutions, particularly universities. Such a ③ _____ exists alongside the culture of the rest of the country. Academic culture includes among other things the rules and ④ _____ for appropriate behavior on the part of professor and student, and the ⑤ _____ that underlies teaching and learning at this level. It is also about the beliefs held by those working within such an institution, such as a belief in original ⑥ _____ and critical ⑦ _____ .

1.3 Use the definition of academic culture to help you discuss the differences between the learning culture where you were previously with that of the institution you are attending.

Task 2 Important words in academic culture

2.1 What do you think is happening in the three photographs?

2.2 Match the terms below with their definitions. Check your answers with other students.

a) continuing education

b) undergraduate

c) academic advisor

d) professor

e) seminar

f) core course

g) social sciences

h) plagiarism

1 a student-focused class with two-way dialogue involving students

2 a person who teaches classes, grades students' work, and leads laboratory sessions

3 the use of other people's ideas or research without appropriate acknowledgement

4 an academic staff member assigned to students for support and guidance

5 courses of study or training, usually not at university, that some people take after they have left high school

6 a mandatory course essential to your degree

7 the study of people in society, which includes politics, economics, law, etc.

8 the first level of study after leaving high school, usually lasting four years

2.3 Select the correct word from the pair of words supplied.

a) class/seminar

The _____ was very crowded, so it was difficult to hear everything.

b) professor/graduate assistant

Xavier stayed in college after finishing his Masters and worked as a _____ while studying for a Masters.

c) research/plagiarism

It is tempting to copy things straight from the Web, but _____ is absolutely forbidden.

d) professor/academic advisor

If you have a problem with choosing your modules, you should make an appointment to discuss it with your _____ .

e) higher/continuing education

My mother left school at sixteen without many qualifications, but she went back into _____ in her twenties to do a photography course.

f) core course/elective course

Jens has decided to take a(n) _____ in Spanish as well as his other subjects. He doesn't need the extra credits, but he wants to go to Spain in the summer.

g) humanities/social sciences

Anna is a _____ graduate. She has a degree in English and Drama.

h) undergraduate/graduate

Leon worked in Australia for a year after he finished his first degree. Now he has gone back to university to study a(n) _____ program.

2.4   You have now worked with the following eight pairs of words. Discuss with another student or in a small group the differences between them.

a) class/seminar

b) professor/graduate assistant

c) research/plagiarism

d) professor/academic advisor

e) higher education/continuing education

f) core course/elective course

g) humanities/social sciences

h) undergraduate/graduate

Reflect

Think about the following points:

- How does academic culture vary from country to country?

- How is the academic culture where you are studying different from the educational environment you are used to?

Student notes for Unit 1

Unit 2 The transition to higher education

At the end of this unit you will be able to:
- identify common challenges for students in the early stages of higher education;
- offer useful advice to these students.

Task 1 Identifying challenges

1.1 The photographs below show the challenges facing students studying at university for the first time. What do they represent? Discuss your ideas in groups.

1.2 Rate the challenges from 1 to 5 (1 = not challenging, 5 = most challenging). Add any other challenges you can think of.

a) _____ making new friends

b) _____ becoming a more independent learner

c) _____ organizing your own time

d) _____ doing research and writing original essays/reports

e) _____ participating in seminars

f) _____ attending classes and taking notes

g) _____ taking three-hour exams

h) _____ participating in teamwork activities

i) _____ adapting to the different expectations of professors

j) _____ _____

k) _____ _____

l) _____ _____

1.3 Discuss your rating with another student, giving reasons for your choices. Explain your five most and least challenging things to the class.

Task **2** Offering advice

2.1　Read comments made by four undergraduates after their first semester at university. Which ones are similar to your own experiences? Write something about yourself at the end.

2.2　Compare your experiences with another student or discuss in a group. How similar/different are you?

2.3　Discuss the best advice for the students below with another student. Present your advice to the class and note down any advice you had not discussed.

❝ I did not organize the time very well, and this ❞ led to not finishing my written assignments.

❝ Like all overseas students, I need to find ❞ ways of increasing my vocabulary.

❝ The reason for my poor performance is that I haven't put in enough effort. ❞ I think many of us have had similar problems because we were not sure what the professors expected from us and what the class required.

❝ I felt really nervous the first time I had to participate in a seminar. Even though ❞ I wanted to contribute, I couldn't find the right words. And some of the other students talked so much and so quickly that I found it difficult to interrupt.

You

Task 3 Asking for help

3.1   Discuss in groups things you would like to discuss with your academic advisor but have not yet asked. Identify several common issues in the group. Note down these issues below and discuss how you would express them to your advisor.

3.2   Discuss as a class some of the issues you raised in Exercise 3.1.

Reflect

Think about how you have adapted to higher education. If there are any particular problems you managed to overcome, think about how you did so. If there are ways in which you have still not managed to adapt, think about why and try to find strategies that might help you.

Student notes for Unit 2

Unit 3 Expectations of higher education institutions

At the end of this unit you will:
- be more aware of expectations about teaching and learning in English-medium universities.

Task 1 General expectations

The expectations you have when you start your program of study will affect the outcome. You may be disappointed by certain aspects as well as motivated by others. You may be shocked or surprised at the way things are done, and this can be upsetting if you are not prepared.

1.1 Think about anything that has surprised you about your program of study so far.

1.2 Decide if these statements are true (T), false (F) or it depends (D). Compare your answers with another student.

a)   Classes are likely to have 100 or more students in attendance.

b)   Exams are normally multiple choice.

c)   A grade of 90% or over is considered very good.

d)   Libraries are poorly stocked, with most books held in the reserve section.

e)   Students are very serious and have little time for relaxation.

f)   Coursework is more important than examined work.

g)   Most students are living away from their families.

h)   Staff members address students by their family names.

i)   Class attendance is mandatory.

j)   Graduating Summa cum Laude is difficult to do.

Task 2 Expectations of professors

2.1 Decide what you think are the main duties of a professor. Discuss your ideas with another student.

2.2 Discuss and decide which of the following you would expect of a professor in a higher education institution. Why or why not? Compare your choices with other students.

  a) teach interesting classes

  b) supply handouts about the class before or afterwards

  c) be available at any time to answer questions

  d) check assignments for language errors before submission

  e) set and grade assignments

  f) organize social events for the class

  g) know students' first names and use them

  h) be known by his/her first name

  i) help students to find jobs after graduation

  j) be flexible about due dates

2.3 Change the statements in 2.2 so that they reflect exactly what you would expect from a professor. Explain your statements to the class.

Task 3 Expectations of students

3.1 Read these statements describing what professors may expect from students in a higher education institution. Discuss with another student which column you would put them in and why. Add anything else you can think of.

a) attend all classes punctually

b) let the professor know if they are going to be absent

c) take notes from the class

d) read around the subject matter of the class

e) participate in seminar discussions and answer questions

f) give presentations

g) use the library for research

h) participate in group and teamwork activities

i) help the professor by cleaning the board or carrying books

j) speak to the professor if they have a personal problem

k) join a university club or society

l) get a part-time job to help with finances

m) buy small presents at the end of the semester to thank the professor

n) ....

o) ....

p) ....

Students are expected to ...	Students aren't expected to ...

Reflect

Think about the things that have most surprised you about life as a student in higher education. These might be things that have shocked you or things that have surprised you. Think about why these things have surprised you and whether or not your attitude has changed towards them as the weeks go by.

Student notes for Unit 3

4 Critical incident analysis

At the end of this unit you will:
- **be more aware of differences between behavior in your own cultural environment and the academic culture in which you are studying;**
- **be better able to handle communication in potentially problematic situations.**

Task 1 What is a critical incident?

The term **critical incident** was originally applied to any serious event that interrupted the ability of an individual to cope with his or her everyday life. The term has typically been applied to events such as illness and bereavement.

More recently, the term has been extended to more commonplace events such as cultural misunderstandings. Although some incidents might not appear "critical" in themselves, they might nevertheless result in a critical outcome.

1.1 Discuss with another student whether you agree that small incidents can have a big impact on our lives. Try to come up with some examples from your own experience.

Task 2 Reflecting on personal experience

Most people remember events in their lives that have left emotional scars or caused changes in their behavior. Many of these will have happened during childhood, where the cultural mismatch is between childhood and adult values of behavior.

2.1 Think about an incident in your childhood that had a big effect on you. If possible, try to think of small events that had a big impact. Discuss the incident with a partner and try to reach a conclusion as to why it had such a big impact on you. For example:

- Being told you were behaving inappropriately in public.
- You made a big effort to do something well but were told you were not good at it.
- You were criticized for doing something wrong when you thought you were helping.
- You were forbidden from having or doing something, but could not understand why.
- Your reasons for doing something were misunderstood.

a b c d

2.2 Look at the following cultural features that might affect the way others interpret your behavior. Identify any that you feel have caused misunderstandings. Add other features you can think of to the list.

gestures

facial expressions

presentation of self: hair, dress, etc.

concept of beauty

concept of time

concept of self

eating habits

work ethic

attitude to family

2.3 Discuss your conclusions with a partner. Then share the results of your discussions with the rest of the class.

2.4 How do the cultural features above transfer to an academic context in a new environment? Think about your attitude to the following. Are they things you would or wouldn't do in a seminar?

- use the professor's first name
- disagree openly with other participants
- accept without question the instructions of the professor
- ask to work with a different student from the one you were assigned to
- agree with the general consensus even though you strongly disagree
- make sarcastic or ironic comments during discussions
- wait to be asked before speaking

Task 3 Critical incident analysis

Studying critical incidents will help you move beyond the individual response and develop an understanding of the bigger picture. In the context of overseas studies, an inappropriate individual reaction is usually the result of a cultural misunderstanding. By analyzing the different scenarios and reflecting on the causes of actions, you will be able to gain a more objective view and adapt more easily to the new environment.

3.1 **Discuss the following four situations with another student. Choose the most appropriate solution from choices a) – d). Justify your ideas with reference to your own experience. Note that more than one answer may be acceptable in each case.**

1) You are 20 minutes late for a lecture. When you arrive, you can see from the door that the lecture has already started. What would be the best thing to do?

   a) Go in, walk up to the professor and apologize.

   b) Wait outside until the class is over and then apologize to the professor.

   c) Knock and wait to be told to enter.

   d) Enter quietly and take a seat, trying not to be noticed.

   Note: Do you think class size makes a difference?

2) You are given an assignment to complete in two days' time. This is very difficult for you because your parents have just come to visit and expect you to show them around. What is the best solution?

   a) Explain the situation to your professor and ask for an extension.

   b) Be absent from class when you have to hand the assignment in.

   c) Go to class without the assignment and say nothing.

   d) Tell your parents they will have to entertain themselves.

3) You need to ask for an extension to your assignment due date because you have not finished an important essay for another class. What would you be most likely to do?

   a) Say you were sick and have a doctor's note.

   b) Say you had problems with your laptop and lost your work.

   c) Say you had too many assignments due in at the same time.

   d) Say you had relatives visiting you.

4) Your professor has asked to see you urgently and has suggested it is about a disciplinary matter. Which of these options is most likely to be the problem?

   a) You haven't returned a library book due a week before.

   b) You lent your lecture notes to a friend who was absent.

   c) You handed in an identical essay to a friend, as you were told to work together.

   d) You broke a test tube in the chemistry laboratory.

3.2 Think of any other similar incidents you have heard of, or that happened to you. Tell a partner/small group and make up your own multiple-choice options like 1) – 4) above. Swap these with another pair/group for them to discuss.

Reflect

This unit should have raised many issues that you have not thought about in any depth before. Think about what you have learned, and continue to reflect on how your attitude to critical incidents will affect your studies.

Student notes for Unit 4

Unit 5 Cross-cultural communication

At the end of this unit you will:
- be more aware of reciprocal speech styles common in English-language academic contexts;
- be better able to participate in academic situations such as seminars.

Task 1 Feeling at ease when you speak

You are judged in universities both by what you say and by what you write. More importantly, you will probably be awarded grades for participation in seminars.

When you write, you have more time to compose your thoughts, whereas participating in class discussions requires more rapid responses and can be stressful for both native and non-native speakers.

As speaking can be stressful, it is worth thinking about how to put yourself at ease before speaking. An important aspect of this is to feel confident about conventions of speaking, especially in a different cultural environment.

1.1 One source of uncertainty is the correct form of address. Which of the following titles have you used with academic staff you have worked with? Discuss with other students.

    a) first name, e.g., Mike

    b) academic title, e.g., doctor, professor

    c) academic title with last name, e.g., Doctor Giddings

    d) surname, e.g., Mr., Mrs., or Ms. Chedzoy

    e) ma'am or sir

    f) dear, buddy, etc.

    g) other

1.2 Your professor is called Dr. Meadows. Your class is a large one and it is the second week of the semester. You pass Dr. Meadows in the corridor one day. How would you greet her?

    a) Good morning, doctor.

    b) Good morning, Doctor Meadows.

    c) Good morning, ma'am.

    d) Good morning, dear.

1.3 Talk about your experiences and conclusions as a class and establish a few criteria for addressing staff. Write your criteria below.

1.4 True or false? Discuss the following with another student, giving reasons.

a) The way you address someone in a hierarchical relationship (such as between professor and student) should be negotiated by the person in the higher position.

b) You should never address a professor by his or her first name.

c) Academic staff may ask to be called by their first names, especially in smaller groups.

d) You won't offend academic staff by addressing them incorrectly. They will understand if you make a mistake.

e) You should ask how someone would like to be addressed if you aren't sure.

Task 2 Reciprocal speech style

Uncertainty about how to express your thoughts can also inhibit your contribution. In a seminar, you are expected to listen to the professor and other members of the group, but also respond immediately (in words) to what they say. This style of exchange can be termed reciprocal speech style.

2.1 The following extract is a typical exchange that you might hear in a seminar. The exchange involves asking and answering questions and adding comments. Identify this pattern in the conversation below by matching 1) – 3) with their functions a) – c).

Student: Do you think the recent climate changes can be attributed to global warming?

Professor: 1) No, I don't actually. _____

2) I think they are part of the normal pattern of climate change. If you look at recorded weather charts kept over the last 200 years, you'll see that in 1857, there were extremely high temperatures in many regions. _____

3) What about you? Do you think global warming exists? _____

Student: Well, ...

a) Ask

b) Answer

c) Add

2.2 Discuss with another student the problems you might have in finding an immediate reply.

Task 3 Giving yourself thinking time

As already discussed, speaking can be stressful, especially in front of others. One reaction to stress is a blank mind. This then adds to the stress, as you feel under pressure to say something. One way of helping to solve this problem is to look for ways of finding stress-free thinking time.

3.1 Match each technique for buying yourself time with the correct picture. Compare your answers with another student. In your pair, evaluate the techniques a) – d), trying to find an advantage and a disadvantage for each one.

a) _____ Pretend you haven't heard.
b) _____ Repeat the question.
c) _____ Use delaying noises.
d) _____ Begin speaking by saying: "It depends ..."

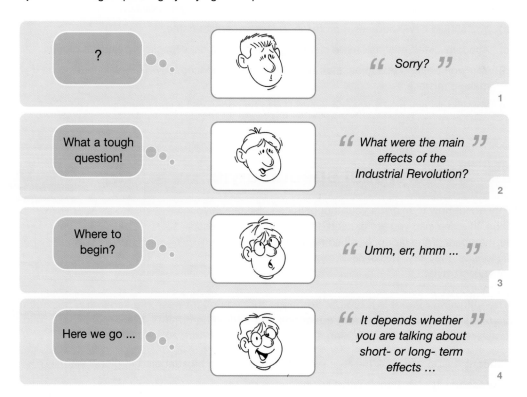

3.2 Think of other ways you can play for time. Write a list below and discuss your ideas with another student.

Task 4 Applying discussion techniques

4.1   What opinions do you have related to the following five questions? Think about each one and then write *Yes* or *No*. Then exchange views with another student.

    a) Do you think capital punishment is a good idea?

    b) Should we ban laboratory testing of cosmetics on animals?

    c) Is it a good idea for tuition fees to be free for all local university students?

    d) Should we make it mandatory for all students to learn at least one foreign language?

    e) Do you think the terminally ill should be able to end their own lives?

4.2   Think about the 3-As reciprocal speech style you looked at in Task 2.1. Your answers to the above questions are the first A (Answer). Which of the following could be the second A (Add)?

    1) Mistakes are possible.

    2) The financial implications would be very important.

    3) We need to consider who would gain what.

    4) All life is sacred.

    5) The decision should depend on what is best for society.

4.3   Think about the following five questions. Which could be the third A (Ask)?

    i) What about the consequences?

    ii) Would that deter people from committing crimes?

    iii) How would this be determined?

    iv) What might the advantages and disadvantages be?

    v) Who would benefit?

4.4   Choose one or more of the questions a) – e) and construct a discussion with another student using the 3-As reciprocal speech style. Use any of the ideas in 4.2 to help, and add your own thoughts.

4.5 Repeat the above. This time try to give your own opinions. Give yourself time to think, using tactics discussed in Task 3.

Reflect

The content of this unit is aimed at helping you participate more fully in discussions during your university study. Much of what you have learned is about feeling more relaxed in spoken discussions. Reflect on your past experience in such situations and to what extent this advice would have helped you. Then think about how you feel it will help you in the future.

Student notes for Unit 5

Unit 6 Philosophy of teaching and learning

At the end of this unit you will be more aware of:
- **what constitutes good teaching;**
- **what is involved in learning a subject.**

Task 1 A good professor?

1.1 Discuss the different professors in the photographs. What kind of professors would you like to have, and why?

1.2 Read the following list of features that you think should be found in a good professor. Rank them from 1 to 10 (1 = most important, 10 = least important), giving reasons for your choices.

A good professor ...

a) _____ explains clearly.

b) _____ takes responsibility for a student passing or failing.

c) _____ knows his/her subject very well and is able to answer any questions students may ask.

d) _____ does not make mistakes.

e) _____ is neat, well-groomed and smart in appearance.

f) _____ has a clean and organized office.

g) _____ gives regular tests to check students' understanding.

h) _____ writes exams that only cover what has been taught in class.

i) _____ makes learning fun.

j) _____ encourages students to be independent and take risks.

Task 2 The good student

a   b   c   d   e

2.1   Discuss the different students in the photographs. What are they doing that is good for study?

2.2   Work in pairs. Read the following list of characteristics that you think should be found in a good student. Rank them in order of importance from 1 to 11 (1 = most important, 11 = least important), giving reasons for your choices.

A good student ...

a) _____ knows the answers to a professor's questions.

b) _____ enters into discussion with the professor if he/she disagrees.

c) _____ is willing to answer in class.

d) _____ is cheerful and popular.

e) _____ prepares for and reviews classes.

f) _____ goes beyond the textbook in the pursuit of knowledge.

g) _____ is able to assess the quality of his/her own work.

h) _____ helps other class members.

i) _____ gets good grades.

j) _____ is able to think critically and creatively.

k) _____ is modest.

Task 3 Professor–student contract

Your success as a student is something you can decide. Complete this section with this fact firmly in mind.

3.1   Think about the discussions you have had in this unit. Then discuss with another student how you can be successful in your studies. How similar are you? Be ready to tell the other students about your decisions.

3.2   Bearing in mind the discussion you had in 3.1, complete the following written undertaking.

I, ... *promise that I will:*

- ....
- ....
- ....
- ....
- ....
- ....
- ....
- ....
- ....
- ....

Signed .... *On this day* .... *20* ....

I, ... *promise that I will:*

- ....
- ....
- ....
- ....
- ....
- ....
- ....
- ....
- ....
- ....

Signed .... *On this day* .... *20* ....

Reflect

You have made a promise to behave in a certain way during your time at university. Over the next few days, think about what this means and how it will affect you.

Student notes for Unit 6

Module 2

Web work

Website 1   Different pond, different fish

http://www.ialf.edu/dpdf/march04page2.html

Review

This website gives access to various issues of a newsletter called *Different pond, different fish*, which was written by Australian academics. In this issue there is advice on negotiating with professors and going to a professor with a problem. There is also advice on life outside the classroom concerning topics such as being polite and making eye contact. This is a fun, informative website, with cartoons illustrating some of the points being made.

Task

This site includes a forum for discussion. Go to the forum and reply to one of the entries as well as posting a comment of your own.

Website 2   Classroom culture

http://www.sfsu.edu/~oip/f1services/SurvivalGuide/SurvivalGuideToLivingInSanFrancisco.html

Review

This website resource, compiled by San Francisco State University, gives lots of useful information and advice on topics such as classroom culture, faculty members, teaching methods, and standards of academic conduct.

Task

Read the section titled *Value of Student Perspective*. Then write one or two paragraphs describing how the classroom culture described here differs from that in your country and/or in the country you are studying.

Module 2

Extension activities

Poster presentation

Prepare a poster presentation that gives some advice on academic culture for a student who is going to be studying in your country for six months.

User guide

Prepare a user guide on academic culture for new students to be posted on the university website.

Glossary

Academic advisor (n) A professor who is assigned to a group of students to provide advice, guidance, and support on personal and study matters within their experience and expertise.

Academic culture (n) The values and *beliefs* that exist in academic institutions, particularly those that inform and influence academic conventions.

Assignment (n) A piece of work, generally written, that is set as part of an academic program and is normally completed out of class and submitted by a set date to be assessed.

Belief (n) Something that is accepted to be right, often by a collection of people, even is it has not been (or cannot be) demonstrated as true. For example, many vegetarians hold the belief that killing animals is wrong.

Continuing education (n) Post-compulsory education at pre-degree level, for example at a vocational, technical or art college or institute. It may offer students the chance to take qualifications also available at the level of compulsory schooling and/or *tertiary* and degree courses.

Core courses (n) Classes that must be completed as part of a general educational requirement, in order to gain a qualification such as a degree.

Coursework (n) Work that is done as part of a course and that is normally assessed to form part of a student's final grade.

Critical incident (n) A problematic or challenging event that may not appear to have an impact at the time, but subsequently has a critical outcome, i.e., an outcome that is insightful and/or changes the views or behavior of those it affects.

Elective course (n) A course that is not mandatory for the completion of a degree. Students may be asked to supplement their core courses by choosing one or more elective courses.

Essay (n) An analytical piece of academic writing that is usually quite short in length. Students are required to write essays as *assignments* and in exams so that their learning can be assessed.

Graduate (n) (adj) 1 (n) A student who has completed a university degree and is studying a higher-level course at post-first degree level. 2 (adj) Used to describe such a student or his/her studies.

Graduate assistant (n) *Graduate* student employed to perform teaching duties such as conducting *seminars*.

Handout (n) Paper-based information that is given out by the professor or speaker in a class. It usually gives a summary, bibliography or extra information connected with the class topic. It may also be a worksheet.

Higher education (n) *Education* that is beyond the level of *secondary education* and that usually offers first and higher degrees. A university is an institution of *higher education*.

Humanities (n) Arts subjects that are concerned with human thought and culture, sometimes known as the liberal arts, such as: philosophy, literature, languages, and history of art. These departments are normally grouped together to form a faculty in a university.

Independent learning (n) Where students take responsibility for their own learning, and are able to develop their personal *learning styles*. It allows students to make decisions and set goals that meet their own needs.

Key concepts (n) Important ideas and *beliefs*. For example, in modern US *academic culture*, *independent learning* is a key concept.

Learning style (n) A style of thinking about, processing and remembering information that you have to learn. Different styles can be classified in a variety of ways. For example, you may have an analytical learning style.

Multiple-choice (adj) Describes a question or task where students are given a set of several possible answers, normally only one of which is correct. They are required to choose the correct answer.

Participate (v) To get involved or take part in something. For example, it is important to participate actively in *seminars*.

Philosophy (n) A system of values or set of *beliefs* that affect how someone lives his/her life.

Plagiarism (n) Presenting someone else's work, i.e., written text, data, images, recording, as your own. This includes:

- copying or paraphrasing material from any source without a citation;
- presenting other people's ideas without a citation;
- working with others and then presenting the work as if it was completed independently.

Plagiarism is not always deliberate, and it is important to adopt the academic conventions of always indicating ideas and work that are not your own, and *referencing* all your sources correctly.

Presentation (n) A short lecture, talk, or demonstration given in front of an audience. The speaker prepares his or her presentation in advance and will often use visual aids or realia to illustrate it.

Reciprocal speech style (n) A description of the speech style where the listener is required to respond immediately to the speaker using a similar style. This is expected in situations such as *seminars* where, for example, a student may respond to a speaker's comments, add information and pose questions.

Reference (n) (v) 1 (n) Acknowledgment of the sources of ideas and information that you use in written work and oral *presentations*. 2 (v) To acknowledge or mention the sources of information.

Research (v) (n) 1 (v) To gather information from a variety of sources and analyse and compare it. 2 (n) Information collected from a variety of sources about a specific topic.

Secondary education (n) Schooling that takes place at middle and high school, usually between grades 6 to 12.

Seminar (n) A small group discussion led by a professor, graduate assistant or guest speaker. Students are expected to take an active part in the seminar.

Social sciences (n) Science subjects that are connected with the study of people in society, including politics, economics, history, anthropology, law, etc. These departments are normally grouped together to form a faculty in a university.

Summa cum Laude degree (n) The highest classification of bachelor degree award that an undergraduate can achieve at a US college or university meaning "with highest praise." Students receive this honor if they score a grade point average (GPA) of over 3.85.

Technique (n) A method or way of doing something that involves skill and/or efficiency. For example, it is possible to learn useful techniques for answering exam questions.

Time management (n) The ability to organize your time so that you use it more effectively and efficiently.

Title analysis (n) The process of breaking an *essay* title into parts in order to identify and highlight *key concepts* and ideas that need to be considered in the *essay*.

Toolkit (n) In academic life, this is a collection of resources, *techniques,* or aids that help you to do something, for example, prepare for an exam.

Undergraduate (n) (adj) 1 (n) A student who is studying for his/her first degree. 2 (adj) Used to describe a first-degree program.

Module 3: Participating in Seminars

Introduction

In higher education, it is necessary to participate in seminars, the smaller group classes that are quite different to lectures. The skills you need to develop in order to lead and participate in group discussions are vital for success at university. They are equally important in many professions and fields of work. The activities and tasks in this module focus on what is involved in effective seminars, and how you can take part fully and effectively.

Units 1 and 2 look at some of the key features of seminars and provide practice in the kind of activities that take place in them. Unit 3 deals with how to plan, research, and discuss a seminar topic, and Unit 4 provides some key language and communication strategies needed for active participation in seminars. Unit 5 looks at the importance of full participation in seminars. Finally, Unit 6 gives an overview of the different kinds of seminars you may meet in higher education, as well as how to get the best out of tutoring sessions.

As you work through this module, you will be able to practice using seminar participation skills, in groups, as you discuss topics such as cloning. After you complete the module, you will be able to participate more confidently in genuine seminars, using appropriate language. You will also be clearer about what is expected of you when you attend seminars in an English-medium university or higher education institute. In addition, you will have better awareness of the differences between the various types of seminar that you may encounter.

Skills Map

Unit 1 — About seminars
Familiarize yourself with the key features of academic seminars.

Unit 2 — What happens in seminars?
Familiarize yourself with some typical seminar activities.

Unit 3 — Subject knowledge
Learn how to prepare thoroughly for the topic through research and reflection.

Unit 4 — The language of seminars
Learn the communication strategies needed to participate confidently and effectively.

Unit 5 — Participation
Practice contributing fully and responding appropriately in an academic environment.

Unit 6 — Different types of seminars
Consider some other types of academic sessions.

Destination: Participating in Seminars

About seminars

At the end of this unit you will be able to:
- **identify some of the key features of seminars.**

Task 1 What are seminars?

Seminars are usually new for people starting out in a university. The experience of most students in high school is of classes led by the teacher, either in a lecture style or a class discussion. The basis for a seminar approach is that students generally learn more when they actively participate in their learning, particularly by listening to each other's views. Not only are students likely to understand the content more fully, but they also remember better what they have learned. Another important point is that seminars provide a forum for finding out the strengths and weaknesses of fellow students and encourage a more supportive atmosphere where views and opinions can be expressed openly.

1.1 **Discuss the words and phrases in the box with another student. Decide what they mean to you, and how they relate to the topic of seminars.**

> active listening   ask questions   clarify
>
> explore a topic   learning experiences   more informal setting
>
> challenge ideas   supporting or conflicting evidence
>
> independent thinking skills   discriminate between facts and opinions
>
> ideas and opinions   actively involved

1.2 **Read and complete the following descriptions with some of the words and ideas you have discussed above. Compare your completed description with another student.**

Seminars provide an opportunity for students to speak, allowing them to ① _____ by asking questions and giving their own ② _____. In seminars, students have the opportunity to meet in small numbers with a professor in a ③ _____, so that ideas can be discussed and complex points can be clarified.

Seminars also encourage participants to develop ④ _____ and speaking skills, and ⑤ _____. These thinking skills include being able to argue, defend, and support a case; being concise and selective in presenting a viewpoint; and being able to ⑥ _____.

Seminars involve groups of students in discussion and study under the guidance of a professor or graduate assistant. An effective seminar requires participants to get ⑦ _____ by contributing appropriately. Skills that participants need in order to contribute well are: being able to ⑧ _____ in order to find out more information or to ⑨ _____ what has been said; to summarize what others have been saying; to listen attentively; to ⑩ _____ at a deeper level; and to give examples of ⑪ _____ .

Task 2 Key features

2.1 **Discuss the following questions with another student. Make notes of your answers and be prepared to present them.**

a) How are seminars different from lectures?

b) What do seminars generally aim to achieve?

c) How are seminars different from debates?

d) What are the advantages of seminars compared with lectures, self-study, or distance learning?

e) What kind of preparation might you need to do to take part in a seminar?

f) What worries do you have as a student about participating in a seminar?

2.2 **Note any questions you have as you listen to other students' ideas. List the skills that you need to use in seminars.**

2.3 Using the information from your discussions, make a list of the DOs and DON'Ts of seminars.

DO	DON'T
Some background reading	Expect to let others do all the work

Reflect

Think about the seminar skills you have experience of from other areas of your academic life so far.

How well do you think you can cope with the aspects of seminars mentioned in this unit?

Decide which skills you think you will have to work on to get the most out of your studies.

Student notes for Unit 1

Unit 2 What happens in seminars?

At the end of this unit you will:
- be familiar with some typical activities that take place in seminars.

Task 1 What exactly are seminars?

1.1   Unit 1 discussed key features of a seminar. With the benefit of reflection, how do you see your role as a student in seminars. Discuss with a partner.

1.2   What do you think these situations describe? Write S for seminar and L for lecture.

a) .... A speaker is using a PowerPoint® presentation, and there are questions, answers, and discussion at the end of the session.

b) .... There is a lot of discussion between the undergraduate students and a graduate student.

c) .... The students all come prepared to make sure they can play their part effectively.

d) .... After the first presentation, the students discuss the ideas in groups before having a feedback session.

e) .... There is not much opportunity to challenge the ideas presented.

f) .... The speaker hands out an outline of notes at the end and then explains what she will do in the following session.

g) .... The students are all eager to listen and participate as this is the only opportunity for input on this important topic.

h) .... It is an enjoyable and interesting overview, so the students are eager to follow up in more depth.

i) .... Notes on the content are sometimes provided in advance.

j) .... A large group of students listen for 45 minutes and take notes.

1.3   Discuss the questions below with a partner.

- Which of the activities and situations described in this task are familiar to you in your college?

- How many hours do you have of different types of classes?

- How useful do you find the different types of sessions, and why?

Task 2 Getting the most out of a seminar

2.1   Seminars may be led by a student rather than a professor. Decide which of the following is true (T) and which is false (F).

a) .... Your role is to teach your fellow students.

b) .... You don't need to cover all aspects of the issue you are presenting.

c) .... You should provoke discussion by giving unsupported opinions.

d) .... It is not a good idea to read from a prepared script.

e) .... You can discuss your own uncertainties.

f) .... Your own view is sufficient as a basis for input.

g) .... A good seminar can be judged by the participation of those attending.

h) .... It takes a long time to prepare a successful seminar.

2.2   How do you think your professors feel about what happens in a seminar? On a scale of 1 to 5 (1 = negative response, 5 = positive response), rate the following points.

Students who:

.... are sometimes absent from seminars

.... never participate

.... dominate a session

.... speak with an accent

.... are good presenters

.... are very well-dressed

.... are frequently absent from seminars

.... have not done the reading for the seminar

.... display their knowledge successfully

.... ask questions

.... are happy to collaborate with other students

.... do not finish assignments on time

2.3 Even if you are not running the seminar, you are still expected to participate fully. Below are some of the skills that you may need to use. Evaluate how good you are at them.

Check the skills you are already good at like this: ✓✓

Check the skills you would like to work on like this: ✓

.... providing a list of sources to help participants do further research

.... researching and reading information about a topic

.... reading aloud from notes or articles

.... reading a page or pages quickly, looking for the main points

.... discussing ideas and solving problems

.... giving a clear presentation

.... arguing a point of view

.... agreeing or disagreeing with other points of view

.... listening and note-taking

.... summarizing the main point of an argument

.... writing a report or summary

2.4 Self-evaluation: Rate yourself on the following skills and compare your answers with another student.

Skill	Weak	OK	Good	Excellent
listening to what other people say				
contributing to an informal discussion				
contributing to a formal seminar				
making a presentation with classmates				
giving feedback to classmates				
asking a professor for help				
knowing how to be an effective group member				
knowing how to deal with difficulties in a group				
receiving criticism				
negotiating with classmates and professors				
planning and presenting a seminar paper				

Reflect

What aspects of participation do you think you need to improve? Make a list of some priority areas for personal development and improvement.

Student notes for Unit 2

Unit 3 Subject knowledge

At the end of this unit you will be able to:
- plan input and prepare for a seminar more effectively.

Task 1 Preparing for a seminar

1.1 Read the advice for new students below. Then say whether statements a) to h) are true (T), false (F) or probably true (P). Where you are not sure, or if there is no information, put a question mark (?). Compare your ideas with another student.

Advice for new students

To get the most from seminars you must prepare well. Make sure that you analyze the topic and think about it so you know what the main issues are, making notes as you go. Fill in any gaps in your knowledge by doing the recommended reading and checking the references. Find out in advance the professor's s exact requirements for a seminar. For instance, you could be expected to:

- do some reading beforehand;
- give your opinions on the recommended reading;
- present a written paper;
- present a paper orally from notes;
- send out a written version of your paper beforehand to everybody who will attend;
- lead a discussion on what the speaker has said;
- take part in a discussion with other students and the professor;
- summarize what has been said orally or in writing;
- hand in a written paper about a week after the seminar.

Remember, seminars are for your benefit! Use summaries and notes to help you to remember information. The more actively you prepare and participate, the more you will learn!

a) _____ Professors organize seminars in advance and provide clear guidelines about what is expected of you.

b) _____ It is better to attend a seminar than miss it, even if you haven't prepared.

c) _____ You are all expected to contribute equally.

d) _____ Lack of preparation means that you probably won't learn anything in seminars.

e) _____ You should memorize what you are going to say before the seminar.

f) _____ You could prepare for a seminar with other students, sharing the work.

g) _____ At some point you will need to do some writing.

h) _____ It is not necessary to do anything after a seminar.

Task 2 Thinking about, researching, and discussing issues

2.1 Imagine you are going to attend the following seminar.

CLONING
FOR and AGAINST

Seminar—everybody welcome

7:00 p.m
Wednesday November 12, 2008
Lincoln Lecture Theater

Analyze the topic. What are the main issues involved? Read the definitions below and underline the important information.

1) **Clone:** An exact copy of an animal or plant that has the same DNA as the original animal or plant, because it was produced from one cell of that animal or plant.

   Longman Advanced American Dictionary

2) **Cloning** is the process of creating an identical copy of an original. A clone in the biological sense, therefore, is a single cell (like bacteria, lymphocytes, etc.) or multi-cellular organism that is genetically identical to another living organism.

   http://en.wikipedia.org/wiki/Cloning

3) **A clone** is a group of genetically identical organisms. Many plants are easily cloned; they can be grown from cuttings. Higher animals are more difficult to clone; the only cells in mammals that are capable of growing naturally into a new mammal are fertilized eggs or cells from very early embryos—up to the stage where the embryo consists of just eight cells.

   http://biotechterms.org

4) Using specialized DNA technology to produce multiple, exact copies of a single gene or other segment of DNA to obtain enough material for further study. This process, used by researchers in the Human Genome Project, is referred to as cloning DNA. The resulting cloned (copied) collections of DNA molecules are called clone libraries. A second type of cloning exploits the natural process of cell division to make many copies of an entire cell.

   www.cdc.gov/genomics/gtesting/file/print/FBR/glossary.pdf

2.2　Read about the PMI method for structuring thought and think about how it could help you make decisions.

PMI stands for Plus/Minus/Interesting and is one of the thinking tools devised by Edward de Bono. It is a method of structuring thought before reaching a decision about an issue or idea. To use the method, you make a list of plus points (P) in favor of the idea, a list of minus points (M) against the idea, and points that are interesting (I) that you wish to consider or discuss. The interesting ideas need not be plus or minus, but simply worth thinking about. The PMI method is to help you explore an issue before coming to a decision.

www.edwdebono.com

P (Plus points, arguments, and ideas for)	M (Minus points, arguments, and ideas against)	I (Interesting points, arguments, and ideas that don't easily fit into the other two columns)
e.g.	e.g.	e.g.

2.3　Read these articles on cloning and make notes.

- http://learn.genetics.utah.edu/units/cloning/whatiscloning
- http://learn.genetics.utah.edu/units/cloning/clissues/
- http://bioteach.ubc.ca/TeachingResources/Genetics/ProsConsCloning/AnticloningBrochure.doc

2.4　Use the PMI method to help you clarify your thoughts on the issue of cloning. When you have completed the table above, think about how it has affected your opinion. Then discuss the issues with another student.

Task 3 Establishing and supporting your opinion

Once you have thought about an issue and done some background reading, you will be able to establish your own opinion on the subject. In other words, are you for or against cloning?

3.1   In no more than three sentences, explain why you are for or against cloning.

3.2   Think back to the issues you identified in 2.1. Have you addressed these in your sentences?

3.3   Work in a group and compare your explanations.

3.4   You need to decide on your point of view on the main issues and then try to provide evidence to support your opinions. You will need to give some:

- explanations;
- arguments relating to your viewpoint;
- examples.

Read the opinion below and complete the first entry in the table.

"In the past, biological diversity has prevented species from being wiped out by diseases such as the Black Death. Clones decrease the diversity of the animal and plant life because they are identical to the parent organism. I believe that cloning would reduce the adaptability and could even threaten the survival of many species."

3.5 Now think of some more arguments for and against cloning. Use the information in the articles to help.

Argument/issue	For/ against	Explanation	Effect	Evidence or examples
cloning would reduce biodiversity		clones are genetically identical to the parent organism so lack diversity	survival will be threatened if organisms have less diversity	

Reflect

What are the steps needed to prepare successfully for a seminar? Make a checklist. Which ones do you think would be most difficult for you, and why?

Student notes for Unit 3

Unit 4 The language of seminars

At the end of this unit you will:
- have developed a range of communication skills and strategies to help you take part effectively in group discussions.

Task 1 Useful language for contributing to group discussions

Your ability to contribute confidently in small-group classes depends on having a wide range of communication strategies. The language you need to use may be more formal, more tentative, or more polite than you are accustomed to using in other situations (e.g., socializing).

1.1 Look at the categories below. What can you think of to say in these situations?

Asking questions in seminars and group discussions
1 Asking a question
2 Asking for repetition when you haven't heard what has been said
3 Asking for clarification when you haven't completely understood the message
4 Asking someone to be more specific

Stating opinions and summarizing

1 Disagreeing with what has been said

2 Adding something to what has just been said

3 Agreeing with what has been said

4 Summarizing what has been said

1.2 Look at these expressions and put them in the correct category in the tables above. Compare your answers with another student.

a) I'd just like to add ...

b) If I might interrupt for a moment, ...

c) X put it very well when he/she said ...

d) Could you explain what you meant when you said that ...?

e) On balance ...

f) I didn't quite catch that.

g) Excuse me, ...

h) I'm afraid I didn't follow your point about ... Could you go over that again?

i) You mentioned X.

j) I see what you mean, but ...

k) Could you go over what you said about ...?

l) Overall ...

m) I have a question about X.

n) To summarize, ...

o) Could you repeat that, please?

p) I would like to ask you something about X.

q) You have a point there, but ...

r) I don't agree that ...

s) X raised some important points.

t) Certainly it's true that ..., but on the other hand ...

u) I fully agree with X.

v) Can I check that I've understood ...?

Task 2 Communication strategies in context

2.1 **Look at the following situations from seminars. Write at least two examples of things you could say. Use the expressions from Task 1, or any others that you think are appropriate, to help you.**

a) You are distracted because you have just remembered something important you have forgotten to do. You realize that people are looking at you, but you have no idea of what has just been said. What could you say?

b) You are trying hard to follow a complicated argument from a fellow student, but he/she is using technical terminology you have never heard before. What could you say?

c) You have followed the speaker's argument, but you need to know the answer to a question before he/she goes any further and you get lost, worrying about your question. What could you say? (Hint: Tell the speaker you have a question, and say what the topic is. Then ask the question.)

d) You completely disagree with the opinions of a speaker. How could you challenge him/her appropriately?

e) You agree with what a speaker has just said, but you have something important that you wish to say.

f) You feel that you have something really important to add to the discussion. How could you interrupt appropriately in order to make your point?

g) You have been asked to give a summary of what has been discussed. How could you do this?

h) You have had a problem understanding some of the ideas in the seminar, and the professor asks you a question. What do you say?

i) You have forgotten to prepare the text before the seminar, and the text is difficult to understand during the session. What could you say in a group discussion?

Task 3 Practice using communication strategies

3.1 You are going to practice using the expressions you have encountered so far, and try out any others that occur to you.

Read the statements below and discuss them with another student. Try to use some of the expressions from Task 2. If you can, record your discussion. Otherwise, try to remember which expressions were used.

1) "The political impact of the use of the English language globally is negligible."

2) "Politics is not important to the average person in the street."

3) "It is more efficient to use translators in international meetings than for everyone to speak one international language."

4) "Space exploration is a waste of money."

5) "The role of the UN is not useful in the modern world."

3.2 Think about the language you used in your discussion and complete the table with the expressions you used.

Agree (reasons?)	Disagree (reasons?)	Clarify questions	Follow-up questions for further discussion

Task 4 Language activation

4.1 Check back and review the language from the unit so far. How well can you do the following?

- agree
- disagree
- give reasons and examples
- ask for repetition
- ask a question
- interrupt
- make an excuse
- summarize points
- introduce a topic to a group
- present a basic argument

4.2 **Look at the following roles.**

- Person A will propose a statement and give reasons why they agree with the idea.
- Person B will challenge the statement and give reasons why they disagree with the idea.
- Person C will ask questions to clarify what is being said.
- Person D will ask follow-up questions and will take notes.

Now, in groups, select roles and choose a statement from the ones below for your first practice. Follow the instructions for your chosen role and discuss the statement for five minutes.

Topic statements

1) Overall, tourism is a destructive force.

2) There should be complete freedom of information on the Internet.

3) Despite a higher standard of living, people in Western societies are becoming more unhappy.

4) Increasing multiculturalism is a threat to stability.

5) The car is the most dangerous invention ever.

6) A country's expenditure on education should be greater than its spending on the military.

4.3 Now change roles for your second and third practices. Follow the instructions for your chosen role (A, B, C, or D) and discuss a different statement for five minutes each.

Reflect

Which role did you find the easiest? Which was most difficult, and why? Which communication strategies are you most and least familiar with, and how can you improve in these areas?

Student notes for Unit 4

5 Participation

At the end of this unit you will:
- **have developed and practiced some communication strategies for seminar participation.**

Task 1 Getting involved

1.1 Look at the following types of academic activities. Have you done these activities before? What skills does each of them involve?

- after a lecture, following up some questions and preparing answers

- after a lecture, reading one or more articles and then writing an essay

- writing an essay before a seminar and then reading or presenting it

- reading a text and making notes before a seminar

- researching a topic and bringing information with you to a session

- making an individual presentation on a topic

- working with a group of other students to prepare a talk or a project

1.2 With your instructor's help, your group or class is going to choose an area that will form the basis of a mini-seminar. You could use one of the topics suggested in Unit 4, or you could choose a topic that you think is interesting or that is relevant to your subject area. You will need to work in groups. Before you practice the seminar, you will need to think about the stages and do some preparation in your groups.

Discuss the following in your groups.

- identify a suitable topic area

- divide the topic into different sections

- choose a group/seminar leader

- decide who is going to look at which aspects

- decide where and how you will do the research (library, Internet, etc.)

- do some background research on the topic (your instructor will help you with some references)

- organize any materials that you will need for the seminar

- prepare materials to bring with you to the seminar

- decide how you are going to work as a team during the seminar

Task 2 More preparation: Roles and stages

Chairing a session

Although all students are expected to participate in seminars, one may be asked to introduce the subject and lead the other students in the discussion, encouraging participation by asking questions or inviting contributions. This is called "taking the chair" or "chairing" the discussion. If you are chosen to be the chairperson, you must be prepared to keep the discussion moving so that the seminar will be a success.

What skills and strategies that you have studied might be needed as a chairperson?

Match and add to the ideas below. (Note: There may be more than one answer.)

a) Ask an individual student ...	**1)** the topic.
b) Paraphrase ...	**2)** a new topic.
c) Summarize ...	**3)** the key issues.
d) Ask for ...	**4)** an answer or an argument.
e) Thank ...	**5)** someone for their answer or ideas.
f) Introduce ...	**6)** clarification of an argument or statement.
g) Outline ...	**7)** the main issues raised in the seminar.
h) Provide …	**8)** an argument and ask for reactions.
	9) for their opinion.
	10) evidence to support an argument.
	11) clear examples.

Other ideas:

2.2 Discuss which strategies the chair could use for each of the situations listed in the table, and then suggest exactly what the chair could say, for example in a seminar on cloning. Refer back to Unit 4 Task 1 for help.

Situation	Strategy What should the chair do?	Statement/Question What could the chair say?
Beginning of the seminar	e.g., introduce the topic	Good morning, everyone. As you know, the topic for today's seminar is cloning. We are going to be discussing the arguments for and against cloning. I'd like to start by ...
No one speaks		
One person dominates		
Someone doesn't say anything or doesn't appear to		
Someone makes a statement but gives no support		
Someone gives a long, complicated answer		
The discussion has focused on only one aspect of the topic		
The discussion wanders off topic		
The end of the seminar		

Task 3 Seminar role play

3.1   Now you have done the preparation for the seminar, you need to carry it out! You should allow a minimum of 20 minutes for your group to present and discuss the materials you have prepared.

Task 4 What kind of contributor am I?

4.1   Think about your contribution to the debate/seminar in Task 3 above. Evaluate how well you do the activities on the left and how you could improve your skills and your performance. Rate yourself, compare your ratings with another student and identify any action/improvement points.

How good am I?	1 = improvement needed 5 = excellent	Action needed
Am I well-prepared?		
Do I contribute?		
Am I a good listener?		
Can I argue a point?		
Do I support others?		
Do I ask relevant questions?		
Do I say enough?		
Are my language skills good?		
Can I chair a session?		
Do I work well with others?		
Can I make a presentation?		
Can I do any follow-up tasks?		

4.2   Monitoring your participation: the observer's viewpoint.

Instructors will be assessing how much and how well everybody participates in a seminar, not just the chair. Seminars help professors to evaluate students' knowledge and academic skills. In some cases, you may be formally assessed on your performance, so it is vital that you take the opportunity to participate fully.

4.2.1 Look back to the discussions and issues in this module. Look at the list below and decide how well you do these things.

Communication and participation

Student …

1   arrives on time.

2   has the necessary paperwork with them.

3   has done the required preparation.

4   uses appropriate language strategies, e.g., asks someone to repeat what they have said or to clarify a point.

5   asks relevant questions.

6   agrees and disagrees and can give full reasons.

7   backs up opinions with suitable arguments.

8   listens well.

9   works well with others.

10   takes notes.

11   presents points fluently and uses accurate English.

12   understands the main points of the seminar.

13   does the required homework.

14   is good with technology.

4.2.2. Which of the points above do you think are most important from the professor's point of view?

List your ideas below.

Reflect

After the seminar, think about your participation. Ask a colleague or instructor about your performance. How effectively did you participate? How could you improve next time?

Student notes for Unit 5

6 Different types of seminars

At the end of this unit you will:
- be more aware of the different types of seminars that you may participate in in higher education.

Task 1 Seminar activities

1.1 Below is a list of some of the main types of activities related to seminars. Make sure you understand what they are and how they are different from one another.

For each one, decide what you would have to do <u>in advance</u> of the session and/or what you would have to do <u>during</u> the session.

Which activities would you find difficult and which would you find easy?

Seminars

a) **Everyone in the group discusses a text they have read.**

Before: *Read text and make notes of key points/questions.*

During: *Listen to others and give opinions, agree/disagree, ask questions.*

b) **You present a paper.**

Before:

During:

c) **Another student presents a paper.**

Before:

During:

d) **A guest speaker gives a talk followed by discussion.**

Before:

During:

e) **You give an informal presentation with several other students.**

Before:

During:

f) You read a text during the seminar and discuss the topic.

Before: ....

During: ....

g) You have to lead a seminar.

Before: ....

During: ....

Task 2 Example activity: Giving a presentation

2.1 Brainstorm six important things you should do in order to give an effective presentation. Make a list. Compare your list with another student.

....

....

....

....

....

2.2 Now look at the following list and divide the advice into DOs and DON'Ts. Fill in the numbers in the appropriate boxes underneath the list.

1 Make sure you write everything down so you can read it out clearly.

2 Organize your presentation into main sections, with a clear beginning and end.

3 Always look at your visual aids when you are talking.

4 Always use PowerPoint®.

5 Make sure you don't run over time.

6 Practice your timing and your breathing.

7 Use prompt cards to help you structure the talk.

8 Give handouts to the audience.

9 Repeat your main points at the end.

10 Give clear examples to illustrate your main points.

11 Arrive in the room at the same time as the audience.

12 You are the most important person in the room.

13 It is better to have too much to say than not very much.

14 Wait at the end for questions.

15 Speak as quickly as you can—that way you cover more material.

16 Practice your presentation once or twice—too many times will make it stale.

Yes	No

For more information on giving presentations see *TASK Module 11: Presentations*.

Task 3 Tutoring sessions and advisee meetings

3.1 Read the list of activities that you might do in a tutoring session or advisee meeting. Discuss what other activities you might do at such meetings and complete the list.

Tutorials

a) **You, a tutor and two other students discuss a topic.**

Before: _____

During: _____

b) **A tutor helps you, on your own, to prepare a piece of writing.**

Before: _____

During: _____

c) **You go to see a tutor about a personal problem.**

Before: _____

During: _____

d) _____

Before: _____

During: _____

e) _____

Before: _____

During: _____

3.2   Tutoring sessions and advisee meetings do not happen in the same way in all institutions, but they are quite common in many higher education institutions. They are often done on a one-on-one basis and can be used for a variety of purposes. Some of these purposes are listed below.

- student support
- individual progress
- academic problems
- personal problems (e.g., health)
- living problems (e.g., accommodation)
- assessment
- assignment support

Think about the following questions.

a)   How often are you likely to have a tutoring session or advisee meeting?

_____

b)   Are such meetings likely to be optional or mandatory?

_____

c)   What experience have you had of academic support in the past and how helpful (or not) has it been?

_____

d)   How much should you participate in tutoring sessions?

_____

3.3   Advisee meetings are often used to help students with personal and study questions and problems. Using your experience, what specific advice could you offer to a student on the following situations?

- bullying by another student
- cheating and plagiarism
- illness
- poor attendance
- help with assignments
- progression questions
- support with academic work
- dissatisfaction with a particular class or professor

Unit 6

Reflect

Think about your past experience of how you have used academic support systems.
Are you the kind of student who needs or likes active support? Which areas of higher education do you think you will need most support with? What are the advantages to you of using the system well?

Student notes for Unit 6

Module 3

Web work

> **Website 1** | **The pros and cons of cloning**
>
> http://www.ornl.gov/sci/techresources/Human_Genome/elsi/cloning.shtml
>
> **Review**
> This website contains a wide range of resources on the topic of cloning.
>
> **Task**
> Use this website to do some background reading on cloning in preparation for the seminar. Be sure to look at both pro- and anti-cloning arguments. If you would like more information, follow the links provided.

> **Website 2** | **Seminars, tutoring sessions, and workshops**
>
> http://www.bbc.co.uk/gloucestershire/students/2002/10/studyskills2.shtml
>
> **Review**
> This website contains more interesting tips on tutoring sessions and seminars.
>
> **Task**
> What other tips can you find for participating effectively in an academic seminar?

Extension activities

> **Activity 1** | **Application of seminar skills**
>
> Present your ideas on a topic that you are studying to the rest of your group. Initiate discussion about the topic. Choose a topic that is relevant to you. For example, you could use an essay topic that you are currently researching.
>
> Preparing for a seminar will allow you to think carefully about the topic and test your own knowledge. Follow these steps:
>
> * make notes on what you already know;
> * do some research and add to your notes;
> * decide on the order in which you want to present your ideas and arguments;
> * think about how other students are likely to respond to your arguments and how to facilitate an interesting discussion, e.g., questions you could ask.

Consider how seminar skills transfer to professional life.

- Make a list of the skills you use when you participate in a seminar.
- In what situations would you apply these skills at work?
- What differences would there be?
- How could you demonstrate your mastery of these skills to a potential employer?

Glossary

Active listening (n) Listening in a way that shows you are giving your full attention to the speaker. The listener is able to demonstrate comprehension and give the speaker the impression that he/she is being understood.

Analyze (v) To break an issue down into parts in order to study, identify, and discuss their meaning and/or relevance.

Background reading (n) Reading around a topic in order to get a general picture or overview of the subject in preparation for a class, *seminar,* or more focused *research* into a specific area. Background reading enables a student to form questions and participate more actively in a seminar.

Bibliography (n) A list of *references* to sources cited in the text of a piece of academic writing or a book. A bibliography should consist of an alphabetical list of books, papers, journal articles, and websites and is usually found at the end of the work. It may also include texts suggested by the author for further reading.

Chair (of a discussion) (n) (v) 1 (n) Someone who takes a controlling role in a formal meeting. 2 (v) To do some or all of the following: take responsibility for the agenda of the meeting, lead the discussion, decide when to introduce new items, call on different group members, and summarize the discussion.

Collaborate (v) To work together with another person (or other people) on a piece of work or an assignment.

Communication skills (n) Skills that enable you to listen, talk, and write to other people effectively. Good communication skills allow you to make a positive impression, participate well in discussions, and convey ideas clearly.

Debate (n) (v) 1 (n) A formal discussion, often about serious issues or problems. A debate is structured so that speakers with opposing viewpoints take turns to state their opinions and answer questions in front of an audience. 2 (v) To participate in a discussion with someone who has an opposing viewpoint.

Distance learning (n) A type of learning in which the student participates from home. The student is more autonomous and communicates with the professor and classmates electronically and/or by mail.

Evaluate (v) To assess information in terms of quality, relevance, objectivity, and accuracy.

Fact (n) Something that is known or can be demonstrated to be true.

Graduate (n) (adj) 1 (n) A student who has completed a university degree and is studying a higher-level course at post-first degree level. 2 (adj) Used to describe such a student or his/her studies.

Handout (n) Paper-based information that is given out by the professor or speaker in a class, *seminar* or *tutoring session*. It usually gives a summary, *bibliography* or extra information connected with the *lecture* topic. It may also be a worksheet.

Higher education (n) Education that is beyond the level of secondary education and usually offers Bachelor's and higher degrees. A university is an institution of higher education.

Lecture (n) A formal talk or *presentation* given to inform or instruct people. In higher education, lectures are usually delivered by academic staff to large groups of students.

Opinion (n) A personal belief that may be subjective and is not based on certainty or fact.

Overview (n) A general summary of a subject.

Personal tutoring session (n) A *tutoring session* that is designed to give advice, guidance, and support to students. It may be requested by the student if he/she has a personal problem, or it may be built in to the program to give feedback on progress.

PMI method (n) A method of structuring thoughts or reaching a decision about an issue or idea. To use the method, you make a list of plus points (P) in favor of the idea, a list of minus points (M) against the idea, and points that are interesting (I) and that you wish to consider or discuss.

Presentation (n) A short lecture, talk, or demonstration given in front of an audience. The speaker prepares his or her presentation in advance and will often use visual aids or realia to illustrate it.

Professor (n) A senior faculty member of staff at a university. A professor is responsible for giving classes and *seminars* as well as conducting *research* in his or her own field.

Reciprocal speech style (n) A description of the speech style where the listener is required to respond immediately to the speaker using a similar style. This is expected in situations such as *seminars* where, for example, a student may respond to a speaker's comments, add information and pose questions.

Reference (n) (v) 1 (n) Acknowledgment of the sources of ideas and information that you use in written work and oral *presentations*. 2 (v) To acknowledge or mention the sources of information.

Research (v) (n) 1 (v) To gather information from a variety of sources and *analyze* and compare it. 2 (n) Information collected from a variety of sources about a specific topic.

Self-evaluation (n) The process of testing and assessing your own performance or progress in order to decide which areas you need to work on, and/or select for future study or employment.

Seminar (n) A small group discussion led by a professor or guest speaker. Students are expected to take an active part in the seminar.

Social sciences (n) Science subjects that are connected with the study of people in society, including politics, economics, history, anthropology, law, etc. These departments are normally grouped together to form a faculty in a university.

Strategy (n) A plan of action that you follow when you want to achieve a particular goal. For example, it is possible to have a clear strategy for passing an exam.

Summative assessment (n) Assessed assignments and/or tests taken at the end of a course to see how much a student has learned, which counts towards a final grade.

Tutoring session (n) A small group discussion or one-on-one meeting with a tutor.

Undergraduate (n) (adj) 1 (n) A student who is studying for his/her first degree. 2 (adj) Used to describe a first degree course.

Module 4: Teamworking

Introduction

Most students will be familiar with the importance of teamwork in everyday life, but many students will be unfamiliar with working in teams in an academic environment. Traditionally, it is your work alone that is assessed at school or in higher education, particularly on an exam or test. Increasingly, however, students are being asked to take part in assessed group work at various levels of study. This reflects a recognition of the value of and need for teamwork, both in the workplace and in everyday life.

This module will take you through some tasks that will clarify the importance of teamwork in various aspects of academic study. It will also encourage you to examine and evaluate your own strengths and weaknesses as a team member.

In Units 1 and 2 you will have the chance to try out some team activities and analyze how effectively you worked together. These units also introduce you to the different roles and skills involved in teamwork and explore the benefits and potential problems that can occur. Unit 3 looks more closely at functions such as making suggestions, agreeing and disagreeing, questioning and summarizing in team discussions. Units 4 and 5 examine interaction patterns and how they differ in various cultures and contexts. They aim to raise awareness of ways of maintaining balanced interaction in team conversations. Finally, Unit 6 looks at how teamwork can aid different study activities.

Participating in and observing various team activities in the module will raise your awareness of the skills, techniques, and strategies that are needed for effective interaction. By the end of the module, you will also have a clearer idea of the purpose and benefits of team collaboration.

Skills Map

Teamwork in action
Find out about the different skills and roles involved in teamwork by taking part in an active teamwork exercise.

Why teamwork?
Explore the benefits and potential problems of teamwork.

Effective team membership
Examine verbal and non-verbal strategies for participating in a team discussion.

Interactive dialogue
Consider differences in culture and interaction patterns that may affect teamwork.

Encouraging interaction
Consider what kinds of strategies and techniques encourage and discourage effective team participation.

Ways of working with others
Become more aware of the benefits of collaborative study.

Destination: Teamworking

Teamwork in action

At the end of this unit you will:
- understand key considerations when working in teams;
- be more aware of how teamworking involves and develops different skills.

There are many advantages to working in a team. In this unit you will be working with members of your class on a variety of tasks and evaluating the benefits of brainstorming and sharing ideas.

Task 1 Factors to consider when working as a team

Robbins (2001) defines a team as a group whose individual efforts result in a performance that is greater than the sum of those individual parts.

1.1 Discuss the following with another student:

    a) what you understand by *greater than the sum of those individual parts*;

    b) factors to take into account when working as a team. (Think about individual abilities, setting, time factors, etc.);

    c) your own preferences for working alone or as part of a team.

1.2 Work in a group of three to five people. Make a list of things that people usually do in teams, for example, playing games and puzzles.

1.3 Once you have established a list, discuss why it is useful or necessary to do the things on your list in a team. Establish a number of criteria.

Task 2 Do a teamwork activity

You are now going to complete some puzzles, working as a team, and then reflect on how effectively your team was able to carry out tasks.

2.1 Work in groups of four or five. Choose one member of the group to be an observer. You have 20 minutes to complete 16 puzzles. Your instructor will time you.

Team task

Work together to find a solution to each puzzle and explain your conclusions.

Observer's task

Evaluate the teamworking skills of your group and make notes on the answer sheet on the next page. Refer to the answer sheet for the puzzles during the observation.

a) This time last week I was the owner of a CD player, 100 CDs, 20 records, and 50 DVDs. On Saturday night I came home to find that a burglar had taken all but ten of the CDs, 12 of the records, and 40 of the DVDs. How many CDs have I got left?

b) What can be found in the middle of Paris, that can't be found in London or Milan?

c) One man carries three sacks of corn on his back, and another has four sacks on his back. Which of them has the heavier load?

d) When the fire alarm rang in the ten-story office where he works, John didn't go down the stairs, but jumped out of the nearest window. How did he survive?

e) If it takes three minutes for an egg to boil in a two-liter pan of saltwater, how long will it take to boil three eggs in the same pan?

f) If you have a bucket of water (A) at 10 degrees centigrade and another bucket (B) at 10 degrees Fahrenheit, and drop a 20-nickel coin into each, which coin will be the first to reach the bottom of the bucket?

g) When asked which half of an apple he would like, 12-year-old Simon replied, "the bigger half". On hearing this, his 13-year-old sister Lucy, who had been studying superlatives at school, replied, "What you mean is the biggest half". Who was right?

h) After passing her driving test, Clare was on her way home, feeling very proud and not really focusing on where she was going. She went straight across a crosswalk and the wrong way up a one-way street. Her driving instructor and a policewoman saw her, but they didn't stop her or seem surprised. Why?

i) The number of bacteria in a large sealed jar doubles every minute. An hour after the first bacterium was put into the jar and sealed in, the jar was full. When was it half full?

j) The verb *to be* is extraordinary in that it has three different singular forms: *I am*, *you are*, *he/she/it is*. Is it ever possible to say *I is*?

k) Even if we never win a gold medal at the Olympics, or get into the *Guinness Book of World Records*, there is one record that each person holds at one point in his or her life. What is it?

l) How many new $10 bills, measuring 5 inches by 2 inches, could you fit without overlapping between pages 33 and 34 of a hardback book measuring 10 inches by 6 inches?

m) There are four pairs of blue socks and three pairs of red socks in a drawer. In the dark, how many socks must you take out of the drawer to be sure of getting a matching pair?

n) What is twice two-thirds of three-quarters of ten?

o) In the first week of the summer harvest, Farmer Smith put six hay bales in one field and five in another. Each week during the four-week-long harvest, he added six hay bales to each field. How many piles of hay would he end up with if, at the end of the harvest, he put them all together in one field?

p) Imagine you are an alien who has managed to learn the English language, but does not know the significance of the days of the week. Think about the English names for days of the week. On which day of the week would you assume:

- you would cook a meal?
- you would have to make decisions?
- you would get married?
- it would be unusually bright?

	Observer's comments
Did all the members of the team contribute or did some members dominate?	
What were the team's strengths and weaknesses?	
What techniques did they use to solve the problems?	
How well did the team keep to time?	
What was the team's score?	

2.2 Debrief: Follow the instructions below.

Observer's task

Give the team the answers and feedback.

Team task

Respond to the comments made by the observer. Use the following questions to help you focus.

- Do you agree with the observer?
- Would the task have gone better if some members of the group had changed their roles?
- How effectively did the group work as a team?

Task 3 What have you learned about roles and teamwork?

3.1 Imagine you are managing a team of five in a business situation. In your teams, decide how you would allocate roles for different members of the team. Choose one of the following situations and give reasons.

a) designing a car

b) finding out about a competitor's product

c) organizing a conference

3.2 Discussion: In your teams, devise a set of five rules for working as a team. Think about the points below to help your discussion.

fairness   competition   motivation   learning styles   goals of activity

Reflect

Think about the team activity you carried out. What do you feel was the most memorable aspect of it? Has it changed any of your ideas about working in a team?

Evaluate your team's performance and how well you participated. Work out what your strengths are and what you need to work on to improve your teamworking skills.

Student notes for Unit 1

Unit 2 Why teamwork?

At the end of this unit you will:
- be more aware of the benefits and potential problems of working in a team.

Task 1 What are the benefits of teamwork?

If we look at the creative, academic, and political worlds, it is clear that teamwork plays an important role. It is useful to focus on the benefits of working in teams to improve your own ability to participate in a team.

1.1 Work in groups of three. Think of a talented individual who you admire, for example, a film star, a musician, or a politician. Fill in the following grid. You have ten minutes.

	Name of individual
1. What individual skills and talents does he/she possess?	
2. How much does he/she rely on others to bring out these skills?	
3. How much does he/she contribute to the overall success of a team?	

1.2 When you have finished, discuss your thoughts with another group. Is there anything that you could add to your grid?

1.3 How have the individuals you discussed benefited from association with a team?

Task 2 What are the problems of teamwork?

2.1 Despite the advantages of teamwork, problems can sometimes occur. In groups, find examples of teams that might have difficulty working together. List reasons why problems might have arisen.

Too many cooks spoil the broth.

Team	Reason
E.g., a political party	Too many people involved who have very different ideas about how a country should be run.
Team 1	
Team 2	
Team 3	

2.2 Discuss your examples with another group and adjust your notes if you wish.

2.3 Back in your groups, discuss the advantages and disadvantages of working together. When might you choose to work alone? When is it better to work in a team?

Task 3 Evaluate a team activity

3.1 Your instructor will provide each group with an object. Think of an alternative use for it and complete the table below. The other teams will vote on the most creative idea.

Name of object	
Use	
Marketability	
Price/value	
Durability	

3.2 Discuss the questions below with your team.

a) What role did you have in the discussion?

b) Who came up with the various ideas?

c) Did you agree with the final outcome, or would you have preferred a different result?

Reflect

Think about how you can work as a team and still be an individual, and how you might avoid having bad experiences working as part of a team. What advice would you give to someone who was having problems working in a team?

Student notes for Unit 2

Unit 3 Effective team membership

At the end of this unit you will:
- be able to identify verbal and non-verbal clues during a conversation;
- have received practice in taking notes.

Task 1 Using verbal and non-verbal information

When we speak to other people we give verbal and non-verbal clues to indicate our thoughts and feelings. This can vary from culture to culture, so it is important to identify commonalities and differences.

1.1   In the left-hand column of the table below is a list of conversational strategies. In the right-hand column is a list of clues. Match the examples in the right-hand column to the actions.

Strategies	Clue
1. Encouraging	a) I think we should develop Yang's idea about ...
2. Building on others' ideas	b) I don't believe that's such a good idea.
3. Including all members	c) Why don't we ...?
4. Showing agreement	d) Do you think that's possible?
5. Showing disagreement	e) That's a good idea.
6. Asking questions	f) We can conclude that ...
7. Making suggestions	g) I agree.
8. Offering information	h) It says here that the most popular form of entertainment is ...
9. Summarizing	i) Does everyone agree?
10.	
11.	
12.	
13.	
14.	

1.2   As a team, discuss the following two questions.

   a)   Are the above strategies used in your culture? If so, how are they communicated?

   b)   What differences did you discover between the various cultures in your group?

1.3   In spaces 10 to 14 of the grid opposite, add more ideas and examples that you think are important to mention.

1.4   Look at the strategies in 1.1 and decide which ones could be communicated in a non-verbal way and how. Then think of five strategies that are usually conveyed non-verbally and how that is done.

Task 2 Group observation

2.1   **Work as a team. Choose one member as an observer and one member as a secretary to write down the conclusions of the team discussion. You have 15 minutes for the discussion.**

   Discussion group: Books shut, discuss the question: Which is the greatest city in the world? Think about architecture, people, food, history, etc. Don't just choose your own city. Be objective. Give reasons for your choice.

   Secretary: Listen to the discussion and complete Grid A.

   Observer: Listen to the discussion and complete Grid B.

   Grid A

| The greatest city in the world -- |
| Architecture |
| People |
| Food |
| History |
| Weather |
| Other |

Grid B

Skill	Group member	Example
1. Encouraging verbally		
2. Encouraging non-verbally		
3. Building on others' ideas		
4. Including all members		
5. Showing agreement		
6. Showing disagreement		
7. Asking questions		
8. Making suggestions		
9. Offering information		
10. Summarizing		

2.2 Debrief: Look at the observer's notes and discuss how the group interacted. Talk about the following points.

   a) Was the discussion restricted or did you talk about different things?

   b) How did group members make it clear that they agreed?

   c) How did they make it clear that they disagreed?

   d) Was anyone very persuasive?

   e) Did anyone try to dominate the discussion?

   f) Were certain people addressed more than others?

Reflect

You were asked to be objective in Task 2. This should have meant that you distanced yourself from the topic rather than being subjective, or personally involved.

Keeping this in mind, do you think it is easier to be objective or subjective about something that interests you? How do you think this affected your contribution to the discussion? Do you feel you were judged fairly by the observer?

Student notes for Unit 3

4 Interactive dialogue

At the end of this unit you will have:
* discussed cultural differences and how to deal with them;
* considered the importance of maintaining balanced interaction in conversation.

Task 1 Cultural differences

1.1 Cultural stereotypes can influence a person's judgment, perception and behavior. With a partner, discuss the following questions.

a) What differences do you notice when you speak to other students from a different culture? Are they quieter? Louder?

b) Is it important to be aware of these differences? Why or why not?

1.2 With a partner, decide whether the following statements are true or false about different cultures. Write T or F next to the sentences.

a) _____ In Chinese society, controversial or potentially embarrassing topics of conversation are often avoided so that no one "loses face."

b) _____ Germans usually make decisions in business discussions more quickly than other Europeans.

c) _____ North Americans stand close to each other when talking.

d) _____ Asian societies tend to use formal terms of address and show great respect towards older people.

e) _____ Japanese students are sometimes reluctant to ask questions in seminars and classes.

f) _____ In Indonesia it can be impolite to say "no" in a conversation.

g) _____ Latin Americans and Spanish people generally like to arrive on time, start promptly and go to bed early.

1.3 Discuss the following questions in groups.

a) Are stereotypes true for everyone?

b) How should we deal with stereotypes?

c) What advice would you give to a student who talked too much or was too quiet?

d) What do you think are the natural characteristics of students of your country?

1.4 What implications do the conclusions you reached in 1.3 have for teamworking in a multicultural group?

Discuss with a partner ways you can minimize misunderstandings. Then write some tips for multicultural discussions below.

Task 2 Talking at or talking to

2.1 Discuss the following sentences with a partner and decide who is talking, a Type A or Type B person.

Type A: to you, i.e., eliciting a response;

Type B: at you, i.e., not interacting with you.

a) Well, when I was at university, blah, blah, blah.

b) I'd love to know what you think of your new residence.

c) You should so listen to the new Eminem CD. Only a nerd wouldn't like it.

d) How's your family?

e) We've spent enough time on this "at you–to you" exercise. Let's do the next one.

2.2 Think about the following questions and how they apply to you. Then discuss your answers with a partner.

- Are you more of a Type A or Type B person?

- Are there any problems with being a Type A person?

- Might it be useful sometimes to be a Type B person? If so, when?

Task 3 Team behavior

3.1 Working individually, match the strategies i) to vii) with the appropriate behavior A) to D).

A) Includes shy, quiet people in your group's discussion.

B) Interrupts the conversation.

C) Keeps the floor to himself/herself.

D) Returns the conversation to something you were talking about earlier.

i) Avoids eye contact.

ii) Says something like "Can I just say something?"

iii) Turns towards another person.

iv) Says something like "If I can just finish what I was saying, …"

v) Makes eye contact with the person speaking.

vi) Says something like "What do you think about global warming?"

vii) Says something like "Back to what I was saying about …"

3.2 Compare your answers with the group. Use the following questions to prompt discussion.

- When might it be appropriate to interrupt a conversation?

- Should shy people have to contribute to a team?

- How can you tell whether someone is shy or simply disinterested?

- What's wrong with wanting to talk all the time?

Reflect

Think about the following two situations.

- Past conversations where you might have talked at a person. Were you aware of doing this? Did the person you were talking to indicate that they were not happy with you?

- Past conversations where there might have been cultural interference. Did either of you get angry or embarrassed? Did you realize at the time what was happening?

Reflect on whether you feel it is important to encourage equal participation in a conversation. If so, how would you encourage shy members of the group to participate?

Student notes for Unit 4

5 Encouraging interaction

At the end of this unit you will:
- be able to identify and use techniques for encouraging and discouraging interaction between people.

Task 1 Listening techniques

1.1 Work in groups. Appoint a note taker, then discuss which of the following strategies would encourage or discourage someone who was talking. The note taker marks the general group consensus for each strategy.

Strategy	Encourage	Discourage	It depends
Fidgeting			
Maintaining eye contact			
Scowling			
Smiling			
Head nodding			
Looking down			
Making non-verbal noises such as uh-uh or mmm			
Using exclamations such as Really! Great! Wow!			
Repeating key speaker words			
Asking questions			
Keeping silent			
Folding your arms across your chest and sitting back in your chair			

1.2   The note taker will have observed your behavior during the discussion. Elicit from him or her whether any of these techniques were used during the discussion.

Task 2 Deploying techniques

2.1   Encouraging techniques: In your group, discuss the food you most enjoy and why. Try to use as many of the encouraging techniques you highlighted in Task 1 as you can.

2.2   Evaluate the discussion with a partner. Use the questions below to prompt your thoughts.

- Did the techniques help?
- Were some strategies better than others?
- Did some strategies actually put you off?

2.3   Discouraging techniques: Take it in turns to describe the food you find most revolting and why you hate it. Stick to a strict time limit of two minutes. (Appoint a timekeeper or use a stopwatch.) The other members of the team should try to deploy the discouraging techniques.

2.4   Evaluate the discussion with a partner. Use the questions below to prompt your thoughts.

- How did it feel to be discouraged?
- Which strategy was the most frustrating?
- Did you manage to speak for two minutes or were the others too distracting?

2.5   Think of situations where you may have inadvertently used these strategies, e.g., a classroom discussion, a conversation with parents, etc.

- Why were you using these strategies?
- How do you think the person who was speaking felt?
- Did you achieve your aims?

Unit 5

Task 3 Interaction issues

3.1 With a partner, discuss the following situations.

What would you do if:

a) someone you were talking to did not maintain eye contact with you?

b) someone kept interrupting you?

c) you felt too shy to join in the conversation?

d) someone kept using negative body language when talking to you, such as fidgeting, yawning, or looking at their watch?

e) someone asked you a question that you could not answer, in a public place, e.g., in a seminar or a class?

3.2 Discuss all aspects of this unit as a class. Try to monitor your own behavior and that of other students during the discussion.

Reflect

Think about the way you talk in your own culture. Do you use all of the strategies discussed in this unit?

Reflect on aspects of body language that are used to show interest or disinterest. Which of these techniques do you think you use consciously or subconsciously?

Student notes for Unit 5

Unit 6 Ways of working with others

At the end of this unit you will:
- be more aware of the benefits of collaborating with a team;
- have discussed different teamwork activities.

Task 1 Examples of teamwork

1.1 List all the different ways that you have worked as a team over the past week. These don't have to just involve study techniques.

E.g., Deciding on a weekend plan with friends

1.2 Did you have much influence on any of the final decisions made? With a partner, discuss what happened. Express how you felt and whether the outcome could have been improved by using different strategies.

Task 2 Studying in a team

2.1 Collaboration with others is an important study resource. Complete the table below to show how comfortable you are with a variety of collaborative study activities. Work on your own, then discuss your answers with another student.

Activity	Happy	Not happy	Indifferent
Talking with others in your group about difficulties you are experiencing.			
Asking others in the group for their opinion on your ideas/work and giving your opinion.			
Giving reading suggestions.			
Discussing books or articles you have read with others.			
Acting as a guinea pig for a fellow student's research.			
Going through lecture notes together.			
Photocopying and reading each other's graded essays.			
Leaving if you feel you are too involved in another group member's problems.			
Copying someone else's assignment.			
Allowing someone to copy your assignment.			

2.2   Compare your answers with a partner. In what ways were they the same or different?

2.3   Discuss the following statements in groups. Do you agree with them? Why? Why not?

1) Two heads are better than one.

2) TEAM = Together Everyone Achieves More.

3) There is no "I" in teamwork.

4) It is amazing how much you can accomplish when it doesn't matter who gets the credit.

5) A successful team beats with one heart.

6) Real teams don't emerge unless individuals in them take risks involving conflict, trust, interdependence, and hard work.

2.4   Discuss the issues raised in relation to collaborative study as a class. Try to resolve any disagreements and build a consensus.

Student notes for Unit 6

Module 4

Web work

Website 1 When teamwork breaks down

http://www.readinggroupguides.com/guides_E/enduring_love1.asp, then click *excerpt*.

Review
An extract from Ian McEwan's *Enduring Love* about a disturbing ballooning accident. This is the first chapter of a novel that explores the consequences of not pulling together as a team.

Task
Read through the chapter and think about what your response would be in this situation. Would you let go? Why? What do you think would happen if you didn't let go?

Website 2 Team building

http://www.agcasscotland.org.uk/esoftskills/tw_introduction_02.html

Review
There is no "I" in TEAM—Scotland's Graduate Careers website. This site interactively takes you through the process of team building. It highlights the importance of working in a team in the workplace.

Task
Work through the interactive online tasks.

Extension activities

Activity 1

Reflect on the various exercises that you have done in this module.

List three skills that contribute to good teamwork.

a) ....

b) ....

c) ....

List three things that contribute to poor teamwork.

a) ....

b) ....

c) ....

Activity 2

Reflect on the various teamwork activities you have tried out.

- What did you find most difficult or challenging?

- What did you find came naturally?

Make a quick note of the skills that other members of your team noticed in you.

- Which skills do you need to improve on?

Glossary

Analyze (v) To break an issue down into parts in order to study, identify, and discuss their meaning and/or relevance.

Body language (n) A form of *non-verbal communication* of feelings and ideas through movements of the body. For example, certain body movements such as fidgeting and yawning may indicate boredom.

Characteristic (n) Unique feature or trait that characterizes a person, thing, place, or group and identifies it.

Collaborate (v) To work together with another person (or other people) on a project or assignment.

Competition (n) A situation where individuals try to do better than each other, rather than cooperating and working together.

Conflict (n) (v) 1 (n) Strong opposition or disagreement within a group or between two or more groups. 2 (v) To clash or have opposing ideas or points of view.

Consensus (n) An agreement or majority decision reached by a group.

Contribute (v) To actively take part in something or give something to a situation, such as time, energy, thought, or money. For example, it is important to contribute ideas when working in a team.

Culture (n) The beliefs, institutions, traditions, arts, and patterns of behavior of a particular group of people that help them structure their lives.

Cultural interference (n) The influence of one *culture* on another.

Custom (n) Something that is done as a habit or because of a long common tradition. Groups of people from the same region, *culture,* or religious group generally share customs. For example, it is a custom to take off one's shoes when entering a Japanese house.

Debrief (v) (n) 1 (v) To talk to or question a group after an activity to find out and reflect on what has been learned, and give participants an opportunity to express their feelings. 2 (n) A meeting or session in which debriefing occurs.

Discourage (v) To try to prevent someone from doing something through words or actions such as *gesture* and facial expression.

Dominate (v) To have a controlling position in a group or strong influence on a situation.

Encourage (v) To support someone and give him/her confidence to do something through words or actions such as *gestures* and facial expression.

Evaluate (v) To assess information in terms of quality, relevance, objectivity, and accuracy.

Eye contact (n) A form of *non-verbal communication* in which people look into, or avoid looking into, each other's eyes when they communicate.

Fairness (n) The ability to make judgments in an honest, unbiased way, in line with accepted standards or rules.

Gesture (n) (v) 1 (n) An action meant to communicate an idea *non-verbally* or to emphasize a thought or feeling. 2 (v) To make such an action. For example, to put one's hand over one's heart to indicate sincerity.

Goal (n) An aim or end purpose that someone tries to achieve or reach.

Implication (n) Something that can be interpreted or inferred but is not directly stated.

Interaction (n) How people or things act together with each other, respond to and affect each other.

Interrupt (v) To enter a conversation or situation without waiting for someone to finish speaking or doing something.

Learning style (n) A style of thinking about, processing, and remembering information that you have to learn. Different styles can be classified in a variety of ways. For example, you may have an analytical learning style.

Motivation (n) The intention and desire to move towards a *goal*. This enthusiasm is affected by different factors and environments. For example, studying with a friend or listening to an interesting lecture may increase your motivation to study.

Multicultural (adj) Describes a community or group that is made up of individuals of different national, racial, or religious backgrounds.

Non-verbal communication (n) The communication of ideas (intentionally or unintentionally) through behavior, body movement, gestures, and facial expression, but not through words.

Objective (adj) (n) 1 (adj) Not influenced by personal feelings or emotions. 2 (n) The aim, or what you want to achieve from an activity.

Outcome (n) A final decision and result.

Participate (v) To get involved or take part in something. For example, it is important to participate actively in *seminars*.

Presentation (n) A short lecture, talk, or demonstration given in front of an audience. The speaker prepares his or her presentation in advance and will often use visual aids to illustrate it.

Role (n) The part someone plays in a group (or any situation that involves interacting with other people). In some situations, these roles may be flexible or unspoken, in others they are well-defined, such as the leader of a team.

Stereotype (n) A simplified and fixed image of a group of people or things. This may be inaccurate, due to over-generalization or incomplete or biased information. For example, the view that Germans are always on time, and Mexicans are always late, is stereotypical.

Strategy (n) A plan of action that you follow when you want to achieve a particular *goal*. For example, it is possible to have a clear strategy for passing an exam.

Subjective (adj) Describes an idea or opinion that is based on someone's personal opinion rather than on observable phenomena.

Teamworking skills (n) The skills needed to *participate* effectively as a member of a group, a team, or a network. They include the following abilities: to work constructively with others, to be assertive without *dominating* too much, to be flexible, and to *contribute* ideas.

Technique (n) A method or way of doing something that involves skill and/or efficiency. For example, it is possible to learn useful techniques for answering exam questions.

Time management (n) The ability to organize your time so that you use it more effectively and efficiently.

Module 5: Problem Solving

Introduction

In higher education, you need to be able to solve problems objectively using critical thinking. The strategies involved in problem solving are also useful life skills that can be transferred to personal and professional situations.

This module will help you develop these strategies by presenting you with tasks that draw on a variety of problems and predicaments, decisions, and deadlines. It takes you through all the steps of the problem solving process, from identifying problem types to using appropriate strategies to solve them.

Unit 1 will introduce you to different types of problems and examine why problem solving is an essential skill for your academic studies. Unit 2 will raise your awareness of the skills and strategies required for successful decision making. Unit 3 looks at problem-solving procedures and techniques and provides a simple model for dealing with the different stages of a problem. Units 4 and 5 tackle the steps of the problem-solving procedure in more depth. You will learn to use strategies and procedures such as breaking down the problem, gathering information and comparing options for a solution. You will then practice using these different strategies by looking at some case studies. Finally, Unit 6 encourages you to analyze the way you have considered options and solutions to problems. It also focuses on useful language for justifying and explaining your choices.

This module encourages you to think creatively in order to analyze and choose solutions to problems. After completing the module, you will be better equipped to use clear strategies to deal with problems. You will also be able to explain and support your approach and solutions to problems, something that is essential when writing academic essays and participating in academic discussions.

Skills Map

What is problem solving

Look at different types of problems and discover why problem-solving skills are essential to your studies.

Problem-solving strategies

Learn how to evaluate different problems and select appropriate strategies for dealing with them.

The problem-solving process

Develop a better awareness of problem-solving procedures and techniques.

Elaborating on the problem

Learn how to break down a problem into steps and gather information to help you solve it.

Finding the best solution

Improve your ability to objectively evaluate a solution.

Creative thinking

Understand how to support and justify reasons for analyzing alternatives and choosing options.

Destination: Problem Solving

1 What is problem solving?

At the end of this unit you will:
- **become more aware of different types of problems and forms of problem solving.**

Life is full of problems. As we grow up, we quickly learn how to deal with many of them. Studying at college or university has its own set of problems, so this is a good time to sharpen our skills in problem solving.

We all possess the ability to solve problems. The purpose of this course is to improve that ability. It is always useful to first identify what you already know, through discussion. The following three tasks will help you.

Task 1 Types of problems

Problem solving involves being clear and precise in our thought processes. It is therefore useful to identify those problems that are relevant. Follow these three steps to help you clarify your thoughts.

1.1 Think about the different types of situations where you face(d) problems in the past, present, or future, for example, at home, school, or college, in the workplace, etc.

1.2 Work in groups and share the different kinds of situations you have come up with, for example:

At school I found it difficult to review for exams.

When traveling I lose things.

1.3 In your groups, divide these problems into the three categories below.

Problems that affected you more in the past	Problems that affect you now	Problems that are likely to become bigger in the future

Task 2 Thinking about problem solving

A good understanding of problem solving will help you in college or at university. The next two tasks will help you think more clearly about the areas where it can help you.

2.1 Discuss the following five questions with another student. Make notes and be prepared to talk about them with the rest of the class.

a) What is the first thing you do when you try to solve a problem?

b) What other stages are involved in solving a problem?

c) What kind of skills do you need to solve problems?

d) Who can help you with problem solving?

e) Why is it useful to study problem solving in college or at university?

Note that you will discover the answers to these questions as you work through this module.

2.2 Problem solving is an essential element of many types of study assignments across all disciplines in higher education. With another student, think of study activities that might pose problems. Add them to the first column of the table below.

Activity	Possible problem	Possible solution
1. Writing essays		
2. Doing research		
3. Giving presentations		
4.		
5.		

2.3 Now discuss problems you might encounter with these activities, for example, lack of time. Add them to column 2 of the table.

2.4 What solutions to these problems can you think of? For example, better time management using a schedule or planner. Make a note of your ideas in the third column of the table.

Task 3 Forms of problem solving

There are a number of different forms of problem solving. To help us think clearly, we need to identify how they are different. Some problems involve finding a correct solution, others involve considering several possible answers, with some more useful than others.

3.1 Discuss the following three problems in groups and the different thinking processes required for each one.

Problem A—What is 2+2?

Problem B—Discuss the rise and fall of the Republican Party.

Problem C—How can we reduce pollution?

3.2   Share your opinions about the differences between the different types of problems with the rest of the class. As part of the discussion, identify which of the three types of problems you can expect on your course.

3.3   By doing the following task, identify how your practical skills in problem solving are progressing. Work in groups to find possible solutions to the following problems that you might face while studying in a foreign country.

   a)   You can't find the books on your book list in the library.

   b)   The professor speaks too quickly.

   c)   You want to go out with your friends but you don't have enough money.

   d)   You have bought a computer so you can have internet access, but don't know how to get it.

   e)   You did poorly in your last essay.

   f)   It's too hot in your room.

   g)   The nearest grocery store is three miles from your house and you don't have a car.

   h)   You are homesick.

   i)   You want to change courses.

   j)   Your visa is about to expire.

3.4   Do the other groups have the same solutions?

Reflect

Think about how you normally approach problems. Do you tend to run away from them or try to face them and look for solutions?

Try to remember a time when you solved a difficult problem and how you felt about it. Then think of a time when you tried to hide from a problem, what the consequences were, and how you felt about that. Then think of how you would deal with such a situation in the future.

Student notes for Unit 1

2 Problem-solving strategies

At the end of this unit you will:
- be more aware of how to evaluate different problems;
- be more able to select appropriate strategies for dealing with them.

Task 1 Expectations in higher education

1.1   Problem solving in higher education requires particular skills and strategies. When you have completed the blanks below with words from the box, you will have a better idea of what is expected of you.

Problem solving in higher education settings refers to a student's ① _____ to identify the main ② _____ of a given problem and to develop appropriate ③ _____ for solving it. You will be expected to ④ _____ a problem, identify strategic options for its ⑤ _____, and evaluate the ⑥ _____ of different strategies. This means thinking ⑦ _____ to produce solutions: considering other viewpoints, looking for evidence and using experience when evaluating alternatives.

> critically   analyze   resolution   features   strategies   ability   success

1.2   Use the context of the text in 1.1 to work out a definition of the words *critically*, *analyze,* and *strategy*. Discuss them with your partner.

Task 2 Problems and solutions

2.1   For every problem, there may or may not be a solution. Discuss the following problems with another student and see how many solutions you can find.

Example: Traffic congestion

  i) Increase highway tolls
 ii) Encourage people to carpool
iii) Improve public transportation

a) Global warming
b) Inflation
c) Overcrowding in cities
d) HIV/AIDS

2.2   Discussion

Think of a problem your country is facing at the moment. Can you think of any solutions to this problem? Discuss with another student and see if you can offer them advice on their problem.

2.3   Rank the following tasks from 1 to 8 (1 = most problematic, 8 = least problematic) with another student. You may disagree!

a) _____ remembering a chemical formula

b) _____ controlling inflation

c) _____ noisy neighbors

d) _____ writing an essay

e) _____ proving a theorem in geometry

f) _____ finding the best route from your house to Fenway Park in Boston

g) _____ finding your keys

h) _____ data analysis

2.4   What strategies would you need to solve the above problems?

2.5   Think of a problem you or your partner have had recently and write down five strategies to solve it. You have 15 minutes.

Problem:

Strategies:

2.6   Living in a foreign country often means that people face cultural problems. Discuss with another student what you would do if you were faced with the following situations.

a) Men and women are not allowed to socialize together.

b) The country you are living in does not celebrate your religious holidays.

c) You have to carry identification with you at all times.

d) You must wear the national dress.

e) The food is very different, and you don't like it. It is difficult to find food that you do like.

f) The mealtimes are completely different from what you are used to.

g) Entertainment is different from what you are used to.

h) People wait in line!

2.7   Discuss your answers with the class. Are the solutions different?

Reflect

Studying in a foreign country can be problematic and stressful. Think about how you approached these problems.

Did you use any particular strategies?

Were any of them the same as the ones discussed in this unit?

How would you interpret this saying? A problem shared is a problem halved.

Student notes for Unit 2

Unit 3 The problem-solving process

At the end of this unit you will:
- be more familiar with language used to describe problems and their solutions;
- have a better awareness of problem-solving procedures and techniques.

When writing in an academic context, it is important to describe the processes involved. This means using specific language associated with the topic. An awareness of problem-solving procedures will also help you structure your essays.

Task 1 The language used in problem solving

1.1 What verbs are usually associated with problem-solving tasks? Hint: Many of them have been used in earlier units. Spend three minutes with another student thinking of as many as possible.

1.2 Using the verbs you have just discussed, fill in the blanks in the following text. There may be more than one answer for some blanks, so check with another student.

When you are faced with a problem it is good to ① _____ ideas in small groups. Together, you can ② _____ the problem, and ③ _____ and ④ _____ possible solutions before ⑤ _____ the best one. You may need to ⑥ _____ up the alternatives and see which is the best option.

Task 2 Steps to solving a problem

2.1 When you are faced with a problem, what is the first thing you do? Put the following steps into a logical problem-solving sequence with another student.

a) _____ Develop alternatives for each major solution. Take the time to think of different options available to you.

b) _____ Choose the best solution for the problem.

c) _____ Weigh the alternatives: evaluate each option carefully. Consider the advantages and the disadvantages.

d) _____ Define the problem clearly. What exactly do you need to do? State your goal. Use practical verbs such as *find out about* …

e) _____ Find major solutions: brainstorm as many possible solutions as you can for solving the problem.

Task 3 A logical approach to problem solving

The following pattern of organization is commonly used in writing when analyzing problems:

Situation → Problem → Solution → Evaluation

- A situation is given.
- The problem of the situation is identified.
- A solution to the problem is presented.
- An evaluation of the solution is given.

The following text discusses the problem of rising sea levels. It follows a logical sequence like the one mentioned above. It illustrates how this pattern of organization is commonly used in writing.

3.1 Read the text and identify and underline the parts of the text that:

- describe the situation;
- identify the problem;
- suggest a solution or solutions;
- evaluate the solution(s).

Recent evidence confirms that global warming is melting the ice in Antarctica faster than had been previously thought. Scientists say the rise in sea levels around the world caused by the melting may have been underestimated. It is thought that over 13,000 square kilometers of sea ice in the Antarctic Peninsula have been lost over the last 50 years. This poses a major problem because its effects will be felt across the globe.

A rise in sea levels increases the level of wave attack and tides, causing changes in the stability of shorelines as well as flooding of lowlands. In many places, a 50-centimeter rise would see entire beaches being washed away by erosion, together with a significant chunk of the coastline. Many island nations will have their supplies of drinking water reduced because seawater will invade their freshwater aquifers. While some islands have sizeable populations, they are insignificant compared with the tens of millions of people living in the low-level coastal areas of Southern Asia. These include the coastlines of Pakistan, India, Sri Lanka, Bangladesh, and Burma.

Since more than 75 percent of the human population live within 60 kilometers of a coast, finding a solution is imperative. While implementation of flood prevention measures on a local level is helpful in the short term, there is no physical capacity that humans have to protect against long-term sea level rise. The key to coping with the rise in sea levels is education about the effects and accurate assessments of hazards for given points in time. In this way, humans can act decisively and appropriately to minimize loss of life and economic and ecological impacts. Education is the only long-term, far-reaching solution to sea level rise.

3.2   Now complete the flow chart below with notes based on the text.

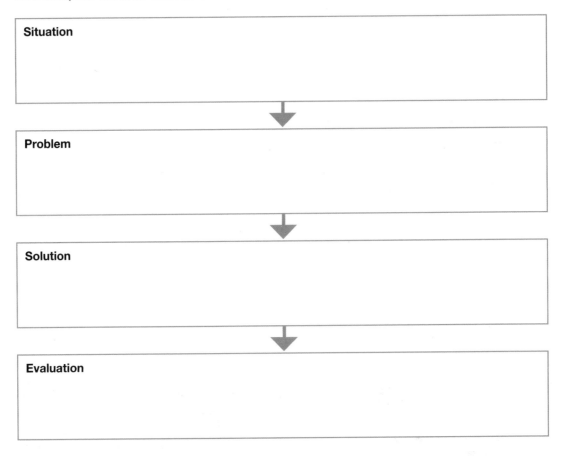

The same steps can be applied to problems that affect you at college or university.

3.3 The model in the table below looks at and evaluates major solutions and alternatives for the problem of how to improve student attendance at university classes. Look at it and decide whether you agree with the ideas. Can you add any more solutions?

STAGE 1 State problem in general terms	STAGE 2 Find major solutions	STAGE 3 Develop alternatives	STAGES 4 & 5 Evaluate options and choose the best one
How to improve student attendance at university classes	**Solution 1** Change teaching methodology	- use interactive whiteboards - be more student-centered - incorporate group activities	- will only work if training is available for professors and there are sufficient resources to buy equipment
	Solution 2 Introduce attendance policy	- check up on persistent absentees - send students with more than 10% absences to the Faculty Dean - expel students with more than 20% absences	- students need to have warning - system needs to be monitored and tracked - could encourage up to 20% absence
	Solution 3 Introduce attendance incentives	- give attendance prize at the end of each semester - add information about attendance to a monthly on progress	- could be expensive to provide prizes - prizes may not motivate all students
	Solution 4		

3.4   With your partner, make notes on the grid below about another problem. When you have finished, be prepared to share your ideas with the rest of the group. Try to be inventive and creative!

STAGE 1 State problem in general terms	STAGE 2 Find major solutions	STAGE 3 Develop alternatives	STAGES 4 & 5 Evaluate options and choose the best one
How to improve my grades	Solution 1		
	Solution 2		
	Solution 3		
	Solution 4		

Reflect

The problem-solving procedures in this unit can help you think more clearly. How did they help you work out a solution to the tasks in 3.3 and 3.4?

Think about other ways that you solve problems, particularly when you are studying.

Student notes for Unit 3

Unit 4 Elaborating on the problem

In this unit you will:
- look at some case studies and apply the points discussed in previous units to them;
- gather information to find solutions to problems in an academic situation.

When you attempt to solve problems, it is not a good idea to act too quickly, without undertaking the initial reflection and preparation. Research shows that people who invest time at the beginning working out exactly what a problem involves have a better chance of success. It is worth spending time reflecting on:

- the kind of problem it is;
- how it is like other problems you have encountered;
- different ways of approaching the task.

It can be useful to apply your own experience to other situations. Pooling experiences and ideas in a group is even more beneficial. In this unit you will use examples from your own experience to help you think of solutions to more general problems.

Task 1 Identifying problems

1.1 In Unit 2, we looked briefly at the cultural problems students face when they arrive in a foreign country. They may also encounter problems associated with the language, food, weather, etc. In groups, make a list of all the problems you have encountered when first arriving in a new country, for example, finding somewhere to live.

1.2 What did you do to alleviate these problems? Are they the same problems that other groups had? Do you have any good advice for fellow students?

Task 2 Defining the task

2.1 You are going to read a short case study about a young female student who has just started her degree in the US. Read the information below and fill in the grid with a partner. Use your own experiences of being a student in a foreign country to help you.

Mini case-study 1

Petra has recently arrived in the US to begin her studies at a large university. She is feeling homesick and misses her friends and family back home. She thought her English language skills were good, but when she attended her first economics class today, she did not understand it very well because the professor spoke too fast for her to follow. What advice would you give to Petra?

What are the problems?	
Write the problems as questions, e.g.: How/What can I ...? + add a verb such as improve, alleviate, increase, reduce, etc. + in order to/so that I (to state your goal).	
Think of some solutions.	

Task 3 Gathering information

In exactly two weeks, you must submit a 3,000-word paper and give a 12-minute presentation on a different subject at a seminar on the same day. You have done some background reading for the paper and taken notes, but you have not written an outline yet, and you have not thought about the presentation at all. Today your parents call to tell you that they will be making a surprise visit to see you in the US in ten days' time. How will you manage to complete your assignments in time to enjoy their visit?

3.1 Fill in the grid as in Task 2. Work in small groups to brainstorm ideas and generate as many solutions as possible.

What are the problems?	
Write the problems as questions, e.g.: How/What can I ...? + add a verb such as improve, alleviate, increase, reduce, etc. + in order to/so that I (to state your goal).	
Think of some solutions.	

3.2 You have ten minutes with another student to create another problem like the two you have just worked on. Use your imagination!

Try to think of at least three points to put in each box. When you have finished, compare your ideas with another group. If your answers are different, explain your reasoning behind them.

What are the problems?	
Write the problems as questions, e.g.: How/What can I ...? + add a verb such as improve, alleviate, increase, reduce, etc. + in order to/so that I (to state your goal).	
Think of some solutions.	

3.3 When you have finished the previous task, swap problems with another group and try to think of some solutions. Use the grid to help you. Be prepared to give a short presentation on your findings.

Reflect

Think about the collaboration you took part in for Task 3. Reflect on the different experiences that other students brought to the task and how this helped to find a solution. Did you feel that the experiences of others helped to draw out your own ideas?

Student notes for Unit 4

Unit 5 Finding the best solution

At the end of this unit you will:
- be more able to objectively evaluate a solution;
- be more familiar with different problem evaluation techniques.

When working towards a solution, you have to be careful not to choose your favorite one, as this may be seen as too subjective. Instead, you should take a step back, remain focused and try to be objective, i.e., choose a solution that is best for everyone.

Task 1 Deciding how to react

1.1　When you are faced with a problem, what is your first reaction? Imagine you have two weeks to hand in a 5,000-word essay (in English). In groups, discuss which of these reactions is similar to yours.

*" I tend to panic and "
my mind goes blank.

a

*" I find someone to "
talk to about it.

b

*" I find somewhere "
quiet to consider
my options.

c

*" I think of a quick "
solution and take
immediate action.

d

1.2 Below is a possible checklist for how to tackle the situation. Decide which of the words in the box below should go into the blanks. There is only one possibility for each solution. Work on your own and then check your answers with a partner.

> conclusions   expertise   problems   ideas   objective
> implemented   drawbacks   matrix   range

a) Consider a ① _____ of options.

b) Discuss your ② _____ with others. Find out how others have approached similar
③ _____ .

c) Do some research. Look for hidden advantages and ④ _____ in each option. What has been tried and didn't work before?

d) Make sure each solution is feasible in the circumstances. Can the solution be ⑤ _____ ?

e) Check your ⑥ _____ . Is your existing knowledge sufficient, or should you consult with experts?

f) One way of ensuring that your final assessment is based on ⑦ _____ criteria is by drawing up a grid or a ⑧ _____ .

g) This will ensure that you do not jump to ⑨ _____ too hastily.

Task 2 Paired comparison analysis

This is a technique that helps you compare each option against all others and is a good way of weighing up the relative effectiveness of different courses of action. Read the example problem below and work out which option was selected.

A student is looking at ways in which she can improve her grades. She lists the options below:

- Study an extra two hours every day.
- Go to the library after each class to review.
- Form a study group.
- Join a study skills class.

She draws up a table that shows these options as both row and column headings. (Shaded cells indicate comparison of an option with itself, and are therefore not used.)

	1 Extra 2-hrs study	2 Go to library	3 Form a study group	4 Join a study skills class
1 Extra 2-hrs study		2	1	4
2 Go to library			2	4
3 Form a study group				4
4 Study skills class				

a) She begins by comparing the advantages and disadvantages of options 1 and 2. Which of these two options is better?

b) After consideration, she writes the better option in the appropriate box, and then does the same with options 1 and 3.

c) She continues until she has filled up all six empty boxes with her best options. The option that has been chosen most often is the best solution to her problem.

Which option did she choose?

Task 3 Subjective versus objective evaluation

3.1 **Read the following two texts and decide which text is objective and which one is subjective.**

Text A: I think studying in the United States is the best option for all students. First of all, it is the best country in the world. The universities provide the best education and the degrees are recognized internationally. While you may find the cost of living high and the food different, don't let that dissuade you. I wouldn't choose any other option.

Text B: It is important to consider the options available when deciding where to study. If you choose to go abroad, various factors need to be taken into consideration. Tuition fees and the cost of living may be a deciding factor. Be realistic about how far away from your friends and family you will be. Also, think about the type of degree you will be studying for. Will it be recognized in the country you eventually decide to work in?

3.2 **Discuss the following questions with another student.**

a) What differences do you notice about the styles of the two texts and the information in them?

b) Which one appears to be more academic? Why?

Task 4 Writing a report

Problems and their solutions often need to be discussed and summarized in written form, often in a formal report. Writing a description of the problem-solving process can also help you assimilate your ideas. In this unit you are going to complete a report as a table.

4.1 **In this module you have looked at the problem of improving your grades. Write a 250-word report for your instructor outlining how you are going to solve the problem. Use the headings on the next page to structure your report.**

Begin your report.	E.g., make notes on points you want to cover in the report. Think of how to order these points logically. Start a new paragraph with each new point.
Define the problem.	
The parameters of the problem, e.g., the time available, resources used, expertise, limitations.	
The different solutions that you considered, with their advantages and disadvantages.	
How you arrived at the decision you made.	
Your method for applying the solution, and what you did.	
The results.	
An evaluation of the outcome.	

Reflect

Think about whether the way you have tackled problems in the past has affected their outcomes.

Was your evaluation subjective or objective?

Think of a problem that you are facing now, or that you might face in the future. Which of the steps, approaches, and techniques from this unit could you use in trying to solve it?

Student notes for Unit 5

6 Creative thinking

At the end of this unit you will:
- be able to support and justify reasons for analyzing alternatives and choosing options.

Task 1 Discussing solutions to problems

1.1 Below are some expressions that are useful when discussing alternative solutions. Match the sentences and then check your answers with another student.

1. I'd rather look at alternatives	**a)** alternatives before we decide.
2. I think we need to try this	**b)** my opinion is number 2.
3. The best option in	**c)** realistic considering the situation.
4. I don't think we should choose that one	**d)** solution, we should try to evaluate which one is best.
5. Let's look at all the possible	**e)** before I make up my mind.
6. If there is more than one	**f)** option because it has had good results in the past.
7. That alternative is very	**g)** we'll have to vote on it.
8. If we can't decide	**h)** if there are better alternatives.

Task 2 Putting techniques into practice

You are now ready to put all the ideas and techniques you have studied into practice. You are going to work in two groups. You will spend some time discussing and solving a problem with your group, while the other group observe you doing this. You will then swap roles and observe the other group solving a different problem.

This task will give you the opportunity to use as many techniques and suggestions from previous units as you can while solving the problem. You will also have the opportunity to observe the techniques and procedures that the other group use and reflect on how effectively they are used.

2.1 In each team, choose a "secretary" who will fill in the grid. The two problems are on the following page. To be effective, you will need to practice some or all of the problem-solving skills that we have identified in earlier units.

Follow the procedure below.

1 Read the two problems in the boxes and decide which group is going to tackle each problem and who will go first.

2 The group that is dicussing their problem should complete Table A during or after the discussion.

3 The group that is observing the discussion should complete Table B.

4 After the discussion, the observers should give feedback on how well they think the other group managed the problem-solving task.

5 The groups should now swap roles and repeat the procedure (completing the other tables).

2.3 Read the problems and make sure you are clear about what you have to discuss. Decide which problem your group is going to discuss.

Problem 1
Imagine you are John Smith. The city where you live is holding local elections to elect a new congressperson. As a group, look at the platform for each of the three candidates below and decide which person you will vote for. Before you make your decision, study John Smith's profile.

John Smith	
Age:	38
Marital status:	Married (Sarah).
Children & dependents:	2 daughters, 11 and 15. John's elderly mother also lives with the family.
Job:	Social worker
Other activities:	Chairman of the neighborhood watch committee. Volunteer work for a drug abuse awareness group.
Spouse's job:	Unemployed (awaiting results of a sex discrimination trial).
Likes:	Going out with friends, European travel.
Dislikes:	Traveling to work on local buses, which are always late.
Is worried about:	Lack of local government spending on education. His mother, who needs a hip operation.

Janet Jones

Improve education

Better welfare and benefits

Equal rights for women, especially in the workplace

Pro-immigration

Raising driving age to 18

Arthur Price

Decrease taxation

Decrease crime

Improve benefits for the elderly

Anti-immigration

Improve transport

James Ellis

Decrease unemployment

Fight racism

Anti-drugs campaign

Increase spending on healthcare

Slight increase in taxation

Problem 2

You are a member of the Research and Development Board for a pharmaceuticals business. The pharmaceuticals company is investigating the viability of three new drugs.

Drug 1: has been demonstrated to aid rapid weight loss.

Drug 2: is reported to delay the aging process in adults over the age of 40 by up to 20%.

Drug 3: claims to offer an effective and nonaddictive alternative to market-leading anti-depressants without any side effects.

Problem: The company is only able to invest in the development of one of the products mentioned above. Suggest and evaluate possible solutions to the following.

a) Which of the three drugs should be selected for development? Provide reasons to support your decision.

b) Which brand name should be selected for the drug?

c) Which special features should be highlighted for the purposes of marketing?

2.4   Use the following table to structure your discussions. Make notes while or after you discuss the problem.

Table 1

Problem	Solution	Alternatives	Final option
1	1		
	2		
	3		
2	1		
	2		
	3		

2.5   While or after you observe and judge the other group's problem-solving skills, complete the table below.

Table 2

Which problem-solving skills did the team practice?	
Which different stages of problem solving did you observe?	
How many different alternatives were considered?	
Can the solution(s) be supported or justified?	
Is the majority of the group satisfied with the solution?	

Reflect

You have now finished the module on problem solving. Think about the different ways you have tackled problems and the techniques you have used. How do you feel these techniques helped you do the final task?

In what way has your approach to problem solving changed as a result of this module? Decide which strategies you will use to help you with your future studies.

Student notes for Unit 6

Module 5

Web work

Website 1 Different approaches to problem solving

http://www.soton.ac.uk/~pw/teach/cheminfo/ss_exam1.html

Review

A useful Web-stop for chemistry students faced with chemistry problems—from the University of Southampton in the UK.

Task

Identify the similarities and differences between this scientific approach to problem solving and the approach outlined in this module.

Website 2 Problem-solving strategies

http://www.une.edu.au/psychology/staff/academicstaff/malouffproblemsolving.php

Review

University of New England: 50 problem-solving strategies are listed and outlined in this site.

Task

You are already aware that there is more than one way to approach a problem. Read through some of the strategies to see if any are particularly useful for your study area.

Extension activities

Activity 1

You have been asked to complete the following assignment:

Prepare a presentation outlining American attitudes to foreign language learning.

1   The problem: How can I investigate Americans' attitudes to foreign language learning?

2   Find major solutions.

3   Develop alternatives.

4   Evaluate options.

5   Choose the best one.

Read the text about the Isle of Lingua and then consider the problems underneath.

The Isle of Lingua is a remote tropical island and has a population of 100,000. 15% of the population are native speakers of English. However, the remaining 85% speak Linguish, the local language. For a number of years, the economy of the Isle of Lingua has been in decline and unemployment is now a major problem.

The culture of the island has a long history, and the location of the region makes it an area of outstanding natural beauty. To boost the island's economy, the government has suggested the implementation of a policy that would make English the official language of the island. The Linguish people have been called to vote for or against the policy in a referendum.

Imagine you are the Linguan Minister for Tourism. You are broadly in favor of introducing English as a lingua franca because this would promote tourism. However, you are also very concerned about local employment and the potential loss of the Linguan cultural identity.

Should the Isle of Lingua adopt English as its official language?

- Consider alternative solutions.
- Evaluate and choose the best solution.

Glossary

Alleviate (v) To improve a situation and/or make it feel better, although not necessarily find a solution to the underlying problem(s).

Alternative (n) (adj) 1 (n) One of two or more possibilities that can be chosen to solve a problem or reach a decision. 2 (adj) Describing a choice between two *alternatives*.

Analyze (v) To break an issue down into parts in order to study, identify, and discuss their meaning and/or relevance.

Approach (n) A way of doing things based on a clear set of ideas or beliefs.

Assignment (n) A piece of work, generally written, that is set as part of an academic program and is normally completed out of class and submitted by a set date to be assessed.

Assimilate (v) To fully process and understand an idea or concept.

Brainstorm (v) The act of bringing ideas together by writing down all the thoughts and ideas you have about a topic without stopping to monitor, edit, or organize them. Brainstorming is a creative process that can be done alone or in a group.

Case study (n) Example case or situation that can be studied and discussed in order to develop skills or illustrate a scenario.

Collaboration (n) Working together with another person (or other people) on a piece of work or an *assignment*.

Critical thinking (n) The academic skill of being able to look at ideas and problems in a considered, critical way in order to *evaluate* them. It also involves the ability to see links between concepts and develop one's own ideas.

Drawback (n) A negative point or disadvantage that hinders or discourages someone from doing something or prevents them from reaching a solution.

Elaborate (v) To go into more detail when explaining something, or look at an issue or problem in more depth.

Evaluate (v) To assess information in terms of quality, relevance, objectivity, and accuracy.

Evidence (n) Information and data that establish whether something is true or not.

Expertise (n) Skill or knowledge in a particular subject area.

Flow chart (n) A diagram that shows a process. Steps or ideas are shown in a structured way (for example, from left to right) and linked by arrows.

Grade (n) (v) 1 (n) A mark for an essay, an exam, or for overall performance. Grades often correspond to a number, letter, or word, such as *70%*; *"A," "C+"* or *"F"*; or *Pass/Fail*. 2 (v) To assess an essay, exam or overall performance and assign a *grade*.

Implement (v) To put an idea or plan into action.

Incentive (n) A prize or goal that gives people encouragement to meet a deadline or do something well.

Initial reflection (n) Time taken to think carefully about a task or problem before tackling it.

Jump to conclusions (v) Decide on a solution quickly without knowing or listening to all of the information and *options*.

Justify (v) Put forward a case for or against a knowledge claim or idea.

Methodology (n) Set of methods and *techniques* based on a clear *approach* or set of beliefs.

Objective (adj) (n) 1 (adj) Not influenced by personal feelings or emotions. 2 (n) The aim, or what you want to achieve from an activity.

Option (n) One possible choice that may be selected when making a decision.

Outcome (n) A final decision and result.

Paired comparison analysis (n) A *technique* where pairs of *options* are compared in turn in order to rank them and then choose the best option.

Parameter (n) Something that defines the scale of a task or project and sets limits such as time, cost and/or number of people available to work on it.

Policy (n) A formalized agreement on which *procedures* and/or *methodology* to adopt and follow.

Presentation (n) A short lecture, talk, or demonstration given in front of an audience. The speaker prepares his or her presentation in advance and will often use visual aids or realia to illustrate it.

Procedure (n) Set of steps that are followed in order to complete a task.

Resolution (n) The successful *outcome* of a *strategy* used to solve a problem.

Seminar (n) A small group discussion led by a professor or guest speaker. Students are expected to take an active part in the seminar.

Strategy (n) A plan of action that you follow when you want to achieve a particular goal. For example, it is possible to have a clear strategy for passing an exam.

Subjective (adj) Describes an idea or opinion that is based on someone's personal opinion rather than on observable phenomena.

Technique (n) A method or way of doing something that involves skill and/or efficiency. For example, it is possible to learn useful techniques for answering exam questions.

Time management (n) The ability to organize your time so that you use it more effectively and efficiently.

Weigh alternatives (v) Consider and compare the advantages and disadvantages of different *options* or possible solutions to problems.

Module 6: Critical Thinking

Introduction

Critical thinking is a fundamental component of academic life in the Western world. It is an essential skill when writing essays or reports, or taking part in seminars and debates, for example. However, this skill is rarely taught explicitly and students are left to guess what their professors mean when they are told to be "more critical." This often results from a misunderstanding of the word "critical" itself. In the context of academic life, it has the positive sense of careful analysis rather than the negative sense of expressing disapproval.

Most of us use some aspects of critical thinking in our everyday lives, but we do not naturally transfer the skill to academic life—especially in the early stages. This module provides you with an introduction to critical thinking to help you recognize sound and strong arguments in academic texts.

Unit 1 will clarify what critical thinking is and help you recognize the difference between fact and opinion. Units 2 and 3 will equip you with the skills to recognize the strength and soundness of an argument. It will also help you spot reasoning that results in a poor argument. You will practice how to build strong or sound arguments using appropriate language and structure. Unit 4 will make you aware of the way that language can be used to manipulate opinion without necessarily following the steps of logical reasoning. You also need to consider the bias that may affect the selection and presentation of information, and this area is addressed in Unit 5. Finally, in Unit 6 you will have the opportunity to put all of your new skills into practice and to reflect on what you have learned in this module.

After completing this module, you should feel more confident about your ability to express yourself in a reasoned way. You will also be able to analyze the arguments of others, and to recognize sound arguments and support or challenge them where necessary.

Skills Map

What is critical thinking?

Familiarize yourself with the basics of evaluation and practice distinguishing between fact and opinion.

Recognizing strong or sound arguments

Learn how to construct strong or sound arguments and how to better recognize these in the work of others.

Recognizing poor arguments

Learn how to recognize faulty reasoning in the arguments of others.

Persuasion through language or pressure

Explore the manipulation of argumentation by the use of a variety of linguistic techniques.

Detecting bias

Consider important questions about authors' selection and presentation of materials.

Putting it into practice

Put into practice the skills you have learned in this module by preparing for and taking part in a seminar.

Destination: Critical Thinking

Unit 1

What is critical thinking?

At the end of this unit you will be able to:
- understand the difference between thinking and critical thinking;
- recognize the difference between a fact and an opinion;
- use a framework to evaluate arguments.

Task 1 Thinking skills

1.1 Working alone, find the "odd one out."

For example:

aba aba aba aba aba (bba) aba aba

a) ✓ ✓ ✓ ✓ ✗ ✓ ✓ ✓ ✓ ✓ ✓

b) ♠ ♥ ♠ ♠ ♠ ♠ ♠ ♠ ♠ ♠

c) ‖ ‖ ‖ ‖ ‖ ‖ ‖ ‖ ‖ IL ‖ ‖ ‖ ‖ ‖

d) ttf tft tft tft tft tft tft tft tft tft tft

1.2 Working alone, fill in the next item in the sequences below.

For example:

✓ ✗ ✓ ✗ ✓ ✗ ✓ ... = ✗

a) ■ ▲ ◆ ● ■ ...

b) ✓ ✓ ✓ ✗ ✓ ✓ ...

c) 1 2 3 5 8 13 ...

d) 2 4 8 16 32 ...

1.3 Now work with a partner and compare your answers. Then discuss what steps you took to find the answers.

Task 2 Critical thinking skills

To answer the two exercises in Task 1, you compared items in a sequence and looked for patterns. These are two examples of thinking skills that you probably use every day, maybe to predict if your bus might be next or to put your clothes away in the right places (socks in a drawer, shirts in a closet, etc.). Critical thinking is based on these everyday thinking skills that you use all the time.

Generally, critical thinking is used to understand and evaluate arguments. It is not important whether you agree or disagree with the arguments. Rather, critical thinking requires you to recognize that an argument is a good one, even if you disagree with it, or that another is a bad one, even if you agree with its conclusions.

2.1   Read the following argument carefully.

> English has become a global language for a number of reasons. From an historical perspective, it spread to many parts of the world when successive waves of English speakers migrated abroad from the UK. In terms of the language itself, it is relatively easy to learn with its vocabulary, which is borrowed from many different languages, and its fairly simple grammar. The economic dominance of English-speaking countries for many centuries has also contributed to its status as a global language. Indeed, English is likely to remain the number one global language forever.

2.2   Discuss the following questions with your partner.

   a)   What does the writer of this argument want you to believe?

   b)   How does the writer try to persuade you?

   c)   What is the writer's conclusion?

   d)   Is the writer's argument logical? Why/Why not?

Task 3 Facts or opinions?

" It's got a powerful engine. "

*" It's too fast to drive "
on public roads.*

In academic work, it is important to distinguish a fact from an opinion. A fact is a piece of information that can be checked and proved. Something is a fact if, for example, we can observe it, test it, or check it against some evidence. In contrast, an opinion is something that someone thinks is true. Unlike a fact, an opinion cannot be proved. However, sometimes the distinction between a fact and an opinion is not clear to us because so many people share the same opinion. Equally, new evidence may disprove something that was once considered a fact.

3.1   **Look at the following statements. Which one is a fact and which one is an opinion? When you have finished, compare your ideas with your partner.**

English is a very easy language to learn.

English is spoken all over the world.

3.2   **Now look at the following statements about English.**
        Underline opinions like this and facts like this.

For example:

English is better than other languages because it has a bigger vocabulary than other languages.

a) English has borrowed many words from a wide range of other languages. Examples include "tycoon" from Japanese, "gong" from Javanese, "slim" from Dutch and "junta" from Spanish.

 tycoon
 gong
 slim
 junta

b) English is spoken in more countries than any other language.

c) English contains vocabulary that is borrowed from many other languages, and this is why it is a global language.

3.3   **Work with a partner. Choose one of the essay titles below and make a note of any opinions that are directly stated in it or that indirectly support it.**

a) Decisions about the practice of cloning should be made by experts who understand the science that is involved, not by the general public. Discuss.

b) Outline the main measures for the prevention of cancer.

c) A knowledge of economics is essential for historians. Discuss.

d) One of the causes of juvenile delinquency is a result of poor attachment from birth. What might other causes be?

Task 4 Questioning opinions

In small groups, discuss what questions you would need to ask in order to accept, reject, or suspend judgment of the opinions you have identified in one of the titles in Tasks 3.2 and 3.3. Write as many questions as you can think of.

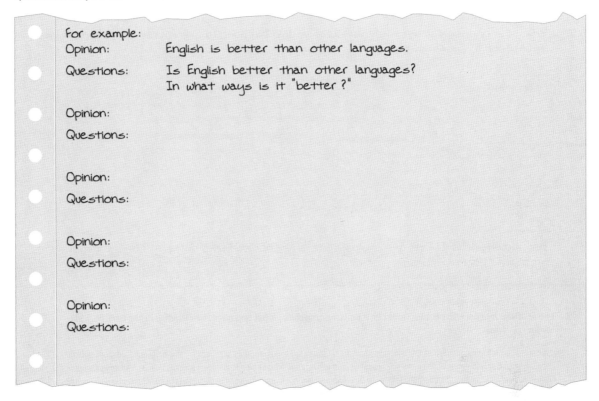

For example:
Opinion: English is better than other languages.

Questions: Is English better than other languages?
                In what ways is it "better?"

Opinion:
Questions:

Opinion:
Questions:

Opinion:
Questions:

Opinion:
Questions:

Task 5 A checklist for evaluating research

The following five questions should be asked when critically evaluating others' or your own work. Some words have been removed. Use the words in the box below to complete the questions.

evidence	unbiased	viewpoints	concepts	reasoning

a) Is the issue under discussion clearly stated in a/n _____ fashion?

b) Is relevant _____, experience, and/or information provided?

c) Are key _____ defined as necessary?

d) Is there a clear line of _____ arriving at logical conclusions?

e) Are alternate _____ presented?

Task 6 Putting evaluation into practice

6.1 Look at the following essay question and, working with a partner, underline the opinion.

> The artificial language Esperanto would be a more appropriate global language than English in the twenty-first century. Discuss.

6.2 With your partner, discuss what questions you would need to ask in order to accept, reject, or suspend judgment of the opinions you have identified.

6.3 Use the checklist in Task 5 to evaluate the essay below. Make notes and then compare your ideas with your partner's.

The artificial language Esperanto would be a more appropriate global language than English in the twenty-first century. Discuss.

Esperanto, which remains one of the best-loved artificial languages to date, was invented by the brilliant Ludwig Lazarus Zamenhof in the late nineteenth century. Zamenhof, a multilingual who spoke Russian, Yiddish, Polish, Hebrew, Latin, Greek, French, German, and English, set out to develop an easy-to-learn universal second language which could help bring about world peace (Crystal, 1987).

How can a language help to bring about world peace? When he constructed Esperanto, Zamenhof hoped it would become a universal second language. He based his new language on a number of Indo-European languages. Its sounds are from Slavic, its vocabulary comes from a mixture of languages, including Latin, French, Spanish, and German (Wells, 1989). As a result, it is not associated with any one nationality and may be considered a truly international language.

Due to its international status, Esperanto is now widely spoken around the world. Although estimates vary widely, it is thought to have between 100,000 and 15,000,000 speakers. By the 1970s, over 60 countries had a national Esperanto association (Crystal, 1987). It is thus a global language.

Given that it is so easy to learn, Esperanto could rapidly overtake English as the global language of the twenty-first century. For example, in the mid-1960s approximately 1,000,000 people in 74 countries signed a petition addressed to the United Nations in favor of Esperanto becoming an official international language (Auld, 1988). Although the United Nations eventually rejected this proposal, the petition is evidence of Esperanto's popularity.

In conclusion, Esperanto would clearly make a better global language than English in the future, as it does not belong to any one group of people, and so its speakers are all equal. Moreover, Esperanto is a popular language, with speakers all over the world. This fact also makes it a better global language than English. Finally, Esperanto is a relatively new language compared with English. Arguably, Esperanto is the language of the future; English is the language of the past.

Bibliography

Auld E.F. Esperanto: the early struggle for recognition. Smiths Press, London 1988

6.4 We use critical thinking skills not only to evaluate other people's arguments, but also to improve our own. Use the checklist in Task 5 to evaluate a piece of your own writing. Make notes and then discuss your ideas with your partner.

Reflect

Consider the general thinking skills you use when you make everyday decisions. What to wear in the morning; what to eat for lunch; how to make use of your spare time. Choose a decision you have made today and try to analyze the process you went through to arrive at the decision. Reflect in the same way on other decisions you have made.

Compare these thinking skills with the critical thinking skills you have discussed in Unit 1. To what extent do you use them already to evaluate opinions and express your own opinions?

Think about your experience of people you know who have graduated from higher education studies. Bearing in mind what you have learned in this unit, do you feel they use critical thinking skills to a greater extent than others?

Student notes for Unit 1

2 Recognizing strong or sound arguments

At the end of this unit you will be able to:
- **identify parts of arguments;**
- **understand the relationship between the parts of an argument.**

In your university assessments, you will be rewarded for recognizing and using strong and sound arguments. It is therefore important to understand what these are and to be able to build your own strong and sound arguments.

An argument can be divided into two parts: premises and a conclusion. A premise gives evidence to support the conclusion. In some cases, the conclusion may not be directly stated, but it can be understood by the reader.

Task 1 Constructing an argument

1.1 Underline the premises and the conclusion in the following argument.
For example:

My tutor is always on time for her lessons, but today she is ten minutes late, so something must have happened to her!

Global warming is definitely happening. I don't care what people say, but it was hotter this year than it has ever been.

1.2 What are the unspoken premises in the following?

a) You can't travel to Bhutan without a visa, so Ali is going to have problems if he intends to fly out there tomorrow.

b) I heard on the radio this morning that the buses will be very disrupted tomorrow, so Natalia will be late for the interview.

1.3 What are the unspoken conclusions in the following?

a) The student candidate who best reflects mainstream opinion is very likely to win the next student election. The policies put forward by Sarah Rollings most closely match popular opinion.

b) The ban on smoking in public places will hit profits in cafes and bars. My cousin owns a large chain of bars.

Task 2 Recognizing sound or strong arguments

There are various types of arguments: valid, sound, and strong.

2.1 The following are examples of the three types of argument. Look at the three examples and underline the premises and the conclusions you find in them.

a) Some manufactured food products contain nuts. Harry is severely allergic to nuts. Therefore, he should avoid certain manufactured foods.

b) My aunt has sent me a check every year since I was five years old. Therefore, I expect to receive a check for my birthday this year too.

c) All Chinese people are good cooks. Ting Ting is Chinese so, as a consequence, she must be a good cook.

2.2 Now read the definitions of the three types of argument. Match an example to each one. When you have finished, check with your partner.

A valid argument
This is an argument where the conclusion absolutely follows from the premise, but the premise may not be true. _____

A sound argument
This is an argument where the conclusion absolutely follows from a true premise. A sound argument is deductive (working from general to particular). _____

A strong argument
This is an argument where the conclusion does not necessarily follow from the premise, but if the premise is strong enough, the conclusion is likely to be true. A strong argument is inductive (working from particular to general). _____

A good argument should ideally be both sound and strong.

Task 3 Checking your understanding

3.1 Are the following statements true or false?

a) Valid arguments are always good arguments.

b) If a strong argument has a false conclusion, then not all its premises can be true.

c) A sound argument can't have a false conclusion.

3.2 Match the type of argument and the example.

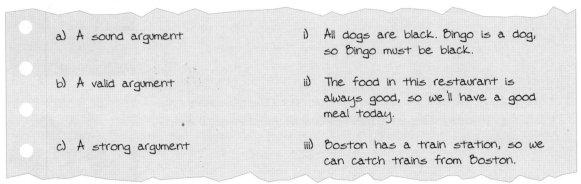

a) A sound argument

i) All dogs are black. Bingo is a dog, so Bingo must be black.

b) A valid argument

ii) The food in this restaurant is always good, so we'll have a good meal today.

c) A strong argument

iii) Boston has a train station, so we can catch trains from Boston.

3.3 Look at some arguments put forward in a seminar comparing the advantages and disadvantages of Esperanto and English as international languages. Decide if the arguments are valid, sound or strong. When you have finished, compare your answers with your partner's.

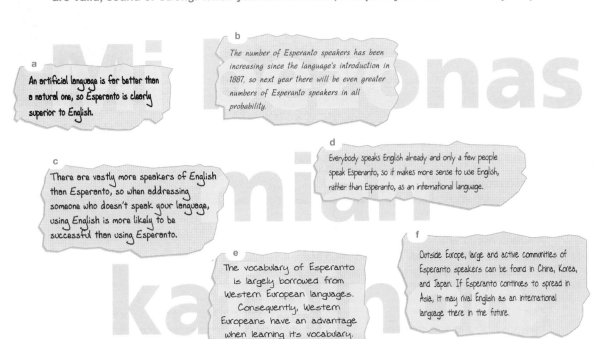

a
An artificial language is far better than a natural one, so Esperanto is clearly superior to English.

b
The number of Esperanto speakers has been increasing since the language's introduction in 1887, so next year there will be even greater numbers of Esperanto speakers in all probability.

c
There are vastly more speakers of English than Esperanto, so when addressing someone who doesn't speak your language, using English is more likely to be successful than using Esperanto.

d
Everybody speaks English already and only a few people speak Esperanto, so it makes more sense to use English, rather than Esperanto, as an international language.

e
The vocabulary of Esperanto is largely borrowed from Western European languages. Consequently, Western Europeans have an advantage when learning its vocabulary.

f
Outside Europe, large and active communities of Esperanto speakers can be found in China, Korea, and Japan. If Esperanto continues to spread in Asia, it may rival English as an international language there in the future.

Task 4 Your examples

4.1   Write two examples of a sound argument based on your field of study.

_____

_____

4.2   Write two examples of a valid argument based on your field of study.

_____

_____

4.3   Write two examples of a strong argument based on your field of study.

_____

_____

4.4   Work with a partner and share your examples. Together, you have four examples of each type
        of argument (sound, valid and strong). Evaluate all four examples for each type and choose
        the best one. Then copy your three examples onto a sheet of paper without saying which type
        of argument they exemplify. Swap papers with another pair. Match each example with a type
        of argument (sound, valid and strong). It may help to underline premises and conclusions to
        do this.

Reflect

Think about how your attitude to argumentation has changed now you have completed this unit.
Reflect on discussions you have had in the past. Do you feel they generally used sound arguments?

Reflect on whether the way you discuss issues varies according to the situation you are in and the
people you are with. Compare a late-night discussion with friends in a cafe or bar with a discussion
with fellow students after class.

Bearing in mind your thoughts on the above, do you feel it is always appropriate to use academic
arguments in daily life?

Student notes for Unit 2

....

....

....

....

Unit 3 Recognizing poor arguments

At the end of this unit you will be able to:
- recognize weak arguments;
- point out weak arguments politely.

In Unit 2, the focus was on recognizing and building strong and sound arguments. Unit 3 turns to the topic of poor or weak argumentation. In academic work, it is important to recognize poor argumentation in other people's work so that you are able to criticize the writers' ideas, and in your own work so that you can improve it.

Task 1 Spotting fallacious arguments

1.1 Arguments where the conclusion does not naturally follow from the premises or is not likely to occur are called fallacies or are fallacious. Look at the example below and underline the premises and the conclusion.

Hablo espanol.

" Pita speaks Spanish, so he must have come from Spain originally. "

1.2 Look at the arguments below. Underline their premises and their conclusions. Then discuss with your partner what is wrong with them as arguments.

a) He hasn't replied, so he must not have received my letter.

b) He does not wear glasses, so he must have excellent eyesight.

c) English is superior to other languages and, as a result, is a global language.

d) I've double-checked my essay, so there can't be any mistakes in it.

Task 2 Poor argumentation strategies

There are certain strategies that can be used in place of proper argumentation. The following exercise examines four of the most common.

2.1   Match the four strategies below with their explanations.

Strategies	Explanations
a) Being subjective.	1 This is where the speaker plays on your desire to conform and be the same as other people, but does not offer any premises or reasons why you should conform.
b) Appealing to common beliefs.	2 This is where the speaker tries to convince you of the validity of their opinion by making you annoyed rather than providing real evidence.
c) Invoking peer pressure.	3 This is where the speaker does not examine the claim critically. Instead, they refer to their own experience. This is an attempt to stop any further discussion.
d) Attempting to make others annoyed.	4 This is where the speaker uses the fact that many people believe something to be true as a reason for you to accept their argument.

2.2   Now match an example below to one of the four strategies. When you have finished, compare with a partner.

Examples

a)   _____   Our taxes are so high and the government is planning to use the extra revenue raised for opening multicultural centers. This is a complete waste of taxpayers' money.

GOVERNMENT TO WASTE MORE TAXPAYERS' MONEY

b)   _____   Everyone knows that living a rural life is preferable to the stresses of urban living.

URBAN LIVING CAUSES STRESS!

c) _____ The idea that we all need to eat five pieces of fruit or vegetables a day to be healthy may be true for some people, but it is definitely not true in my case.

FRUIT 'N VEG BAD FOR YOU!

d) _____ Harry Potter novels are childish and unsuitable for adults, so you should not read them.

HARRY DRIVES ADULTS MAD!

2.3   How could each of the arguments above be made into a strong or sound argument? Work individually and then compare your ideas with your partner's.

Task 3 Checking your understanding

3.1   Read the excerpts from a seminar on the advantages and disadvantages of English and Esperanto as international languages. Label examples of poor argument strategies as:

a) being subjective

b) appealing to common beliefs

c) invoking peer pressure

d) attempting to make others angry

1   People who think that Esperanto is better than English are a bit strange.

2   Listen, I know what I'm talking about. I've been an Esperanto speaker for years, and I can tell you it is far easier to learn than English. It's a fact. End of discussion.

3   I'm sure the CIA has been involved in making English the international language. It's America's way of dominating the world. Doesn't it make your blood boil?

4   Nobody thinks that Esperanto will ever rival English as an international language.

3.2   In seminars, it is important to point out when someone is using poor argumentation. We often do this by using a negative question form and softening language, e.g., *a little* + negative idea adjective. Write a reply to the poor arguments given in Task 3.1, using softening language.

> " Aren't you exaggerating a little? "

> " Haven't you got that slightly wrong? "

1   _____

2   _____

3   _____

4   _____

Reflect

Consider what you have learned about poor argumentation. Try to notice examples of poor argumentation over the next few days. Listen to informal and class discussions, and the arguments used in radio and TV debates.

Student notes for Unit 3

Unit 4 Persuasion through language or pressure

At the end of this unit you will be able to:
- recognize when language, rather than reason, is used to persuade;
- recognize when pressure, rather than reason, is used to persuade.

In English-speaking cultures, argument often occurs in contexts where there is opposition, for example in Congress or in the law courts. In these places, an issue is explored through two or more people taking opposing viewpoints and "attacking" each other's arguments. In this sense, the discussion is like a "fight" or a "duel." However, there are (unspoken) rules about what is acceptable, just like in a duel.

Words are very powerful. We need to be aware of how others may use words, as their words are like "weapons" in an argument. These language weapons may be used to manipulate us unfairly. Ideally, however, we should be persuaded by logical reasoning.

Task 1 Making an idea sound better or worse

Euphemisms are used when we want to make an idea that might have negative connotations more neutral or positive.

Euphemisms can be used in situations when we feel the need to be sensitive to others' feelings. For example, when we are talking to a friend whose father has died recently, we may prefer to say, "I'm sorry to hear about your loss," rather than, "I'm sorry to hear that your father has died."

When we are talking about people fighting against a government, we can show our viewpoint by describing them as either *terrorists* or *freedom fighters*. When we choose one of these descriptions, we are painting the fighters in a bad light (terrorists) or a good light (freedom fighters). This choice of language may affect the listeners' viewpoint without them realizing.

Freedom fighter or terrorist?

1.1   **Work in a group of 3–4 students. Discuss the following questions.**

    a) Do euphemisms exist in your language?

    b) Does your language have an expression like "freedom fighter?"

    c) In what sort of contexts do people use euphemisms?

    d) Why do people use euphemisms?

    e) Why should you avoid using euphemisms in academic argument?

Dysphemisms are used when we want to make a word more negative.

The word *terrorist* has a negative meaning, while the expression *freedom fighter* has a positive one, as we saw above. *Terrorist* is used by a person who is strongly critical of the soldier. In contrast, *freedom fighter* is used by someone who strongly approves of the soldier. Thus, the different choice of vocabulary indicates the speakers' different attitudes to the soldier.

1.2 Divide the following words into two lists according to whether they are euphemisms or dysphemisms. (They are all words and expressions that describe a person's appearance.) When you have finished, compare your answers with your partner's.

| skinny | slim | willowy | bony | svelte | skeletal | small-boned | scrawny |

Euphemisms:
The speaker approves

Dysphemisms:
The speaker disapproves

1.3 What is the best way to find out if a word indicates a neutral, approving or disapproving attitude on the part of the speaker? Discuss with your partner.

1.4 Working with your partner, give a euphemism or dysphemism for the following:

(i) a toilet

(ii) to kill someone or something

(iii) being overweight

Task 2 Making something sound less important or serious

No! I'm fine! Just a few scratches.

When we downplay something, we try to make it seem less important or significant in order to further our own ends.

2.1 Add each word or punctuation mark in brackets to its sentence. Pay attention to its correct position in the sentence.

a) He is a teacher. (just)

_____

b) It costs $30 a month to insure your life. (a mere)

_____

c) She got her degree from a Southern university. (" ")

_____

2.2 Working with a partner, discuss what each of the rewritten sentences means.

Task 3 Making something seem more important or serious

Hyperbole is a huge overstatement that may be used to persuade people of our viewpoint. The strength of the overstatement may persuade us to believe what someone has said, even though they may not have given us any premises.

For example:

Bob Dylan is the most inventive musician who has ever lived.

The use of hyperbole in the above is designed to leave the reader thinking Bob Dylan must be a very good musician, even if he is not the most inventive musician who has ever lived.

3.1 Discuss the hyperbole in the following statements in groups of 3–4 and speculate why the speaker has used it.

a) "I can't come to work because I have a serious illness. I have a headache."

b) "My parents won't let me stay out later than midnight. They're such fascists."

c) "It's the most boring film in the world!"

3.2 Working individually, write two more examples of hyperbole. Then read your examples to your group, and see if the other group members can decide why each piece of hyperbole might be used.

Task 4 Pressuring the audience

Speakers and writers can push their audiences to agree by using pressure. They can suggest that:

a) <u>all people</u> would find their arguments logical and reasonable;

b) all people <u>who are like the listener/reader</u> would find their arguments logical and reasonable.

4.1 **Read through the following statements and decide which category described above (a or b) they belong to. After you have finished, compare answers with your partner.**

“ *Anyone with half a brain understands that a natural language is better than an artificial one.* ”

“ *It is clearly the case that Esperanto is easier to learn than English.* ”

“ *Any educated person understands the value of English.* ”

“ *Anyone can see that Esperanto could be learned in weeks.* ”

“ *As is universally acknowledged, English will always be the best global language.* ”

“ *All intelligent people naturally recognize Esperanto's superiority over English.* ”

Task 5 Checking your understanding

5.1 **Read the following transcript of a discussion between two students about Esperanto and English. Underline the words and phrases they use to try to influence their listener unfairly.**

A: *Anyone with half a brain can see that Esperanto is an easier language to learn than English. It doesn't have any irregular verbs ... and it has the smallest vocabulary ever of any language.*

B: *But the "language" [the speaker makes a gesture with both hands] of Esperanto is totally unknown. Who speaks it? No one.*

A: *Unknown! It has one or two fewer speakers than English, but the difference in numbers is minimal.*

B: *You're joking! Esperanto has a handful of speakers and there's a reason for that. It's OK for chitchat, but you can't have a serious conversation in it.*

A: *Well, we're speaking English now and I wouldn't call this a serious conversation!*

5.2 **Compare your answers with your partner's. Discuss what happens to a discussion when language is used to persuade unfairly.**

Reflect

In this unit, we have studied the use of indirect language by English speakers. Think about the problems that this style of communication causes speakers from cultures that prefer direct expression.

Can you remember any situations where someone has used euphemisms, dysphemisms, hyperbole, or pressure in an argument? How did you respond?

Student notes for Unit 4

Detecting bias

At the end of this unit you will be able to:
- consider sources of bias in evidence in academic research;
- identify possible reasons for researcher bias.

A critical thinker must ask him- or herself questions about who has written a text or which body might be funding the research in order to decide whether or not the text may have been affected by things such as personal agendas or vested interests.

Task 1 Detecting possible bias—Interviews

In some academic disciplines, interviews are used to collect evidence. These interviews can provide detailed information that is difficult to obtain from other sources. However, the information given by the interviewee may not be accurate.

1.1   Working in a small group, brainstorm reasons why interviewees may not give a totally accurate picture. Write the list of possible reasons in the space below.

1.2   Discuss the following questions with your group. During your discussion, think about the following.

- the content of the questions
- choice of vocabulary and language style
- question types *Wh-* or *Yes/No* questions
- differences in age, gender, or culture

a) An interview is an interaction between two or more people. How might the interviewer affect what the interviewee says?

b) What can the interviewer do to minimize his or her impact on the interviewee?

Task 2 Detecting possible bias— Researchers and sources of funding

The relationship between a researcher and the research or the source of funding for the research might also affect the findings.

2.1 Working in a small group, discuss what *possible* bias might be involved in the following situations.

   a) A research report on nicotine and tobacco sponsored by the Tobacco Manufacturers' Association.

   b) A study on student library use conducted by a library threatened with closure.

   c) An ethnography of migrants living in Los Angeles written by an American person.

   d) A research report sponsored by a cereal manufacturer on the impact of fiber on a diet.

   e) Analysis of a questionnaire on student satisfaction with a class carried out by the professor.

2.2 Working with a partner, discuss the following questions.

   a) What could the researchers involved in the projects described above do in order to deal with the problem of possible bias?

   b) What could a student do to find out whether a writer or source of information might be biased?

Task 3 Avoiding bias

Researchers are starting to reflect more on who they are and how their identity affects their beliefs and actions. They then share this information with their audience. This is known as reflexivity. Reflexivity has two benefits: it allows the reader to assess the work in question more easily, and it reduces the possibility of the writer being criticized for being biased.

3.1 Imagine you are going to write a report on how successful non-native students are at American universities. If you included this type of description of yourself in your report, which of the following elements might it be useful for your reader to know?

   a) Your age
   b) Your religion
   c) Your star sign
   d) Your political affiliation
   e) Your nationality
   f) Your weight
   g) Your marital status
   h) Your gender
   i) Your sponsorship (if any)

j) Your hobbies

k) Your class

l) Your educational background

m) ....

n) ....

o) ....

3.2   Discuss with your partner any further elements to add to the list and write your ideas above.

3.3   Using the elements you selected, write a brief description of yourself that outlines how your personal identity impacts on your practice.

Reflect

In this unit, we have studied the problem of bias. Think about your own area of study. Is it possible to be entirely objective?

You will need to convince others of your objectivity both during your studies and after you graduate. How do you think you will do this?

Student notes for Unit 5

Unit 6 Putting it into practice

At the end of this unit you will be able to:
- use your critical thinking skills to construct your own arguments;
- evaluate your own and others' arguments using your critical thinking skills;
- recognize different styles of arguing;
- put together the skills you have developed in the earlier parts of the module.

The outcome of this unit will be a discussion of the following question: can local cultures be preserved despite the globalization of culture?

Task 1 Understanding the question

1.1   In small groups, discuss the following questions, taking notes on your discussion.

    a) How can you define "culture?"

    b) What do you understand by the phrase "globalization of culture?"

    c) What examples can you give of "local cultures?"

    d) What does the word "preserve" mean?

    e) What attitude towards culture does the word "preserve" suggest?

    f) What does the word "can" mean in the context of this essay title?

1.2   Working in pairs, write a list of statements that the discussion question presents as facts. Then compare your list with another pair's list and discuss whether, in your opinion, the statements are facts or not.

1.3 Working individually, try to rewrite the following statement in your own words. You can use more than one sentence if you wish.

Local cultures can be preserved despite the globalization of culture.

_____

_____

Task 2 Your view

It is important to be clear about your views on the discussion question.

2.1 Working individually, read the following statements and put a cross on each line to show how far you agree or disagree with the statements.

Culture is becoming globalized.

| 1 | 2 | 3 | 4 | 5 | 6 | 7 | 8 | 9 | 10 |
Completely agree   Completely disagree

Local cultures are valuable.

| 1 | 2 | 3 | 4 | 5 | 6 | 7 | 8 | 9 | 10 |
Completely agree   Completely disagree

It is possible to preserve local cultures.

| 1 | 2 | 3 | 4 | 5 | 6 | 7 | 8 | 9 | 10 |
Completely agree   Completely disagree

It is desirable to preserve local cultures.

| 1 | 2 | 3 | 4 | 5 | 6 | 7 | 8 | 9 | 10 |
Completely agree   Completely disagree

2.2 Compare your opinions with those of your partner. Give reasons for your opinions.

2.3 Work in a small group and discuss the following questions.

a) What are the alternatives to preserving local cultures?

b) What would the consequences of these alternatives be in your opinion?

c) Would these consequences be desirable? For whom?

Task 3 Gathering information

3.1 Working in a small group, discuss what questions you need to research in order to discuss this topic. Add them to the list below.

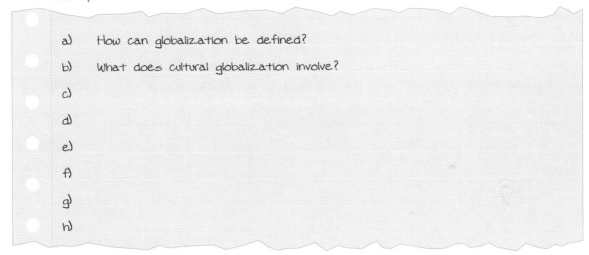

a) How can globalization be defined?

b) What does cultural globalization involve?

c)

d)

e)

f)

g)

h)

3.2 Divide up all the research questions between the group. Use the resources available to you to research the questions and take notes. When you are reading, practice applying the criteria given in Unit 1, Task 5 of this module.

3.3 Share the following with the other members of your group:

- the information you have collected;
- your evaluation of the arguments you have read.

Task 4 Developing your argument(s)

You are now going to prepare for the final discussion. It is important to develop your argument(s) so that the discussion helps you to broaden your understanding of the issue, rather than just exchanging opinions. To do this, you need to be clear about your general argument and the more specific arguments that support it.

4.1 To think about your general argument, put a cross on the line below to show where you stand on this issue.

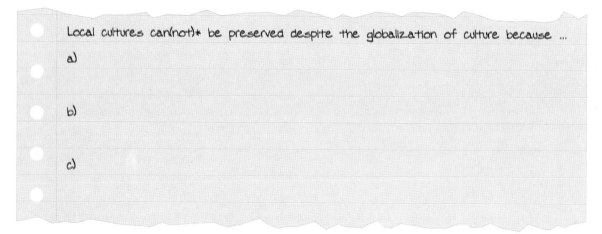

Local cultures can be preserved despite the globalization of culture.

| 1 | 2 | 3 | 4 | 5 | 6 | 7 | 8 | 9 | 10 |

Completely agree   Completely disagree

4.2 Now think about why you hold this opinion and write your answers below.

Local cultures can(not)* be preserved despite the globalization of culture because ...

a)

b)

c)

*delete as appropriate

4.3 For each point you wrote in Task 4.2, add a supporting reason. When you have done this, add one or two examples that you have discovered through your group's research.

4.4 Now work with a partner. Explain your overall argument and more specific arguments to each other, and make notes on your partner's ideas.

When you have completed your discussion, evaluate your partner's arguments. Check:

- the premises support the conclusions in the specific arguments;
- the specific arguments support the main argument in turn.

Give your partner feedback in a helpful and supportive way.

Task 5 Developing counter-arguments

Predicting how an argument might be countered is a useful exercise. It helps you to strengthen your arguments and prepare a defense of your ideas.

5.1   Take the specific arguments you developed in Tasks 4.2 and 4.3 and predict how another person might counter them.

5.2   Now work with a partner. One of you gives one of your specific arguments with supporting reasons and example(s). The other listens and then gives a counter-argument, with supporting reasons and possibly an example. You then swap roles.

Task 6 The discussion

6.1   Now discuss the question in a small group, keeping notes of the arguments put forward by the various speakers.

Task 7 Evaluating the arguments

7.1   Work in a group of three or four students. Use your notes from the group discussion to answer the following questions.

    a)   Which three arguments you heard in the discussion were most persuasive, and why?

    b)   Which three arguments you heard in the discussion were least persuasive, and why?

    c)   Did participating in the discussion change your overall opinion?

7.2 Now work in a new group of three or four students. Discuss the following questions.

a) Can you think of any examples where speakers used euphemisms or dysphemisms in the discussion? (*Look at Unit 4, Task 1.*)

b) Were there any examples of something being downplayed in the seminar? (*Look at Unit 4, Task 2.*)

c) Were there any examples of overstatement being used? (*Look at Unit 4, Task 3.*)

d) Were there any times in the discussion when you felt a speaker was pressuring you to agree with him or her? (*Look at Unit 4, Task 4.*)

7.3 Finally, discuss with a partner what you learned from participating in the seminar.

Reflect

In this unit, you discussed with other members of your class whether local cultures can be preserved despite globalization. Imagine various different settings and think about how differently the discussion might have progressed: for example, with your family, or with a group of environmental activists.

Then think about how this might be influenced if the participants were all of one nationality that had very different cultural values to your own.

Student notes for Unit 6

Module 6

Web work

Website 1 Critical discussions

http://www.criticalthinking.org/resources/articles/

Review

This website provides an excellent discussion of definitions of critical thinking, articles to read, and various other resources.

Task

Go to the ARTICLES link and then on to *Becoming a Critic of Your Thinking*. Look especially at the *How to* list for dysfunctional living. How many of these statements could apply to you? How can your study of critical thinking help you to change some of those statements?

Website 2 Critical thinking quiz

http://www.cof.orst.edu/cof/teach/for442/quizzes/q1003.htm

Review

This site takes the form of a fun quiz that should inspire you to think critically. A discussion of the answers is also provided.

Task

Using the quiz as a model, create three questions of your own that also require critical thinking. Try these questions out on a fellow student.

Extension activities

Activity 1

Choose from the resolutions below and conduct in-class debates where different groups take turns supporting or refuting the resolution in question. The audience should vote on which team has carried the resolution.

Resolutions:

a) It is better to work for a small company than a large corporation.

b) Foreign vacations are preferable to vacationing in one's home country.

c) All undergraduate students should be required to live in a residence hall throughout their time in college.

d) Voting should be mandatory.

When you are planning your arguments, keep in mind the exercises you have completed on what makes a good argument and avoid the pitfalls of poor argumentation.

Find a recent journal in your subject area and critically evaluate one of the articles in the journal, using the checklist from Unit 1.

Listen to an edition of "Any Questions" on the UK's BBC Radio 4 and see if you can note any examples of speakers trying to persuade the audience by using euphemisms or dysphemisms, or by downplaying or overstating a point.

You can listen to and find the tapescript of the show at:

http://www.bbc.co.uk/radio4/news/anyquestions.shtml

Glossary

Analyze (v) To break an issue down into parts in order to study, identify, and discuss their meaning and/or relevance.

Bias (n) An attitude you have, or a judgment you have made, based on *subjective opinion* instead of *objective fact*. It can make you treat someone or something in an unfair way.

Common beliefs (n) Ideas that are accepted as true by many people even though there is no evidence for them.

Concept (n) The characteristics or ideas associated with a class or group of objects. For example, the concept *city* brings to mind traits common to all places classed as *cities*. *Paris* is not a concept as it refers to a single, specific place.

Conclusion (n) The final part of a piece of academic writing, talk, or presentation that summarizes ideas and reaches a final result or judgment.

Counter-argument (n) An argument that opposes or makes the case against another argument.

Critical thinking (n) The academic skill of being able to look at ideas and problems in a considered, critical way in order to *evaluate* them. It also involves the ability to see links between concepts and develop one's own ideas.

Dissuade (v) Make someone stop believing an idea or argument, or prevent them from doing something, by *reasoning* with them.

Downplay (n) Make something seem less important or significant in order to support our own ideas.

Dysphemism (n) An offensive and emotive term or expression that is used to replace a neutral term when we want to make a description sound more negative. For example, *brat* is a dysphemism for *child*.

Euphemism (n) A neutral or inoffensive expression that is used to replace a more negative or offensive expression when we want to make something sound more positive. For example, *pass away* is a euphemism for *die*.

Evaluate (v) To assess information in terms of quality, relevance, *objectivity* and accuracy.

Fact (n) Something that is known or can be demonstrated to be true.

Fallacy (n) A false belief that is due to faulty reasoning.

Hyperbole (n) Huge overstatement that may be used to *persuade* someone of a *viewpoint*.

Manipulate (v) To influence or control someone else's *opinion* in a dishonest way.

Objective (adj) (n) 1 (adj) Not influenced by personal feelings or emotions. 2 (n) The aim, or what you want to achieve from an activity.

Opinion (n) A personal belief that may be *subjective* and is not based on certainty or *fact*.

Overstate (v) To exaggerate or state in terms that are stronger than necessary.

Paraphrase (v) To alter a piece of text so that you restate it (concisely) in different words without changing its meaning. It is useful to paraphrase when writing a summary of someone's ideas; if the source is acknowledged, it is not plagiarism. It is also possible to paraphrase your own ideas in an essay or presentation; that is, to state them again, often in a clearer, expanded way.

Peer pressure (n) The pressure on someone to conform, look, behave, or think in the same way as other people.

Persuade (v) Make someone believe something (such as an idea or argument) or do something, by reasoning with them.

Poor argumentation (n) An argument that is not strong or sound because the *conclusion* does not follow from the *premise*, or because the *premise* is faulty.

Premise (n) A statement that is assumed to be true by an author or speaker who is presenting an argument.

Reasoning (n) The arguments or logic one uses to form *conclusions* and judgments.

Sound argument (n) An argument where the *conclusion* absolutely follows from true *premises*. For example: All cats are carnivores: tigers are cats; therefore, tigers are carnivores. A sound argument is deductive (working from general to particular).

Strategy (n) A plan of action that you follow when you want to achieve a particular goal. For example, it is possible to have a clear strategy for passing an exam.

Strong argument (n) An argument where the *conclusion* does not necessarily follow from the *premise*, but if the *premise* is strong enough the conclusion is likely to be true. For example: Tigers sometimes eat people; therefore, this tiger is likely to eat us. A strong argument is inductive (working from particular to general).

Subjective (adj) Describes an idea or *opinion* that is based on someone's personal opinion rather than on observable phenomena.

Valid argument (n) An argument where the *conclusion* absolutely follows from the *premises*, but the *premises* may not be true. For example: All birds can fly; penguins are birds; therefore, penguins can fly.

Viewpoint (n) The mental position that someone sees things from. For example, the viewpoint of a child is different to that of its parent.

Weak argument (n) An argument that is not *valid*, *strong* or *sound* because the *premise* is wrong and/or the *conclusion* does not follow from the *premise*.

Module 7: Introduction to IT Skills

Introduction

A practical understanding of office-based software packages is more and more important for students in continuing and higher education. In almost all academic disciplines and subjects, students now have to submit essays and reports using word processing and spreadsheets. This may be difficult for some students at first, but there are many benefits, especially for editing and storing information.

Although contemporary students are increasingly IT literate, coping with IT skills in an unfamiliar context can be challenging. This is particularly the case when adapting to the academic expectations of a new institution or department at the start of a program of study.

Unit 1 focuses on creating a document and shows you many of the choices you can make. Unit 2 focuses on using tools and utilities that help you manipulate texts and documents. Unit 3 looks specifically at using word processing in an academic environment. Unit 4 helps you understand how to save and store documents, as well as send them to other people. Unit 5 focuses on the use of spreadsheets in your university studies. Finally, Unit 6 will help you to select and create appropriate graphs and charts to complement your work.

After completing this unit, you should feel more confident in using a wide variety of features of *Microsoft Word* and *Microsoft Excel* in your college or university studies.

Skills Map

Unit 1 — Creating a document

Study menu options to understand the choices you can make when creating a document. Learn how to use the toolbar effectively.

Unit 2 — Modifying and manipulating text

Learn more about the choices you can make when creating a document. Practice highlighting text in order to modify and move it around.

Unit 3 — Word processing academic documents

Become more familiar with academic conventions. Learn how to use headers and footers effectively. Gain confidence in using the spell and grammar check to edit your work.

Unit 4 — Filing and sending documents

Gain confidence in storing documents on different drives. Practice sending attachments by e-mail.

Unit 5 — Understanding and using spreadsheets

Explore the benefits of using spreadsheets for certain operations. Become familiar with tabulating numerical information and applying formulas to tables.

Unit 6 — Creating charts and graphs

Learn how to create appropriate charts and graphs.

Destination: Introduction to IT Skills

Creating a document

At the end of this unit you will:

- know more about choices you can make when creating a document by studying the menu options;
- be able to use the toolbar effectively.

Task 1 Getting ready

1.1 Switch on the computer. It will open with a view of the desktop. Click on the *Microsoft Word* icon if there is one on the desktop.

Alternatively, click on the *Start* menu on the bottom left-hand side of the screen. Click *Start*, then click the *Word* icon.

You are now ready to start. Although you may be familiar with some of the functions that can help in your typing and word processing, this unit will show you some of the utilities, or word-processing options and facilities, which can help you to improve the presentation of your work.

Task 2 Menu options

At the top of the screen there is a *menu* bar with a list of categories. The categories are indicated by words. Each menu at the top of your screen opens a drop-down menu with a list of options.

Sometimes you will only see the most common options plus an arrow at the bottom. By clicking the arrow, you can get more options (you do not need to see the extra options at this stage). You will notice that some options are in black writing and others are in gray. If they are gray, it is because options are not active at this time—but they can become active when you do other operations.

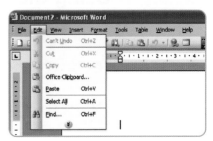

2.1 Look at the list of words on the menu bar. Click each of the following menus: *File, Edit, View, Insert, Format, Tools, Table* and *Window*. Read the list of options for each one. Decide which menu you would use for:

   a) checking the spelling of a word;

   b) formatting in double-spacing;

   c) adding a hyperlink within a document to a web page;

   d) finding out general information about *Microsoft Word*;

   e) inserting a table;

   f) adding a header to the page.

2.2 Discuss your findings with another student.

2.3 See how many of the utilities you can list for each of the options, without looking at the screen.

Menu option	Sub-menu utilities
File	New, Open, …

2.4 Work in small groups. Discuss which of the above functions you: a) already use; and b) might use in your future college or university studies.

Task 3 Using the *Help* menu

For utilities you do not know, you can use the *Help* option to find out more.

3.1 Practice using the *Help* option by following these steps. Then compare what you have found with another student.

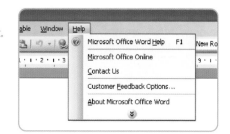

a) Open the *Help* menu and look at the drop-down menu that appears.

b) Find two different ways of getting help from the utilities.

c) Find some help on how you can check your spelling and grammar.

Note: The explanations in the *Help* option are sometimes complex. You might find it easier to complete the whole module before making use of *Help*.

Task 4 Learn more about menu options

4.1 Look at the *File* menu below. Write the correct letter in the chart and then check with another student.

a)
b)
c)
d)
e)
f)

g)
h)
i)
j)
k)
l)
m)
n)

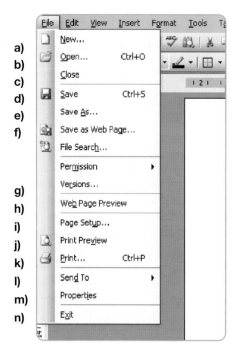

What the menu option is for	Key commands
choose a name for your document	
print a document	
close the active document without exiting Word completely	
save a document for later use	
find out who wrote the original document and other details	
save a document for viewing on a web browser	
create a new document	
change the margins and layout of your page	
see what the printed version of your page will look like	
preview a web page	
close down Word after prompting you to save	
send your document to someone by e-mail	
open an existing document	
find earlier versions of the same document	

4.2   Add key commands in column 3 where appropriate, e.g., *Ctrl+N*.

4.3   Work in pairs or small groups, and prepare your own short oral descriptions for each menu option or utility.

Remember to use the *Help* option for utilities that you do not know.

4.4   Choose one menu that you did not know before and write some notes to explain the purpose of each option.

4.5   Find a student who has chosen the same menu to write about. Compare your descriptions of
       the different menu options.

       Help each other to work out the most memorable descriptions. When you do this, it's a good idea to
       think about how you will make use of these options in your university study.

Task 5 Practical work

5.1   Practice some of your new skills with another student by using the utilities together.

5.2   Complete the table below to show the five most important or useful things you've learned.

I have learned how to ...	... by using ...	I need it to ...

5.3   Now add what you would still like to know.

I want to know how to ...	... because ...

Student notes for Unit 1

2 Modifying and manipulating text

At the end of this unit you will:
* **understand more about the choices you can make when creating a document;**
* **be able to highlight, modify, and move text around.**

In Unit 1, you looked at the menu options. These gave access to a variety of utilities. You also looked briefly at a second way of accessing these utilities using shortcuts on the keyboard, for example Ctrl/P for *Print*.

We will now look at a third way—using icons. These show utilities in picture form. They allow you to do certain tasks more easily than using the menu options, once you get used to using them.

When the main groups of icons are open, they are displayed directly below the menu options. They may or may not be open on your computer.

Task 1 Familiarize yourself with toolbars and icons

1.1   Click on the *View* menu, then the *Toolbars* sub-menu, and answer these questions.

    a) How many toolbars can you find?

    b) How many have a check next to them?

Notice that the toolbars that have been selected (✓) appear on the screen.

1.2   Using the mouse and cursor, make sure the following toolbars have been selected by checking (✓) the boxes.

* Standard
* Formatting
* Drawing
* Tables and Borders

Which of the four toolbars normally appear under the menu options and which one at the bottom of the page?

1.3 Match each of the toolbars in 1.2 with the correct description below.

i) The *Drawing* toolbar supplies a range of image sources that can add to the visual impact of the document you are creating. This toolbar offers a series of instruments for creating boxes and artwork to enhance the written word.

ii) The *Standard* toolbar gives you alternative access to many of the basic utilities available in the *File* menu option. You can use this toolbar to print or save a document.

iii) The *Formatting* toolbar allows you to change the appearance and layout of the text on your screen. This toolbar helps you by providing a selection of fonts and a choice of formatting for the text you are creating. (You should have explored these options in Unit 1.)

iv) The *Tables and Borders* toolbar is a set of tools for the ordering of information in tables and charts. This toolbar has all the devices you will need for creating spaces, called cells, and ordering data efficiently.

1.4 Compare your answers with a partner and discuss any difference of opinion you may have. Check with your instructor if necessary.

Task 2 Explore ways of using icons

2.1 With another student, identify the icon you need to click on to carry out the following tasks.

a) undo the task you have just done

b) insert an arrow

c) change the font style

d) see what the page looks like before printing

e) write bullet points

f) underline a word

g) center your text

h) change the text to bold

Task 3 Navigating in a document

If you have written a long document, you need to understand how to navigate (move around) in the text and find things easily. There are various ways of navigating a text.

3.1 Follow the procedure below and compare your findings with another student.

a) Click on *Microsoft Word* to open a new document.

b) Use the return key to make your document two or more pages long.

c) Look at the scroll bars at the side and bottom of the screen and try to find different ways of moving around your document. Use the scroll bars and the computer keys.

Unit 2

3.2 What are the following buttons and keys used for? Discuss your ideas with a partner.

Task 4 Highlighting and moving text

Highlighting text is the first step in making many different changes to your documents, including moving text within a document or from one document to another. You will practice this in the following tasks.

4.1 Create a document in *Word*, and then type the following.

Bibliography
Morris, J. & Winn, M. (1990). *Housing and social inequality.* London: Longman

Now follow these instructions.

a) Place the cursor at the beginning of the word *Bibliography*.

b) Click the left mouse button and hold it as you drag (or move) the cursor to the right. This will *highlight* (or cover) the word.

c) Release the mouse button when the cursor has reached the end of the word *Bibliography*.

The word *Bibliography* should now appear with a black background (Bibliography). This means that you have successfully highlighted a piece of text.

Practice highlighting different pieces of the text, one after the other.

4.2 Move highlighted text by following the steps below.

a) Highlight the word *Bibliography* again.

b) Place the cursor anywhere on the highlighted text.

c) Keep the mouse depressed and drag the cursor to the end of your text, i.e., after the word *Longman*.

e) Take your finger off the mouse.

The word *Bibliography* should now be after the word *Longman*. If so, you have successfully moved a piece of text from one place to another.

4.3   See what happens to highlighted text if you do the following operations. Discuss how you can perform the same operations in another way.

   a)   Click on *Ctrl+C*.

   b)   Click on *Ctrl+X*.

   c)   Click on *Ctrl+V*.

Task 5 Using the horizontal ruler

Another important tool is the horizontal ruler. This may or may not be open on your computer. Click on *View* and see if the *Ruler* option has been checked. If not, click on it now.

You will see the following symbol on the left

and the following symbol on the right.

5.1   Put the curser on the left-hand marker.

When it looks like this, left-click and move to the left. Notice that all the writing moves to the left.

5.2   Click on the word *Bibliography*. Then click on the small square on the bottom of the left marker and move it to the right. Notice that the word moves to the right, but the sentence below stays where it is.

   Bibliography
   Morris, J. & Winn, M. (1990). *Housing and social inequality*. London: Longman

   What do you think happens if you highlight both lines, then move the small square to the left?

   You can experiment more with the ruler as you gain experience in layout.

Task 6 Using what you have learned

6.1 Practice using some of the actions you have learned about in this unit. Follow the steps below.

a) Click on the *Word* icon to open a new document.

b) Choose a font and a font size that you like.

c) Write a text of 20 lines or more giving information to another student about computer menus and icons.

d) Experiment with the spacing and layout.

e) Experiment with moving the different sections of your text to different places.

f) Click on the *Save* icon and type in a name for your document.

g) Swap texts with another student and make some changes to their text.

h) Go back to your original text and undo the changes the other student made.

6.2 Discuss the following with another student.

a) What you have done.

b) Ways in which *you* can use this skill (think about your future university studies).

Reflect

Think about what you have learned about using icons. Consider the difference between using icons and using the menu options. Which would you use to carry out a complex task? Which would you use to carry out a simple task?

Reflect on when you are likely to use the operations you have practiced in this unit for writing your academic assignments.

Student notes for Unit 2

Unit 3 Word-processing academic documents

At the end of this unit you will:
- **be more familiar with academic conventions;**
- **be able to use headers and footers effectively;**
- **be more confident about using the spell and grammar check to edit your work.**

Higher education institutions do not expect all assignments to be written in exactly the same format. However, each department will probably expect you to follow its own *in-house format*. This will include a particular kind of font, line spacing, bold, italics, front page, and headers and footers.

Task 1 Understanding house style

1.1   Discuss these questions with another student.

a)   Why do you think universities and colleges expect students to follow their house style?

b)   Have you been taught to use a particular format at educational institutions that you have attended? If so, what?

1.2   Which of the following does your institution ask you to use when writing assignments? If you are not sure of any points on the list, discuss with your instructor.

a)   double-spacing

b)   a specific margin width

c)   justified text

d)   a header or footer

e)   page numbers

f)   indented quotations

g)   a particular font or size of letters

h)   footnotes

1.3   Work with another student. Check that you know how to do all the operations in the list.

Task 2 Formatting an academic assignment

You have been told to write an assignment entitled *Overseas Students in the US*. Your professor wants you to write a document using:

- Times New Roman;
- double-spacing;
- centered title (18-point size, bold, capital letters);
- heading on the left: *Introduction* (12-point size, bold, lower case).

2.1   Write the title and headings requested by your professor.

2.2   Compare your work with another student's version.

Check that your final "product" looks exactly like the other student's layout. If it doesn't, discuss what went wrong. If one of you finished much more quickly, discuss why (it's possible one of you followed a quicker procedure).

Overseas Students in the US

Task 3 Setting headers and footers

Your professor has asked you to include a footer on each page of your assignment as follows: your first name, last name and the full title of your assignment (12-point size, bold).

3.1   Discuss with another student how to do this. Then complete the task.

You will now have the same footer on each and every page of the document.

3.2   Look at the *Header and Footer* toolbar and check to be sure you know what each icon represents. Experiment with using some of the icons.

Task 4 Using the spell and grammar check

You may be asked to use the spell and grammar check before you submit a written assignment at university.

4.1 How do you do each of these operations? Discuss with another student.

a) Check the spelling of a complete document.

b) Check the spelling in *part* of a document.

The grammar check will normally be activated when you click on the ABC icon, unless it is disabled for some reason. The grammar check is useful for correcting tenses, noun + verb agreement, word order, etc. Sometimes, however, it will suggest changes to things that do not need to be altered.

4.2 Find examples of: a) *useful*; and b) *useless* information you can get from the grammar check. If you are unsure, ask your instructor.

4.3 Type the following (correct) sentences into your computer and see if the grammar check marks problems with any of them. Discuss with a partner whether what the grammar check marks is useful or not.

a) The more documents you create, the more untidy your *My Documents* page will look.

b) A database consists of information that has been ordered and presented in a particular way.

c) Quickly carry out the following operations.

d) You should write a short user guide that could be used by another student.

4.4 Now plug in your memory stick, go to a document stored there and practice using your spell and grammar check for five minutes (on documents of your choice). Decide if the check has told you something useful or not.

If you have a recurrent problem with spelling and/or grammar, e.g., the difference between plural and singular verbs, you may find the check is very useful.

Although it is useful to use the spell and grammar check, always *proofread** your documents before handing them in to your instructor. When you do this, consider particular spelling or grammar problems that you have.

*Proofreading means reading very slowly for accuracy rather than meaning.

Reflect

Think about the opportunities a computer gives you to format documents in different ways. Then reflect on the reasons for using a house style.

Think about how you can you use word-processing features to help you create documents in the most time-efficient way. Make a note to set aside time each week to learn new features that will help you work more efficiently.

Student notes for Unit 3

Unit 4 Filing and sending documents

At the end of this unit you will:
- be more confident about how to store documents in files on different drives;
- be able to send attachments by e-mail.

Task 1 Filing documents

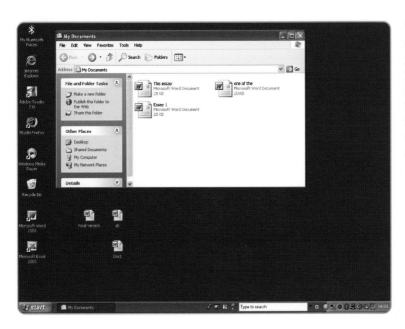

You already know how to create and save a document. However, if you have too many documents on your desktop or in the *My Documents* folder, it will look untidy and be difficult to find them. It is therefore important to create folders in which to save and organize your documents.

1.1 The easiest way to create a folder is to use the mouse. Practice as follows on the desktop.

- Right-click with the mouse.
- Click on *New*.
- Then click on *Folder*.

A folder called *New folder* will appear on the desktop. Rename the folder as follows:

- Left-click once on the folder.
- Then left-click again on the name.
- Finally, type *General work folder*.

1.2 The best place to keep your documents is in *My Documents*. Access this by clicking on *Start* (bottom-left of the screen). Right-click on *My Documents* and click *Show on Desktop*. A shortcut to *My Documents* will appear on your desktop for easy access.

Tidy up your documents as follows.

- Left-click a document on the desktop.

- Hold the left button down and drag the document into *General work folder*.

- Do this for all the documents on the desktop.

- Then left-click *General work folder* and drag it into *My Documents*.

Double-click *My Documents* and you will find *General Work Folder* is now there. Double-click *General Work Folder* and you will find all the documents from the desktop.

If you now go to *My Documents,* you should be able to see your new folder. If so, you have successfully created a folder.

1.3 Discuss the questions below in small groups.

You have a folder named *Philosophy* and you have just created two documents named *Descartes* and *Plato*. If you go to *My Documents*, you will see the folder and the documents stored there.

a) What is the easiest way to move your documents into your *Philosophy* folder?

b) If you create a sub-folder called *Modern Philosophy*, how can you put it into the main *Philosophy* folder?

c) There are several ways of viewing your documents in the folder. How can you view them:

- alphabetically?

- as a list?

- together with information about their size, etc?

Task 2 Saving to a folder

Now you know how to create folders, you need to make sure you save your documents in the right folder.

2.1 Discuss the following menu with another student. How do you make sure you save to the right folder?

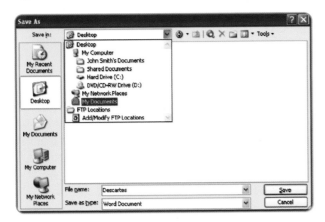

2.2 Write the procedure for saving a document into *My Documents* for the first time.

a) Click on the .... menu options.

b) Click .... within the *File* menu.

c) If the name of the folder next to *Save in* is not .... , click on the arrow next to the folder name. Then click the .... folder.

d) Type the .... of document you wish to save.

e) Click ....

Task 3 Using a memory stick

If you are working on a computer that is not your own, you will need to save a copy of your work to take away with you. You may also wish to give or send your work to an instructor or another student.

3.1 A memory stick is a very useful way of transferring data. How many other ways can you think of to transfer your work to a different computer? Discuss your ideas with another student.

3.2   What are the advantages and disadvantages of each form of transfer? Write them below.

3.3   Follow the directions for transferring a document onto a memory stick. How similar is the procedure for saving a document onto a CD or external hard drive?

- Insert your memory stick in the port (note that you should hear a noise to confirm that it has been correctly installed).

- Right-click on your document.

- Click on *Send to*.

- Click on the name of the memory stick (usually in drive *E*).

Note: When you remove a memory stick, you should click on the following icon to make sure it is removed safely.

3.4   Practice this procedure a few times. Save at least three documents onto your portable storage.

Task 4 Sending attachments

Another important way of transferring data is by e-mail. The latest utilities make this a very easy operation. You can even send a document that you are still working on.

4.1   Look at the following two procedures for sending a document by e-mail. How are the procedures different and how are the results different?

Procedure 1

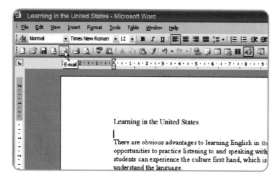
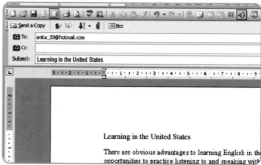

Procedure 2

 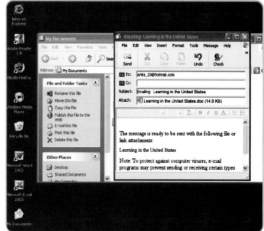

4.2   Complete Procedure 2 for sending an e-mail.

Right-click on the _____ you wish to send.

Select _____ .

Then left-click on *Mail* _____ .

Type the e-mail address of the recipient.

_____ the subject if you wish.

Write a _____ to the recipient if you wish.

Left-click on _____ .

4.3   With another student, discuss different ways of sending documents by e-mail. Write one
        procedure below.

4.4 Collect the e-mail addresses of all the students in your class and type them in the *Address Book* of your mail service. Send attachments to various students from different places on your computer.

4.5 Follow the instructions below for extra practice in sending e-mails with attachments.

a) Work with another student. Imagine that one of you is an instructor and the other is a student. The "student" should send an e-mail with a document attached to the "instructor."

b) The "instructor" should read it, write comments on it, and make alterations as necessary before sending it back (as might actually be the case between instructor and student).

c) The document can go backwards and forwards as many times as you like. Make sure that you then reverse roles.

Note: You may wish to do this outside the class.

Reflect

Think about what you have learned about filing and sending documents. In particular, think about ways in which you can save valuable time.

Reflect on the need for carefully organized backup for your key documents. Think about how you can use the information in this unit to organize backup.

Student notes for Unit 4

Unit 5 Understanding and using spreadsheets

At the end of this unit you will:
- understand the benefits of using spreadsheets instead of word-processing programs for some operations;
- be familiar with how to tabulate numerical information and apply formulas to tables.

As with the previous units, we assume that you are using the *Microsoft Excel* spreadsheet software, as it is the most common. You may have to adjust some tasks if you are using different software.

Task 1 What spreadsheets are for

A spreadsheet is basically a table that can be used for ordering and presenting information in a particular way for a particular purpose. Spreadsheets are often used as databases, although for commercial use it is generally better to use dedicated database software.

1.1 In groups, discuss the following questions.

a) Electronic databases are widely used. What are their advantages for:
- individuals?
- organizations?

b) What other uses can you make of spreadsheets?

Task 2 Using *Excel*

Opening a new spreadsheet is similar to opening a word-processing document. Click on the *Excel* icon or select the appropriate option from the *Start* menu.

When you open a blank spreadsheet, you will see many similarities between the menu options and toolbars in *Word* documents.

Microsoft Excel 2008

2.1 Identify toolbar icons that are not used in *Word*. Discuss what you think they may be for with another student.

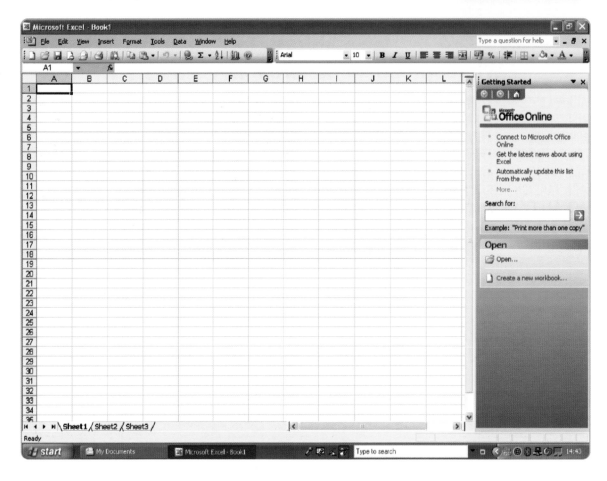

2.2 Look at the main menu options at the top of the page. Which one is different from the menus in *Word*?

2.3 Make a list in the table opposite of the main features and utilities in the spreadsheet that do not appear in *Word*. Use the *Help* option to find out about any features that you are not sure of.

Note: You may need to look at a *Word* document to do this.

Menu option	Features that do not appear in Microsoft Word	Functions
File	Print area	Allows you to choose parts of the spreadsheet that you want to print

2.4   Compare the contents of your chart with your partner.

Task 3 Creating cells

Spreadsheets use a system of *cells*, like boxes in a table. These can be used to make a table of data with columns and rows. Usually, the top row is used to label the columns.

Look at the information about four companies and three countries below. The information shows the net income for each company from exports to each of the three countries in 2004.

Apollo Inc.: **Canada** $2,000,000 **Mexico** $2,010,000 **Japan** $1,000,500

Bangles Inc.: **Canada** $3,000,000 **Mexico** $500,000 **Japan** $1,250,000

Corgi Inc.: **Canada** $1,800,000 **Mexico** $1,900,000 **Japan** $800,500

Davis Inc.: **Canada** $2,000,500 **Mexico** $2,020,000 **Japan** $2,030,500

3.1   Follow the instructions below to input information into the cells in your spreadsheet.

   a) Label the first cell *Company* (Column A, Row 1).

   b) Label the next three cells in the same row: *Canada*, *Mexico,* and *Japan* (Columns B, C, and D). Use the cursor and/or the arrows on your keyboard.

   c) Now add the data, starting with the heading *Company* in Column A. In the second row type *Apollo Inc.*, in the third row type *Bangles Inc.*, in the fourth *Corgi Inc.*, and in the fifth *Davis Inc.*

   d) Add the figures for Canada in Column B. Exports for Apollo Inc. were $2,000,000, so type 2,000,000 into Row 2. Continue in the same way for the other three companies. Make sure commas are in the correct place.

   e) Finally, add the figures for Mexico and Japan in Columns C and D.

   Note: Column B, Row 1 is cell B1, etc.

3.2   Compare your table with Columns A–D of the table on page 215.

   Note that you can refer to specific information by identifying the cell that contains the information. Cells are referred to by the letter and number: A1 = Column A, Row 1. For example, you can find the income from Mexico for Corgi Inc. in cell C4 ($1,900,000).

3.3   Discuss what the other cells in the spreadsheet show with another student. Then check with your instructor.

Task 4 Using formulas

Some of the most useful tools in database software are *Formulas* and *Functions*. These help you to make calculations using the data in your table or worksheet.

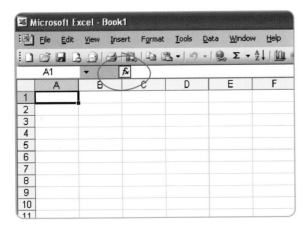

4.1 Discuss with your partner whether the formula below is correct.

> The formula to find the total income for Apollo Inc. is B2+C2+D2, i.e., you need to add cells B2, C2, and D2.

4.2 Follow the steps below to see how the spreadsheet can do the calculation automatically.

a) Give Column E the title *Total* (cell E1).

b) Type the formula =B2+C2+D2 into cell E2 and press *Enter*. The total income for Apollo Inc. will now appear.

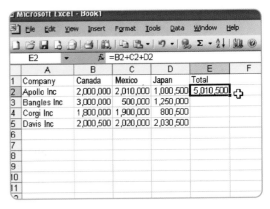

c) Right-click on the tiny black square at the bottom-left corner of the highlighted cell, E2. The cursor changes to a small +.

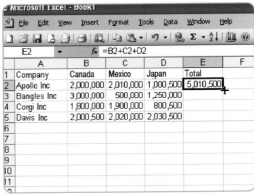

d) Hold the mouse button down and drag the corner over cells E3, E4, and E5. The formula will transfer automatically to these cells; the data in Rows 3, 4, and 5 will then be added up to give a total for each company.

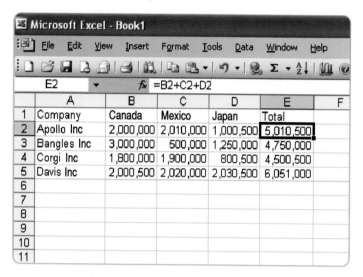

Task 5 Creating your own formulas

The following symbols are used in formulas:

Add	Subtract	Multiply	Divide
+	-	*	/

5.1 Write the formula you would use to calculate the average income per country that each company earned from exports.

5.2 Follow the steps below to test the formula.

a) Type the formula into cell F2.

b) Drag the formula down the rows to calculate the averages for all the companies.

Task 6 Using functions

Functions help you to manipulate your data, so you can work with it more efficiently. They can be used instead of formulas.

6.1 Discuss with another student which of the three functions below is likely to be the correct one to replace the formula =B2+C2+D2.

=SUM(B2:D2) =SUM(MAX B2+C2+D2) =SUM B2/C2/D2

Try the one you think is correct.

6.2 Apply the function to add up columns.

By changing the cell references, you can use the above function to calculate the total value of exports to Canada. Instead of B2 to D2, you now want to add B2 to B5.

a) Type the function into cell B6 and press *Enter* to get the total exports to Canada.

b) Use your mouse to drag the formula across the columns from B6 to D6 to calculate the total value of exports to Mexico and Japan.

Task 7 Exploring functions

Different types of functions can be used with different data for different needs and types of analysis.

7.1 With another student, explore the *Function* facility using the *Insert* menu.

Alternatively, you can use the toolbar icon.

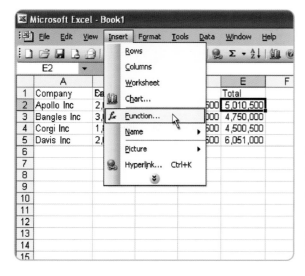

Decide which function categories are likely to be most useful to you in your academic studies.

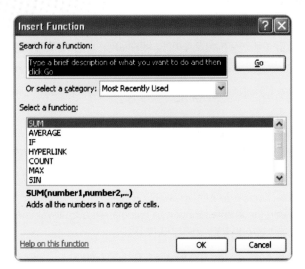

Reflect

Spreadsheets are considered to be very useful tools for business, study, and even for personal use. Reflect on how you can use them to make more efficient use of your time.

Make a list of as many possible uses you can think of. Then decide which ones would be of genuine help to you.

Student notes for Unit 5

Unit 6 Creating charts and graphs

At the end of this unit you will:
- **feel more confident about choosing the appropriate chart or graph to represent your data;**
- **understand how to create a chart or graph using *Excel*.**

When you present and explain data in reports or presentations, it can be difficult for your audience to get a clear picture of trends or patterns from a table of data or a spreadsheet. This is especially true if there is a lot of data.

It is, therefore, often useful to convert spreadsheet entries into a chart or graph form that shows the information more clearly. Fortunately, there is a facility in all spreadsheet software that can convert data into charts and graphs. This is easy to use once you understand the basic procedure.

Task 1 Choosing the right chart

The first decision you have to make is how to represent your data. As the purpose is to represent your data in visual form, you naturally want to choose the one that represents it most clearly.

1.1 Match the charts or graphs below to the correct labels.

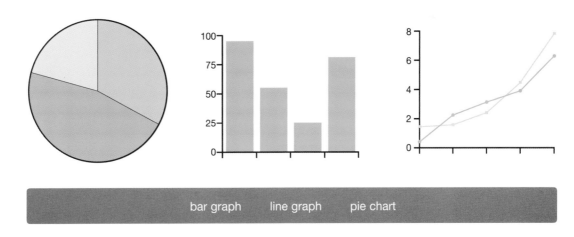

bar graph   line graph   pie chart

1.2 Read the following descriptions of information in three different spreadsheets. Choose the most appropriate chart or graph to illustrate the information provided. Discuss the reasons for your choice with another student.

a) A person's spending and potential savings expressed as a proportion of total income over one year.

b) Daily calorie intake over a period of 12 months.

c) Number of hours spent on four different leisure activities by American teenagers in 2004 and 2005.

1.3   Discuss the best way of graphically displaying the data you entered into the exports database in Unit 5, Task 3.

Note: Sometimes the choice is obvious, but at other times it depends on what aspect of the data you are highlighting, or simply on personal choice.

Task 2 Creating a chart

Probably the most effective method of displaying the data collected in the exports database is with a bar graph. This enables the viewer to compare each company's income gained from different countries.

You are now going to create the chart below by following five simple steps.

2.1   Follow the steps below to create the graph.

a) Select all the data in the database that you created on exports and drag the mouse over it so that it is highlighted in another color.

b) Click on the charts icon, which can be found in the toolbar above the cell screen. The *Charts Wizard* will appear.

c) Select *Column Chart* and choose one of the chart sub-types.

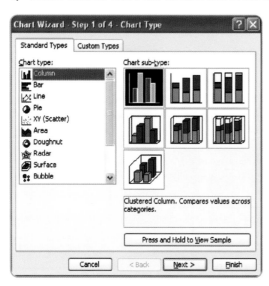

d) Complete each section of the wizard, moving on to each stage by clicking *Next*. When you are asked to provide a heading, type: *Net Income from Exports*.

e) When you reach the end, click on *Finish*. Your chart will now appear. You can change the size of the image by clicking and dragging the edges.

Your chart can be copied and pasted into a word-processing document or even used in presentation software. (See Module 11: *Presentations*, for information on how to prepare a PowerPoint presentation.)

Compare your completed chart with those of three or four other students. Have you chosen the same sub-types of graph and labeled them in the same way?

Your chart should look similar to the one below.

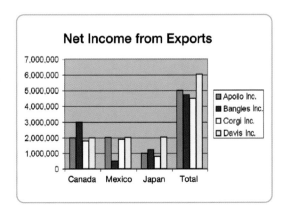

Note: Your chart might have the data presented differently, i.e., grouped by company instead of country on the x axis. If this is the case, change as follows: Click on *Chart* and then *Source Data*. In the window, choose *Series in: Rows*.

Task 3 Refining your chart

3.1 In groups, discuss what you could add to your chart to make it clearer to your audience.

3.2 Click on the menu option *Chart* and then *Chart Options*. Change the settings in all five tabs and watch what happens to your chart.

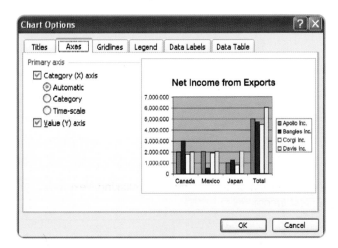

3.3 Now right-click on the values in the Y axis. Click on *Format Axis* and then the *Alignment* tab. Change the setting to *45 degrees*, then click *OK*. See what has happened to your chart.

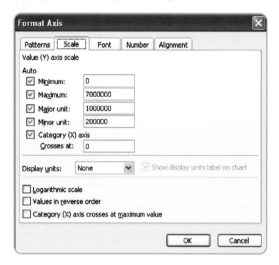

Note: You can right-click on any area of your chart and carry out similar formatting. Alternatively, you can double-click with the left button on the mouse to get similar results.

3.4 Use the utilities you explored in Tasks 3.2 and 3.3 to carry out the following operations.

- Add a label to the Y axis: *Income in dollars*.
- Add $ signs to the data on the Y axis.

Task 4 Explore other types of charts and graphs

4.1 Use the *Chart Wizard* to display the data from your exports database in other chart formats. Think about how this affects your interpretation of the data. Discuss your conclusions in groups.

4.2 Make a list of other types of chart in the left-hand column of the table below.

Chart type	Useful for ...
Pie chart	showing proportions of a whole

4.3   Refer back to the *Chart Wizard* and use the *Help* utility to compare your explanations of each type of chart.

Reflect

You have now completed the *Introduction to IT Skills*. Think about what you have learned and how you can use it effectively.

Now you understand the basic operations, it would be a good idea to buy a manual for using *Microsoft Office* and use it for reference purposes. It is a good idea to do the following:

* Look up how to do something you want to learn about as soon as the need arises.
* Set out to learn something new at least once a week.

Student notes for Unit 6

Module 7

Web work

| Website | Word Tutorial |

http://www.baycongroup.com/wlesson0.htm

Review

This website provides a detailed tutorial of *Microsoft Word* and guides students through the various tools that are available. Pictures and screen shots make these pages a useful and practical guide.

Extension activities

To consolidate your understanding of the facilities available to you in the menu options, focus on one of the options and write a short user guide that could be used by another student. If possible, put your user guide together with those for other menu options that may have been written by other students.

When you have finished, see what you can learn from the full set of guides produced by you and your fellow students.

Glossary

Attachment (n) A document or file that is attached to an e-mail message and can be downloaded, opened and read by the recipient.

Bibliography (n) A list of references to sources cited in the text of a piece of academic writing or a book. A bibliography should consist of an alphabetical list of books, papers, journal articles, and websites and is usually found at the end of the work. It may also include texts suggested by the author for further reading.

Bold (adj) A typeface with thick heavy lines.

Browser (n) A software application that is used to find and display Web pages and information on the Internet, including texts, graphics, and video. Microsoft Internet Explorer and Netscape Navigator are two popular browsers.

Bullet (n) A dot, star, or other symbol that appears at the beginning of each item in a list.

Cell (n) A box in a table or spreadsheet into which you enter data.

Cursor (n) A symbol on a screen that shows where the next entry will be inserted. It is usually a blinking line or a solid rectangle. The cursor can be moved to different parts of the screen using the arrow keys or mouse buttons. See also pointer.

Cut and paste (v) To remove text from one part of a document and place it into another part. In word-processing programs, the cut and paste facilities are normally represented by icons of a pair of scissors (cut) and a clipboard with a document next to it (paste).

Data (n) Pieces of information, such as numbers in a table or addresses in an address book.

Database (n) A collection of data, for example, an address book.

Disk drive (n) A machine that can read data from and write data onto a disk. There are different types of disk drives—such as CD and DVD drives—which may be inside the computer or external.

Download (v) (n) 1 To copy files and other data from the Internet or a computer to another device such as a computer. 2 A file or data that has been copied in this way.

Drop-down menu (n) A menu that opens on a computer screen beneath a command you have selected. For example, in word-processing software, if you select *File*, a drop-down menu appears with *New*, *Open*, *Save* and other actions for you to choose from.

Drag (v) To move an icon or selected piece of text to another part of the screen or document by clicking and holding the mouse and letting go when the pointer is over the spot where you want the item to appear.

Edit (v) To select, rearrange, and improve material to make it more suitable for its final purpose. Editing material involves reorganizing it, correcting errors, improving the wording or content, and changing its length, by adding sections or taking them out.

E-mail (n) (v) 1 Short for *electronic mail*, a system of transmitting communication between computers over a network such as the Internet or a local area network (LAN). 2 To send someone communication via such a system.

File (n) A collection of information (data, text documents, or programs) that is stored on a computer and has a name.

Folder (n) A location on a computer where files are stored.

Font (n) A set of characters (letters, numbers, punctuation, etc.) of the same style, size, spacing, etc.

Format (n) (v) 1 The style and arrangement of text in a document. For example, the font, margins, and layout of the text. 2 To arrange text in a uniform format.

Formula (n) An equation, fact, or rule expressed in symbols and sometimes numbers, for example, πr^2 (pi r squared) is the formula for the area of a circle.

Function (n) A computer operation or command. For example, cut, paste, save, delete.

Highlight (v) To draw attention to something. For example, when using a computer, the highlighting facility enables you to mark text using a different font color or background so that it stands out from the surrounding text.

Hard drive (n) The device in a computer that reads and writes and stores data to a hard disk.

Hyperlink (n) A piece of text, an icon or an image in a document that, when clicked on, moves you to another part of the document or to another document. Text hyperlinks are usually underlined and/or a different color from the surrounding text. When your pointer passes over a hyperlink, its icon often changes to a pointing finger. Often shortened to *link*.

Icon (n) A small image that represents a function, document, or program. For example, the *save* function is normally represented by an icon of a floppy disk.

Memory stick (n) A small flash drive that can store data and transfer it to and from other computers, digital cameras, mobile phones, etc.

Menu (n) In computer terms, a list of functions a user can choose from, for example, *cut*, *paste*, or *undo*.

Mouse (n) A hand-held device used to control the pointer without having to use the keyboard. A mouse has buttons that can be clicked to select functions.

Option (n) A choice in a menu or dialogue box.

Pointer (n) A symbol, usually an arrow, that can be moved around a computer screen using a mouse. Using a pointer, you can move around a document, select text, and perform functions without using the keyboard.

Scroll (v) To move up and down or left and right within an on-screen document using the mouse, arrows on the keyboard, or scroll bars.

Software (n) Programs that make a computer work and enable you to do different types of work on a computer. For example, Word® is a common piece of software for working on text documents and PowerPoint® is popular presentation software.

Spreadsheet (n) A document made up of cells, useful for manipulating data like financial figures, addresses, and lists of text. Microsoft Excel is a popular spreadsheet program.

Template (n) A basic pattern that can be followed to insert data into a document, spreadsheet, or other application in a standard format.

Title bar (n) The bar at the top of a window that displays the name of the document.

Toolbar (n) A box containing icons that represent functions that you can perform on a document. For example, the drawing toolbar enables you to select shapes, colors, etc., for drawing.

Undo (v) To cancel one or more actions you have just performed in a document, such as adding, deleting, or moving text or changing the font. The icon for undo is usually a curved blue arrow pointing to the left.

Utility (n) A program that performs a specific task, usually related to managing the computer system; e.g., the recovery utility recovers lost text and unsaved documents.

Window (n) A rectangular frame on a computer screen in which a program or document is displayed. Using windows, you can have several different tasks running on your computer at the same time. Windows can be moved around, minimized, and resized depending on what task you want to work on at any time.

Module 8: Essay Writing

Introduction

In higher education, it is necessary to be able to structure and organize essays in an appropriate way, according to academic conventions. This module provides an introduction to academic essay writing. It guides you through the process of structuring an essay so that you are prepared for the kind of writing you will have to do in a typical US or Canadian academic institution. You will have the opportunity to develop your ideas and to produce detailed essay outlines on topics such as traffic congestion (covered in the Problem Solving module), English as a global language and urban overcrowding.

Unit 1 looks at some basic principles of writing academic essays. You will analyze essay questions and practice strategies for organizing your ideas and gathering information on a topic. Unit 2 helps you get started by showing you how to write a thesis statement and begin an essay with an interesting introduction. Unit 3 deals with the main part of the essay and how to plan and write effective paragraphs, while Unit 4 deals with the conclusion. Unit 5 examines the language of essays; you will identify the features of academic style and practice using formal, objective language. Finally, Unit 6 looks at some basic principles to help you in the future with academic writing, including redrafting and what professors expect from an essay. A sample essay is included in this unit to demonstrate essay structure and presentation.

By the end of the module, you will be more able to interpret essay questions and understand what professors expect from you. You will be able to tackle the process of writing an essay in a more organized and systematic way, moving from a clear plan and outline to a well-organized and well-written essay with an effective introduction and conclusion.

Skills Map

Getting organized

Learn some basic principles of academic writing: essay structure; analyzing essay questions; brainstorming ideas and issues.

Getting started

Understand how to plan your writing. Learn to create effective introductions and write thesis statements.

The body of the essay

Practice arranging your arguments in a logical sequence. Learn effective paragraphing. Practice supporting your arguments.

Summaries and conclusions

Learn how to close your argument and draw conclusions.

Academic style and register

Practice using appropriate language: formal vs. informal style and some important aspects of academic written language.

Guidelines for the future

Remember some important points: professor expectations; producing a detailed essay outline. Study a model essay.

Destination: Essay Writing

1 Getting organized

At the end of this unit you will:
- understand more about the requirements of writing an academic essay;
- have learned how to produce a clear outline.

Task 1 Basic principles of essay writing

There are several different types of academic essay. For example, you might have to write:

- a descriptive essay
- an argumentative essay
- an analytical essay
- an evaluative essay
- a personal experience essay
- a reflective essay

Some essays may be a mixture of different approaches and types, but you need to be clear about what kind of essay you are writing.

1.1 Match the following titles with the essay types above. Note that sometimes you will need to combine categories.

Title	Type
Using your personal experience, describe a particularly interesting cultural encounter.	
What are the main arguments for and against the implementation of very high rates of taxation?	
How good do you think the author is at creating the characters in this story? Analyze the characterization and give examples.	
The most efficient form of transport is the train. Discuss.	
Using the statistics in the accompanying table, write an analytical description of the rise in the number of American households.	
The World Trade Organization is far too powerful. Discuss.	
Learning a language is one of the best forms of educational activity. Do you agree?	

1.2   Whatever the essay type, the structure of an essay is generally similar. The purpose is to help the reader understand what the writer wants to say.

Write down what you think form the three main parts of an academic essay.

a)

b)

c)

1.3   In pairs or groups, discuss the following aspects of an essay. Make notes of your discussion and present the conclusions to the class.

The introduction:	What is it for?
	What makes a good introduction?
The essay structure:	What is a paragraph?
	How do you show where a paragraph begins and ends?
	How do you decide the order of paragraphs?
The conclusion:	What is it for?
	What makes a good conclusion?

1.4   The purpose of this module is to improve your essay-writing skills. As a starting point, it would be useful to evaluate your current skills in specific areas.

Do the questionnaire below. Grade your competence in each area on a scale of 1 to 5 (1 = poor, 5 = excellent). Compare your answers with another student.

Skill	Score
Writing correct and accurate English	
Planning an outline of an essay	
Drafting and redrafting my writing	
Editing and proofreading	
Organizing information	
Organizing my time	
Finding and using source material	
Paraphrasing other people's words	

Note: You will be able to think about the basic principles of academic writing in more depth in Unit 6. However, it is useful at this stage to think about what you can do already.

Task 2 Analyzing the essay question

2.1 The instruction verbs in the box below are commonly used in essay questions. Think about their meaning. Then discuss your ideas with a partner.

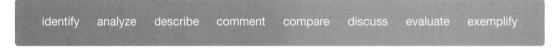

> identify   analyze   describe   comment   compare   discuss   evaluate   exemplify

2.2 Read the following essay question. Find and underline the key ideas it asks you to write about.

Discuss the problems associated with traffic congestion. Suggest possible solutions and evaluate their effectiveness.

2.3 What *exactly* does the essay question want you to do? Circle the instruction verbs in the question. Then think carefully about the kind of essay you need to write. Discuss your conclusions with the rest of the class.

2.4 Ask yourself questions related to the three key elements of the essay. Begin with Discuss the problems associated with traffic congestion. Think about the three questions below. Then add one more question.

a) What exactly is traffic congestion?

b) Where would you find traffic congestion?

c) What are the main causes of traffic congestion?

d) ....

congestion caused by bad weather

congestion caused by maintenance work

congestion caused by weight of traffic

2.5　　**With another student, discuss the rest of the question:** Suggest possible solutions and evaluate their effectiveness, **using the same procedure as above.**

2.6　　Discuss your questions and answers in groups. Present your conclusions to the class.

2.7　　In groups, discuss possible solutions to any aspect of traffic congestion. Choose three possible solutions and write them on a piece of paper. Exchange your solutions with another group and evaluate the effectiveness of the other group's solutions.

Task 3 Brainstorming ideas

Brainstorming involves *free association*, or rapidly generating ideas on a topic. Try these two different ways of brainstorming.

Free writing
This is where you quickly write down every idea you have that could be relevant to the topic. You can write a list or draw an idea web. The aim is to produce lots of ideas, so the form is not important. You do not need to worry about correct spelling or grammar—it is the ideas that are important.

Group brainstorming
This is where all the members of a group contribute their own ideas on the topic, "bouncing" their ideas off each other.

3.1　　Use free writing to brainstorm the following topic:

Transporting goods by road.

You have two minutes.

3.2　　Now carry out a group brainstorming activity.

a)　Start individually. Think about the topic Banning trucks from towns and cities. Accept any ideas that come into your head.

b)　Work in groups. Appoint a chairperson to write down ideas. Then brainstorm the topic.

Task 4 Organizing your ideas

Now that you have a set of ideas, they need to be put together in an organized way. One method is to use a mind map to try to represent your ideas in a visual form. This can be very useful when you want to quickly see the relationship between your main topic, main ideas, and supporting ideas (see essay title, Task 2.2).

You write the main topic in the middle of the page and place the main ideas around it, connected with lines or arrows. Similarly, you write the supporting ideas around the main ideas, connected with lines or arrows.

4.1 Below is a skeleton mind map of the essay topic you are developing. Complete the mind map with your ideas so far.

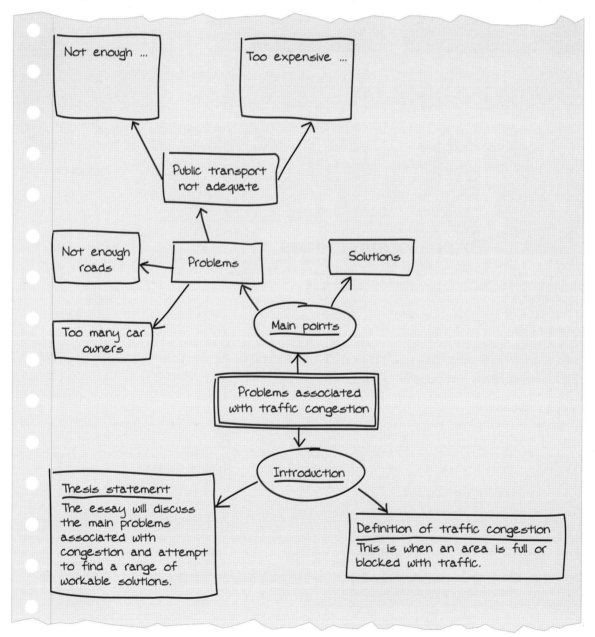

4.2 Using your mind maps, work in groups to discuss the possible content of your essay, the introduction, and the main points.

Reflect

Think about the ideas you have discussed in this unit. How have they changed your attitude to essay writing?

Apply these insights to an essay you have to write, or think of a topic you are interested in and imagine you are going to write about it. Reflect on the process you will go through, from understanding the question to organizing your ideas. Think about how to ensure you fully answer the essay question.

Student notes for Unit 1

2 Getting started

At the end of this unit you will:
- be better equipped to start writing an essay;
- understand how to write a thesis statement;
- have ideas on how to make the introduction interesting for the reader.

Task 1 What to include

Once you have begun to organize your ideas in a logical way, you need to decide:

- how to structure your essay;

- how (and where) to include these ideas.

For example, you need to make decisions about the main sections of your essay.

1.1   You might want to include the following points in your essay on traffic congestion. Think about the importance of each item in the list. Label them I, U, or NI (important, useful, not important). Add any other items or topics you can think of.

a) A definition of traffic congestion.

b) An explanation of the causes of traffic congestion.

c) Your views on traffic congestion.

d) A list of solutions to the problem.

e) Examples of traffic problems in your hometown.

f) Arguments in favor of or against possible solutions.

g) _____

h) _____

i) _____

1.2   Decide in which order the ideas should appear in the essay. Which ones will you need to spend most time on? Compare your ideas with another student.

Task 2 Information gathering

In academic writing it is not enough to use your own ideas without any supporting evidence. It is essential to include relevant information from academic sources to give them "academic weight." You should obtain this information by thoroughly researching the topic, using a variety of sources.

It is important to make clear notes of any information you find. You can then use this information, with references, to support your argument. (See *TASK*, Module 10: *Research and Referencing*.) Keep a record of all your sources when you collect the information, as it is easier to do this at the time, rather than later.

Sources of information

_____

_____

_____

_____

2.2   Number the following points in the order of difficulty for you.

_____ Finding appropriate references

_____ Paraphrasing in your own words

_____ Understanding how much use to make of external sources

_____ Referencing in an appropriate way

2.3   Discuss your answers as a class.

Task 3 Arousing interest: The introduction

The introduction acts as a window to the rest of your writing. A good introduction should make your reader want to read your work. You can encourage interest by using a variety of different techniques. For example, you can use one or more of the following:

a)   a surprising or interesting fact

b)   a question

c)   a quotation

d)   a definition

e)   some important background information

3.1   Which of the above, a) – e), has the author used in the introduction to an essay entitled:

The education system in your country?

> According to a recent survey, a significant proportion of the population in my country has serious literacy problems.

3.2   Look at the four essay titles below. Think of a sentence to use as an introduction to each one, using any of the above, a) – e). Try to interest the reader so as to encourage him/her to read the rest of the essay.

a) Family structure in your country

b) The criminal justice system in your country

c) Imports and exports to and from your country

d) Transportation in your country

Task 4 Writing a thesis statement

An introduction should also contain information on how you will develop the topic in the essay title. You write this in the **thesis statement**, a statement of your standpoint, or the view taken in the essay. It should be concise and convincing. Your thesis is the controlling idea of your essay that you will develop in the main body.

You normally follow the thesis statement with a clear indication of how you will structure the main body of your essay in support of your thesis statement.

4.1   The controlling ideas can be stated in many different ways. Identify the controlling ideas of the following thesis statements.

a) The criminal justice system in my country functions in a variety of ways.

b) Although the Big Bang Theory is widely accepted, it will probably never be proved, and it therefore leaves a number of difficult and unanswered questions.

c) The key to coping with the rise in sea levels is education on its effects and the accurate forecasting of its hazards.

4.2   How do you think the rest of the essay will be developed in each case? What areas will be covered? Continue each statement with a sentence outlining the structure of the essay, beginning: "This essay will ...."

4.3 Look back at the ideas you brainstormed in Unit 1 on traffic congestion. What is your own view about possible solutions to the problems? Identify your main idea and write it as the controlling idea in a single sentence. This will be your thesis statement.

4.4 What will you focus on? How will you develop your thesis in the main body of your essay? Write a follow-on sentence beginning: "This essay will ...."

Task 5 An effective introduction

An introduction should generally move from the general to the specific. The following example is an introduction to an essay about the problems associated with urban overcrowding.

5.1 Arrange the five sentences in the correct order.

a) .... As a result of this migration, modern-day cities face a number of serious problems related to overcrowding.

b) .... People were therefore drawn towards living in towns and cities for simple economic reasons.

c) .... The purpose of this essay is to identify solutions to these problems of urban overcrowding and attempt to evaluate their feasibility.

d) .... The most critical problems include homelessness, inadequate healthcare and education, unemployment, and secondary effects such as rising crime and drug abuse.

e) .... The twentieth century saw a major increase in the world's population and, at the same time, the emergence of a society driven by the forces of economics and industry.

5.2 Discuss the following three questions with another student.

a) Mark the general statements G. How do they attempt to interest the reader?

b) Mark the thesis statement with a check. How do you expect the rest of the essay to be organized?

c) What are the minimum number of paragraphs you would expect in this essay? What can you predict about their content?

5.3 The questions below can act as a checklist when writing an introduction. Look at the checklist and think about how helpful this will be for you.

_____ Is it likely to interest the reader? Why?

_____ Does it start with a general statement related to the topic and gradually become more specific?

_____ Is there a thesis statement that tells the reader what the essay will be about? Can you easily identify it?

_____ Does the introduction give an overview of the essay structure?

_____ Are ideas clearly linked between sentences or is the linking sometimes confusing?

_____ Does it include a definition? Do you think a definition is necessary or would be helpful?

5.4 Using the checklist as your criterion, evaluate the following introduction to a student's essay. Complete the table of strengths and weaknesses below the introduction.

The advantages and disadvantages of genetically modified crops

New developments in the field of genetically modified (GM) agriculture are reported almost daily as exciting new discoveries are made. These new developments have generally been welcomed by consumers. Recently, however, people have begun to realize how rapidly GM agriculture is spreading, so questions are being asked about its effects on our environment and health. Needless to say, farmers generally feel that high production levels and top-quality crops are more important than the possible negative side effects. In the light of such advantages, the influence of GM agriculture on the environment and on our health is, in my opinion, unimportant.

Strengths	Weaknesses

5.5   Choose one of the following essay titles and write a possible introduction. Discuss the content and structure with another student before you start writing.

- Food additives should be banned. Discuss.
- What are the main benefits of investing money in space research?
- Euthanasia should be made legal. Discuss.
- Outline the different types of alternative energy sources.
- What would you do to improve the lives of the elderly in your country?

Essay writing: Points to remember

- Planning and organization are key skills.
- Keep a close eye on your title: always answer the question.
- Word processing is very useful. For example, you can change text or move sections about very easily. (See Module 7: *Introduction to IT Skills*.)
- Keep a note as you go along of all references or sources that you use.
- Redrafting is an essential skill.

Reflect

Sometimes writers prefer to write the introduction after they have finished writing the essay. Bearing in mind what you have been studying, do you think this is a good idea? Why or why not?

Think about the main criteria for a good introduction and why they are so important. Can you add any more? Reflect on ways that you can make these criteria important for you and how they will help you throughout your student life.

Student notes for Unit 2

The body of the essay

At the end of this unit you will:
- **have a clear idea of how to structure the main part of an academic essay;**
- **know how to plan and write effective paragraphs.**

Remember, if you want to write a successful academic essay, you need to have the following:

- an outline plan

- a clear structure

- a strong introduction

- logical and meaningful paragraphs

- a development of an argument or discussion

- a conclusion

The organization of your essay will depend to some extent on what sort of essay you are writing. The body of your essay can be arranged in various logical ways, for example:

- Reasons for and reasons against

- Causes followed by effects

- Problems followed by solutions

Task 1 Paragraph organization

1.1   Decide whether the statements below are true or false. Discuss your answers as a class.

a) _____ Each main idea should be presented separately in a new paragraph.

b) _____ Each paragraph in the body of your essay will usually begin with a topic sentence stating the main idea of the paragraph.

c) _____ The topic sentence should be followed by several sentences that support the main idea.

d) _____ To add support or evidence, you should use examples, figures, or statistics.

e) _____ You should always use quotations to support your ideas.

f) _____ You should have a strong concluding sentence in each paragraph to link the reader back to the topic sentence or provide a link to the next paragraph or section.

1.2   Look at the following extract from a descriptive essay on
       the origins of Coca-Cola. Can you divide the text into
       paragraphs?

The first episode in the Coca-Cola story is an important part of the rise of capitalism in the United States. Towards the end of the nineteenth century, America gradually began to transform itself from a nation of farmers to a city-based industrialized society. The industrial revolution was epitomized by new communications and the arrival and spread of the railways. This produced a new kind of capitalism, a distinctive American variety where the ethos centered firmly on the image of individual immigrant struggle. The world of US business was on its way. One of the most important changes that helped business success was population growth. The American population almost doubled in size between 1880 and 1910, and a large proportion of the increase was created by the new immigrants from Europe and the rest of the world. Success came from ambition and hard work, and anybody could make large amounts of money provided they tried hard enough. Helped by the success of some, immigrants flocked to the USA. By 1890, there were already over 4,000 American millionaires and Andrew Carnegie, who had made a fortune from railways and iron and steel, was spreading the "Gospel of Wealth." There were, however, some disadvantages to the new business environment. In many parts of the USA, there was more than an element of the Wild West. Con men, thieves, and swindlers came to the new towns that were appearing, looking for suitable victims. A second major disadvantage was that Coke was originally a patent medicine, and only about two percent of the medicines that were produced ever became well-known—most inventors and salesmen failed miserably. Third, although large profits could be made from all kinds of medicines, many of which often cost almost nothing to produce, by the late 1880s the market for medicines was already saturated. Patent medicines, therefore, were not an easy commercial area to break into. Another important aspect of the story is that the world of medicine was not advanced at this time. Nineteenth-century American doctors were not numerous, nor were they very good (anesthetics were still to be invented and some of the primitive methods used by the medical profession were terrifying, killing more patients than they saved). This was the reason why many people turned to alternative remedies, the so-called patent medicines, to solve their health problems. By the end of the century, there were thousands of cures on offer for every imaginable ailment, from the common cold to malaria, all of which required extensive advertising in newspapers and public places to promote their superior values over their competitors. To conclude, it is not surprising that many would-be tycoons were attracted by the rising numbers of consumers and that the field of patent medicines was an attractive starting point for some. In 1869, Dr. John Pemberton, a Georgia pharmacist, had moved to Atlanta searching to make his fortune by the discovery of the perfect patent cure. In 1886, after long years of research, he finally launched his new invention. It was into this very crowded and over-competitive market that Coca-Cola was to emerge as a highly successful product.

Task 2 Linking words and phrases

It is important to develop and link your ideas in each paragraph so the reader can follow your line of argument clearly. The Coca-Cola essay uses words and phrases to help the reader follow the sequence of events.

2.1 Match the words and phrases in the text that function in the same way as the following link words.

First _____

Second _____

Third _____

Fourth _____

Finally _____

2.2 Look at the following link words and match them to their function.

> on the other hand   as shown by   for instance   in the same way   as a result
>
> equally important   like   another important aspect   therefore

Showing similarity _____

Comparing or contrasting _____

Adding something _____

Giving reasons _____

Showing cause and effect _____

Giving an example _____

Note: There is a large variety of link words and there are complex rules regarding their use. You should ask your instructor for a good source of reference to learn more about how to use them effectively.

Task 3 The topic sentence and supporting sentences

The topic sentence is usually at the beginning of a paragraph, but it does not have to be. When you write a paragraph, you should try to develop this initial idea and not change or add too many new ideas.

3.1 Consider the following possible topic sentences for a paragraph on The benefits of immigration to industrialized countries. With another member of your group, discuss which sentence is most suitable.

a)

> Immigration is a very difficult subject to discuss because there are many possible different viewpoints.

b)

> One of the major problems of immigration is that people in the host country may disagree with such a policy.

c)

> Immigration can offer several clear advantages for industrialized countries.

3.2 Read the following two paragraphs. In each paragraph, the topic sentence has been underlined. Decide which paragraph develops the idea given in the topic sentence better. Discuss your reasons with your group.

Example A

There are obvious advantages to learning English in the US. Every day there are opportunities to practice listening to and speaking with American people. In the first place, students can experience the culture firsthand, which is a great help when trying to understand the language. This is especially true if they choose to live with an American family as exchange students, for example. In addition, if students attend a language school full-time, the instructors will be native speakers. In this case, not only will students' speaking and listening skills improve, but attention can be given to developing reading and writing skills as well.

Example B

Immigration to industrialized countries poses a number of difficult challenges for incoming families. They may need to learn a new language, they may face racism and discrimination, and they frequently have problems adjusting to the new culture. In France, for example, unlike in the US, it is illegal for Muslim schoolgirls to wear headscarves to school. Already, five Muslim schoolgirls have been expelled from school for wearing headscarves. The ban is perceived by many as intolerant, undermining the integration of France's Muslims. Feminists say the Islamic scarf is a repressive symbol, but many French Muslims say the ban is racist and against their human rights. "Everyone has the right to freedom of thought, conscience, and religion; this right includes freedom to manifest their religion or belief in teaching, practice, worship, and observance" (Article 18, The Universal Declaration of Human Rights).'

3.3   There are three thesis statements below. Write a topic sentence for each of them. Then write a supporting sentence or two for the paragraph. Remember to focus on the main idea. The first has been done for you.

A)   Thesis statement

Young people who live at home while studying at university have several advantages.

Paragraph 1
Topic sentence

First of all, they can focus on their studies without worrying about domestic matters.

Supporting sentence(s)

Students living away from home have to learn how to do their own laundry and may have to shop and cook for themselves. Those who live at home do not have such concerns.

B)   Thesis statement
What is the focus here?

The causes and effects of global warming will be briefly outlined in this essay.

Paragraph 1
Topic sentence

Supporting sentence(s)

C)   Thesis statement
What is the focus here?

Personal computers have revolutionized communication and business practices in the past twenty years.

Paragraph 1
Topic sentence

Supporting sentence(s)

Task 4 Organizing an essay

4.1   Here are the opening words of the paragraphs from the original Coca-Cola essay in Task 1.
       Identify the topic and put the paragraphs into the correct order.

Paragraph begins	Topic	Order
Another important aspect of the story is that the world of medicine was not advanced at this time.		
There were, however, some disadvantages to the new business environment.		
To conclude, it is not surprising that many would-be tycoons were attracted by the rising numbers of consumers and that the field of patent medicines was an attractive starting point for some.		
One of the most important changes that helped business success was population growth.		
The first episode in the Coca-Cola story is an important part of the rise of capitalism in the United States.		

4.2   Look at the list of essay titles below. Discuss the following for each of them.

a) How would you structure your essay? e.g., *Reasons for and reasons against, causes followed by effects, problems followed by solutions*

b) What are the main points that you would include in the essay?

c) What sort of research will you have to do on this topic?

1) There is too much advertising on television.

2) Discuss the advantages and disadvantages of English as a world language.

3) How has education improved over the last one hundred years?

4) Marketing is the most important aspect of a business's activities. Discuss.

5) Every individual has a responsibility to prevent global warming.

4.3   Choose one title and make a plan for it, listing the topics you would cover in each paragraph.

4.4   Practice writing the first paragraph for your essay. Make sure you start with a clear topic sentence.

Reflect

When you understand how to structure an essay, you will begin to notice whether other writers have been successful in doing this well or not. By sharpening your critical skills, you will find your own writing skills will automatically grow.

Look through examples of essays you or other students have written, with a view to developing your ability to recognize good organization.

Student notes for Unit 3

Unit 4 Summaries and conclusions

At the end of this unit you will:
- have a clear idea of how to finish an academic essay with a successful conclusion.

The main aim of the conclusion is to show the reader that you have successfully answered the question that was set. It does not include any new information, but it summarizes the main points made in the body of the essay. It should draw your argument to a close and it also needs to link back to the thesis statement in your introduction.

Task 1 Restating the thesis

You need to repeat the main ideas in the conclusion, but you do not want to simply write the same sentences again. One way of linking back to the thesis statement is to rewrite it (that is, to paraphrase the ideas and the language). You can use synonyms to do this, or you can rearrange the order and also change some of the grammar.

1.1 Look at the extract from an introduction below. Think of synonyms for the underlined words and write them in the table.

Lack of investment in public transportation is having serious consequences for travelers in the United States today; this is the major point that will be discussed in this essay.

Original	Synonym
lack of	
consequences	
travelers	
major point	
discussed	

1.2 Rewrite the sentence, using synonyms and different word order to make a good concluding statement. Think about the grammar that needs to change (e.g., *will be* is not appropriate for a conclusion).

Task 2 Organizing the concluding paragraph

2.1 Rearrange the following sentences to form an effective conclusion for an essay on the topic of **Urban overcrowding**.

a) .... Government policies aimed at solving these problems are too often very simple measures that offer only short-term solutions.

b) .... In conclusion, urban overcrowding causes problems on all levels.

c) .... It is a model that aims for improved social conditions and offers a high quality of life for city dwellers, whatever their number.

d) .... This essay has argued for the implementation of a long-term policy that needs to provide an economically sustainable, resource-efficient model of city design.

e) .... The creation of such a model will help to resolve many of the current and future problems of urban life.

Task 3 Finish with a clear statement

Remember that your conclusion needs to be clear and relevant to the question you are answering. A strong conclusion should refer back to the introduction. Ideally, it needs to leave a strong impression on the reader.

3.1 Read the following thesis statement and the concluding sentences of the same essay. Discuss the following questions.

a) What is the subject of the essay? Think of a title for it.

b) How is the conclusion similar to and different from the introduction?

Thesis statement: The growth of a fast food culture has generated unexpected problems, including rising obesity levels and, more importantly, the loss of our gastronomic heritage. This essay will examine the role of fast food in the development of an increasingly unhealthy society.

Conclusion: Fast food outlets cannot entirely be blamed for our increasingly unhealthy dietary habits. Fast food evidently responds to a need in our modern society, and reflects changes in our modern lifestyle. It is, rather, our lifestyle that needs to be changed if we hope to become a healthier nation.

3.2 Look back at the thesis statement you wrote in Unit 2, Task 4.3 (page 239), in which you stated the focus of your essay. Draw your argument to a close with a concluding sentence that refers back to your introduction. Try to use synonyms, paraphrases, and different grammatical structures.

3.3 Sometimes it may be useful to draft a rough conclusion first, so that you know what you will say at the end of the essay. Can you think of any advantages or disadvantages of this approach? Discuss them and write them in the table.

Advantages	Disadvantages

Task 4 Professor expectations

4.1 Professors have clear ideas of what they want to see in the conclusion to an academic essay. Look at the list below and make sure that you understand the expectations. Identify whether you think you are strong or weak in these areas.

Concluding: professors expect ...	I am good, OK, weak at ...
clear links between the introduction and conclusion	
a strong concluding paragraph	
the ability to say the same thing in different ways (paraphrasing)	
accurate use of vocabulary	
accurate grammar	
a relevant concluding statement	
an answer to the question set (task completion)	

Reflect

You can make a comparison between writing a good conclusion and finishing other things you are faced with doing. Think about how satisfying it can be to complete a task to your satisfaction and how writing a good conclusion can be equally satisfying. Reflect on how the effort put into a conclusion will help you think more carefully about the assignment as a whole.

Look at an essay you or another student has written and think about how you can improve the conclusion to reflect the content of the essay. Think about how this process helps you focus on what the essay is saying.

Student notes for Unit 4

5 Academic style and register

At the end of this unit you will:
- be more familiar with the language of essays and able to identify some of the features of academic style;
- have practiced using formal, objective language.

Task 1 Formal or informal register?

Academic essays usually require a formal style. You need to remember what to avoid in an academic essay.

1.1 Compare the following two definitions of geography. Write the differences between them in the table below. Discuss your findings with a partner.

Informal/spoken: *Geography? Well, I think it's basically just some sort of mix of physical and social sciences and how they interact together. You know, like, for example, how global warming has an effect on the economy, um, of a region … but you can also look at these things individually too … er … so you could just study things like sea-level rise that'd be physical, or you could look at … say … how people, human beings, adapt themselves to the environment, that's human.*

Formal/written: *Geography is the study of the surface of the Earth, the location and distribution of its physical and cultural features, and the interrelation of these features as they affect humans. In the study of geography, two main branches may be distinguished, physical geography and human geography.*

Feature	Informal/spoken examples	Formal/written examples
Use of contractions, isn't, don't, etc.		
Use of fillers: Well, er, etc.		
Use of passive voice		
Impersonal and objective		
Personal and subjective		
Punctuation		

1.2   Do you notice any other features of formal or informal discourse in the texts? Add these features to the table.

1.3   Read the following sentences and decide if they are formal (F) or informal (I). Explain why, and add any further examples to the table above.

a) I don't believe this is true at all. It sounds like nonsense.

b) New regulations will come into effect next year.

c) The study was conducted with a group of school-age children.

d) We're definitely going to have to follow those stupid new rules next year.

e) Further analysis is required before conclusions can be drawn.

f) It really puzzles me why some students don't get better grades.

g) Our experiments were OK—they just proved that his argument didn't stand up.

h) He'll have to have a better look at the findings before making his mind up.

i) It has been proved that the claims are unfounded.

j) We went down to a school and chatted with some of the kids.

k) It isn't clear why quite a lot of students don't get really good grades.

l) A major aspect of the investigation involved research into social housing trends.

Task 2 Cautious language

Another typical feature of academic writing is the need to be careful or cautious. Unless you are quoting a fact or a statistic, or there is evidence that shows 100% certainty, statements and conclusions are often qualified in some way to make them less assertive or positive. The reason is partly academic style, but it is also to avoid making any false claims. This use of cautious language is sometimes called "hedging."

2.1   Compare the following sentence pairs. What sort of language is used in the second sentence of each pair to make it less assertive or positive?

2.2   Underline the hedging expressions used in the second sentence of each pair and then write the example in the appropriate place in the table below. The first one has been done for you.

A) i) Some colleges and universities in this country have large numbers of international students.

  ii Some colleges and universities in this country <u>appear to have</u> large numbers of international students.

B) i) Instead of coming here, international students should study in their own country.

  ii) It could be argued that, instead of coming here, international students should study in their own country.

C) i) This is a misapplication of government policy.

  ii) This would seem to be a misapplication of government policy.

D) **i)** This is true.

   ii) To a certain extent, this may be true.

E) **i)** Erlichman's findings prove that the amount of independent study is directly related to higher performance levels.

   ii) Erlichman's findings suggest that the amount of independent study might be directly related to higher performance levels.

F) **i)** Inflation will not rise next year.

   ii) Evidence indicates that inflation will probably not rise next year.

G) **i)** The survey demonstrates that American schoolchildren don't like learning foreign languages.

   ii) The survey tends to indicate that American schoolchildren are apparently not in favor of learning more foreign languages.

H) **i)** There are situations where this is the only solution.

   ii) There are undoubtedly situations where this would seem to be the only possible solution.

Hedging feature	Example
Hedging verbs	Some colleges … appear to have …
Use of modal verbs	
Qualifying expressions	
Adjectives and adverbs	
Set expressions	

Task 3 Register in use

Informal English uses everyday spoken forms (colloquialisms) that are inappropriate for formal written English. It is important not to mix styles in academic writing.

3.1   Here is a paragraph from the Coca-Cola essay you looked at earlier, rewritten in a much more informal style. Find and underline the parts that are too colloquial. Look particularly carefully at the vocabulary and the sentence structure.

A massive change—one that really helped business—was more people arriving in the USA. There were two times as many people who got here between 1880 and 1910, and lots of them came from all sorts of different places like Europe. If you wanted to be successful you had to work really hard; however, you could get rich quickly if you did this. Lots of immigrants made it, and because of this, lots more wannabe millionaires turned up in the US. By 1890, there were maybe around 4,000 millionaires. One of the best was Andrew Carnegie, who got rich through trains and iron and steel. His message was called the "Gospel of Wealth."

3.2   Go back and check your answers with the original paragraph in Unit 3, Task 1.2.

3.3   The following extract from an essay is written in a mixed style with colloquialisms and other inappropriate words. Rewrite it in a more academic style using:

Electric Powered

- appropriate vocabulary and grammatical structures;
- cautious language (Unit 5, Task 2, page 255).

Another kind of useful alternative fuel is electricity. This isn't really a very efficient fuel right now, because the technology is somewhat limited; however, it's fair to say that recent advances in the production of electric cars could maybe make this a reality in the future. But it is possible for cars powered with electricity to release little or no emissions, so if we want this alternative fuel to become a reality, we'll need it in lots of cars. Maybe then it'll make some sort of a difference. If we want this to happen, i.e., to knock a big chunk out of the pollution problem all around the world, it'll take a while.

Reflect

Read through an essay that you have recently written, looking carefully at the language you used. Bearing in mind what you have learned about the appropriate level of formality, do you feel that you could improve the way you express yourself?

Also make sure that the tone of the essay is not too assertive and explore whether it would benefit from more hedging expressions.

Student notes for Unit 5

Unit 6 Guidelines for the future

At the end of this unit you will:
- understand the editing and redrafting processes in essay writing;
- have a clearer understanding of what professors expect from a piece of academic writing.

Task 1 Things to remember

1.1 In Unit 1, Task 2, we looked at some basic principles. You should now be familiar with some of the main principles of essay writing. Look at the following and decide which areas you will need to work on in the future.

- understanding the task
- checking the title carefully
- answering the question set
- getting organized
- keeping to deadlines
- writing a plan
- collecting and recording sources and important information
- keeping useful phrases and examples of "essay language"
- reflecting on what you have written
- checking and redrafting language and content
- writing a final draft
- presenting your essay in a clear and acceptable form

Task 2 Redrafting

> source?   Sp.   gr.   tense
> It was <u>forcast</u> that the number of robbery would <u>have risen</u> by 29% in London
>   wrong word
> between april 2001 and march 2002 but the <u>real</u> figures show that the overall
>   tense
> number of crimes <u>was falling</u> watch punctuation

2.1   Think about the answers to these two questions.

a) How many drafts of an essay should you write?

b) What do you need to consider and work on when you redraft an essay?

2.2   Make a list of the answers to 2.1 question b). Some examples are given below to help you.

Redrafting: things to work on	Considerations
paragraphs	• the right structure • each paragraph has a main idea • paragraphs are in the right order
grammar	
length of essay	

Task 3 How to get a better grade

Remember that your grade will depend not only on how good your writing is, but also on how successfully you have completed the task. It is important to make sure you read and understand the feedback that your professor gives you to help you with your next essay. It is also important to understand the grading criteria.

For instance, robbery might be decreased, whereas murder has increased so the
total number of crimes has decreased. This is because the <u>goverment</u> always shows

Sp.

its performance in a positive way.   *good to include e.g.*

ref?—this is rather a generalization!

3.1 Here are some comments that professors sometimes make about students' writing. Which ones indicate that the professor thinks you have done what was required?

a) You have written a competent answer, but unfortunately it is an answer to a different question!

b) Your essay would be improved by checking the grammar and spelling.

c) You have answered the question very well; you show a good understanding of the issues and have provided some excellent examples.

d) There is little evidence in the essay of reflective and evaluative thought. Your conclusion is rather weak.

e) The essay needs to be word-processed—in general, the presentation is very poor.

f) You have made good use of personal reflection and have clearly done a lot of background reading on the topic.

g) You have described the situation well but have not analyzed the advantages and disadvantages as the question asked you to do.

3.2 Can you add any other comments that professors have made about <u>your</u> writing?

3.3 Look at the grading criteria on the following page for essay writing and match them with the appropriate percentage bands below (NB: 60% is the pass grade in this scheme).

70%+
60–69%
50–59%
40–49%
30–39%

Grading criteria	Grade
ideas generally not made clear and often irrelevant; weak paragraphs; small range of vocabulary; grammatical structure is very limited	
ideas generally clear but not always very relevant; some lack of paragraphing; limited range of vocabulary; limited grammatical structure at times	
lacks any satisfactory organization or development of ideas; vocabulary use very weak; unsatisfactory use of grammatical structure; generally fails to meet the required pass standard	
excellent text organization; clear paragraphs with well-expressed ideas; wide range of vocabulary; good use of grammatical structure	
good text organization with generally relevant ideas; adequate range of vocabulary and grammatical structure	

Task 4 A model essay

4.1 Read the essay title below and underline the instruction verbs.

Essay title: Discuss the problems associated with urban overcrowding and evaluate possible solutions.

4.2 Read the introduction to the essay and answer the questions.

a) How does the writer arouse your interest?

b) What is the thesis statement?

Introduction:
The twentieth century saw a major increase in the world's population and at the same time the emergence of a global society driven by the forces of economics and industry. People were inexorably drawn towards living in towns and cities, migrating from rural communities out of economic necessity. As a result of this influx, modern-day cities across the globe face serious problems due to overcrowding. The most critical include poverty and homelessness, unemployment, the provision of adequate healthcare and education, and secondary effects such as rising crime and pollution. The purpose of this essay is to identify solutions to some of these problems of urban overcrowding and attempt to evaluate their feasibility.

Main body:

Urban overcrowding is not a recent phenomenon, but it has recently become a global demographic problem. The rise of the world's "megacities" such as Tokyo, Jakarta, São Paulo, and Cairo, with populations approaching 20 million, is one of the most marked trends of recent decades. In 1950 for example, New York City was unique among the world's cities in having more than 10 million inhabitants. By 1975 that number had grown to 15 million. By 2015 it is estimated it will reach 21 million. (UNO 2005). Two principal reasons for this phenomenon can be identified, one economic and the other sociocultural.

People migrate to the cities in search of both economic security and improved social conditions. As the economy of a nation develops, its cities develop as centers of industry, investment, and education, providing plentiful job opportunities for those in search of a higher standard of living. Sydney, São Paulo, and Frankfurt are all thriving modern cities that have developed exponentially since the Second World War. A further example is Tokyo, the hub for Japan's rapid economic development in the 1960s and 70s. Its population grew quickly as people moved there to find employment, and it is now the most populous city in the world (population 35.3 million).

Not all developing nations, however, are equipped to cope with such rapidly expanding city populations. The overriding problem associated with overcrowding is poverty and its attendant social deprivations—homelessness, unemployment, and insecurity. Immigrants to cities from rural areas are typically the poorest members of urban society, and in many cities are often forced to live in shantytowns or slums on the periphery of the city without access to clean drinking water or safe sanitation, in cramped and unsanitary conditions. Examples of such poor living conditions can be seen across the continents, from Caracas to Bombay. Unemployment is widespread as families fight to survive. Transmission of infectious diseases is very common in such conditions, resulting too frequently in high infant mortality rates (UNESCO 2002). Furthermore, access to vital social services such as hospitals and schools may be restricted as authorities try to cope with large numbers of people, thus denying children adequate education and healthcare.

Inevitably, there is no one best solution to a problem of such magnitude. Two solutions are proposed, both of which seek to move people away from the cities. The first is that of resettlement, where government-led housing initiatives seek to rehouse families on the outskirts of cities. The Shanghai housing resettlement project, begun in 1987, is an example of successful urban renewal where living conditions have been measurably improved. Resolution of the housing shortage has promoted long-term social development and stability, resulting in social and economic benefits. This measure does not, however, address the problem of urban sprawl as the city spreads outwards, but it does relieve the pressure of urban overcrowding.

The second solution encourages the relocation of businesses, factories, and warehouses to rural areas. It exploits brownfield sites in the countryside that are developed as business parks. Policies of industrial relocation have been successful in Canada and the US, where industrial expansion of cities has been curtailed. However, people are not willing to leave the cities unless they are guaranteed better housing, schools, and transport facilities, so long-term government investment in these areas is crucial. Furthermore, such projects are disputed by environmentalists, who see the developments as a threat to the balance of the countryside.

a) Underline the topic sentence in each paragraph in the text and make a note of its key words below.

b) How much support does the writer give for the topic sentence in each paragraph? Make a note (key words) of the support below.

Paragraph 1
Topic sentence key words: Urban overcrowding = has become a global phenomenon

Support examples and evidence:

....

....

....

Paragraph 2
Topic sentence key words:

....

Support examples and evidence:

....

....

Paragraph 3
Topic sentence key words:

....

Support examples and evidence:

....

....

Paragraph 4
Topic sentence key words:

....

Support examples and evidence:

....

....

Paragraph 5
Topic sentence key words:

....

Support examples and evidence:

....

....

4.4 Now compare your answers with another student. Decide which paragraph(s) do the following:

a) describe the situation and causes _____

b) suggest solutions _____

c) describe the problems _____

4.5 Read the conclusion and answer the questions below. (While you read, remember the important verbs in the essay title and the thesis statement in the introduction.)

a) Is there any new information in the conclusion?

b) How does the conclusion link back to the introduction?

Conclusion:
In conclusion, urban overcrowding causes problems on all levels. Government policies aimed at solving these problems are too often simple stopgap measures offering only short-term solutions. This essay has argued for the implementation of a long-term policy that potentially provides an economically sustainable, resource-efficient model of city design. It is a model that fulfills a universal desire for improved social conditions and ultimately offers a high quality of life for city dwellers, whatever their number.

4.6 Look through the whole essay and decide where you could make changes from assertive to more cautious hedging language. Write your changes in the table below.

Change from	To

Task 5 Write an essay outline

The sample essay in Task 1 was an example of the Situation-Problem-Solution-Response model (see Unit 3, page 243).

5.1   Prepare an essay outline for the following essay question (or one of the other questions in this module). Follow the steps below.

English has become a global language because it is both easy to learn and superior to other languages. Discuss.

- Analyze the question: How many general statements are there? What is the main instruction verb?

- Brainstorm ideas using one of the techniques from Unit 1, Task 3, page 233.

- Write a thesis statement to show how your argument will develop through the essay.

- Decide which essay pattern to use (Unit 3, page 234).

- Link your ideas into a logical sequence and decide how many paragraphs you will use.

- Write a topic statement for each paragraph.

- Note the supporting evidence and examples for each of your main points.

- Refer to TASK Module 10: *Research and Referencing*, if you are including quotations.

5.2   Discuss your essay outlines in small groups.

Reflect

You should now feel more confident about what is required in writing a formal academic essay. Think about your own skills and what you have learned in this unit. How will you use the information for the future? What do you need to do to become a better essay writer?

Student notes for Unit 6

Module 8

Web work

Website 1 — ABC of academic writing and essays

http://owl.english.purdue.edu/handouts/general/gl_essay.html

Review
The Online Writing Lab is a site run by Purdue University that offers comprehensive support on academic writing.

Task
Write down useful words and terms connected with essay writing, together with their definitions.

Website 2 — Andy Gillett's academic writing

http://www.uefap.com/writing/writfram.htm

Review
This is a very useful study skills site written by a well-known academic at the University of Hertfordshire, in the UK.

Task
This link takes you to the writing section. Try the exercises at the end of each section, then check your answers. Begin with Understanding the Question and apply your knowledge from this module.

Extension activities

Activity 1 — Write another essay outline

Prepare an essay outline for the following essay question. Use the same steps as you did in Unit 6, Task 5:

Discuss the problems associated with the melting of the polar icecaps and evaluate possible solutions.

Activity 2 — Write an essay

Expand one of your essay outlines into a full essay. Although you may have a number of essays to write over the year, it is useful to write one immediately on completing this module.

You can complete one that you have been working on in this module, or choose an area to write about that you are particularly interested in.

Glossary

Academic writing (n) Writing that students and academics produce. It normally involves research, demonstrates learning or knowledge, and follows clear conventions in its style and organization. For example, essays and assignments, reports, dissertations, theses.

Analytical essay (n) An essay that involves analyzing a text, theory or set of ideas.

Analyze (v) To break an issue down into parts in order to study, identify, and discuss their meaning and/or relevance.

Argumentative essay (n) An essay that involves building a case for an idea or thesis statement. This entails giving reasons for your thesis statement and providing evidence to back it up.

Brainstorm (v) The act of writing down all the thoughts and ideas you have about a topic without stopping to monitor, edit, or organize them. Brainstorming is a creative process that can be done alone or in a group.

Colloquial (adj) Used to describe informal spoken words and expressions used in conversation, or informal written language used in letters to friends and family or e-mails. For example, in American English, a colloquial way of saying "Don't be angry!" would be "Don't blow your top!"

Deadline (n) The date or time by which an assignment or project needs to be completed.

Descriptive essay (n) An essay that describes a process or sequence of events rather than arguing, interpreting, or evaluating.

Draft (n) (v) 1 (n) An early version of a piece of academic writing that is used as the starting point for further work. 2 (v) To create an early version of an essay, knowing that you will go back afterwards and develop and edit your language and ideas.

Edit (v) To select, rearrange, and improve material to make it more suitable for its final purpose. Editing material involves reorganizing it, correcting errors, improving the wording or content, and changing its length, by adding sections or taking them out.

Evaluate (v) To assess information in terms of quality, relevance, objectivity, and accuracy.

Evaluative essay (n) An essay that requires you to either compare and evaluate a range of things in relation to one another, or to look at the arguments for and against one thing, and come to a judgment in your conclusion. It is asking for your personal opinion, backed up with facts, examples, and explanations.

Exemplify (v) To illustrate a belief, statement, or theory with examples. You may be asked to do this in an essay.

Free writing (v) To write without deliberate or conscious thought so that ideas flow freely. This is sometimes done as an exercise to stimulate ideas and creativity in preparation for a written assignment.

Grading criteria (n) A list of criteria or qualities that the person who grades an assignment or exam is looking for, including aspects of the style, presentation, and organization of the work. For example, one criterion for an assignment that is graded above 90% (an A) is likely to be that it must include original ideas.

Hedging (n) The use of deliberately vague, uncertain language in order to avoid asserting something as a fact that may not be true. In the context of academic writing, hedging language is often used to discuss theories and possible solutions.

Key skill (n) A skill that it is important to master in order to be successful in a certain area (such as academic life or employment).

Mind map (n) A diagram used to represent words, ideas, tasks, or other items linked to, and arranged radially around, a central key word or idea

Objective (adj) (n) 1 (adj) An opinion or idea that is not influenced by personal feelings or emotions. 2 (n) The aim, or what you want to achieve from an activity.

Outline (n) A brief plan that shows the order in which you will deal with the main issues or ideas in a piece of academic writing.

Paraphrase (v) To alter a piece of text so that you restate it (concisely) in different words without changing its meaning. It is useful to paraphrase when writing a summary of someone's ideas; if the source is acknowledged, it is not plagiarism. It is also possible to paraphrase your own ideas in an essay or presentation; that is, to state them again, often in a clearer, expanded way.

Personal experience essay (n) An essay that asks you to describe and draw conclusions about something that you have experienced.

Proofread (v) To read through a piece of writing and pick out and correct errors in it. It is useful to ask someone else to proofread your work. This should be done before the final draft of a piece of academic writing is submitted.

Redraft (v) To write out a new draft of an essay, incorporating changes and making additions. This is done after you have read through, edited, and/or had feedback on the first draft.

Reference (n) (v) 1 (n) Acknowledgment of the sources of ideas and information that you use in written work and oral presentations. 2 (v) To acknowledge or mention the sources of information.

Reflective essay (n) An essay that involves thinking about a statement or idea and deciding whether you agree with it, and giving reasons for your decision.

Register (n) The style of speech or writing that is used in a specific context and/or by a specific group of people. For example, a student will use a very informal, colloquial register to text or e-mail a friend, but a formal scientific register to write a chemistry report.

Restate (v) To paraphrase or say something again in a different way. This is often done in essays to help clarify an idea or issue. The conclusion of an essay will often restate the original thesis statement in more depth.

Source (n) Something (usually a book, article, or other text) that supplies you with information. In an academic context, sources used in essays and reports must be acknowledged.

Structure (n) (v) 1 (n) A framework or arrangement of several parts, put together in a particular way. 2 (v) In academic writing, to put together ideas, arguments, or thoughts in an organized, logical way. It is important to structure essays and presentations as you work on them.

Subjective (adj) Describes an idea or opinion that is based on someone's personal opinion rather than on observable phenomena.

Supporting evidence (n) Information from academic sources that should be included in a piece of academic writing. This evidence illustrates and backs up your ideas and adds "academic weight" to your work.

Supporting sentences (n) Sentences that usually follow and systematically develop the idea contained in the topic sentence.

Synonym (n) A word or phrase that has a similar meaning to another one and can replace it in a sentence without changing the meaning of the sentence.

Technique (n) A method or way of doing something. For example, it is possible to learn useful techniques for answering exam questions.

Thesis statement (n) A statement that explains the controlling idea or main argument (thesis) in a piece of academic writing. It is stated in the introduction and supported by reasons in the body of the essay.

Topic sentence (n) A sentence that states and sometimes summarizes the topic/main idea of the paragraph and the standpoint taken by the writer. It usually comes at the beginning of each paragraph.

Module 9: Scientific Writing

Introduction

As a science student in higher education, you need to write scientific reports of experiments and field work. You will need to write these reports in a way that is clear enough for other scientists and readers to follow and repeat your experiments, if necessary. This means you will need to organize and structure your report in a conventional way, using conventional style, language, and layout. The aim of this module is to help you learn the conventions and skills required to write a good scientific report.

Unit 1 looks at how to organize your report and schedule your work up to your submission deadline. In Units 2 and 3, you will learn conventions for writing the Method and Materials and Results sections of your report. These skills include using the passive and past tenses, and presenting and writing about tables and figures. In Unit 4, you will review conventions for writing numbers in scientific papers. Unit 5 deals with the Discussion section of the report, as well as the Bibliography, Title, and Introduction. Editing and revision are essential to good writing, and you will develop these skills by doing the exercises in Unit 6. In addition, the editing checklist presented in Unit 6 will be a useful guide when you come to writing full scientific reports.

Skills Map

Structure and schedule
Find out how to structure and schedule your report in a logical way.

The *Materials and Methods* section
Learn how to include appropriate content and write in a suitable style.

The *Results* section
Learn how to write a Results section, including how to present and describe tables and figures.

Writing numbers and abbreviations
Familiarize yourself with conventions for writing numbers and abbreviations in scientific reports.

The *Discussion, Introduction, Bibliography,* and *Title* sections
Find out how to write the other sections of a report effectively.

Editing and revising your report
Practice editing and revising your report using an editing checklist.

Destination: Scientific Writing

Structure and schedule

At the end of this unit you will be able to:
- structure your report and include appropriate scientific report sections;
- organize your time appropriately.

Task 1 Organizing a scientific report

When you do laboratory or field work, you will be asked to write a scientific report of your experiment or investigation. Scientific papers and reports are typically divided into five sections.

1.1   Discuss the following questions in small groups. Use your answers to complete the table below.

   a) What are the sections in a report?
   b) What order do the sections come in?
   c) What questions should be answered in each section?

Sections	Questions
1	
2	
3	
4	
5	

1.2   Feed back as a class. Discuss the reasons for your choices.

Task 2 Organizing your time

When you write your report, you will not only need to write each section, but also allow time for additional research, revision, and possibly discussion with your peers. You will probably have to do all this by a set deadline.

2.1   To meet deadlines, it is important to manage your time. Imagine you and your partner have to submit your reports in seven days' time. Working individually, read through the steps below and put them into a logical order. When you have finished, compare your work with your partner's.

a) Revise first draft

b) Write first draft of the *Introduction*

c) Hand in revised draft

d) Write first draft of the *Discussion*

e) Write first draft of the *Materials and Methods* section

f) Research background information

g) Meet with another student to discuss peer review (have a writing conference)

h) Start *Bibliography*

i) Give first draft to another student to review, using list of "Points to check"

j) Complete practical laboratory work

k) Write first draft of the *Results* (do calculations, draw up tables, graphs, charts)

2.2 **Now that you have decided on a logical order of steps, think about how to time each step. Write your answers in the *Activity* column of the table below and give a reason for your timing, wherever possible, in the *Reason* column. Work individually.**

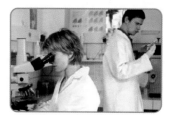

Time Frame	Activity	Reason
Day 0	Complete practical laboratory work	
Day 1		
Day 2		
Day 3		
Day 4		
Day 5		
Day 6		
Day 7		

Remember, you can adjust the time frame according to your own deadlines.

2.3   Discuss your tables in small groups. You may have your own reasons for doing things in a different way from others in the group. Give reasons for your choice.

Reflect

Think about reports you have written or read. Did they include the five sections discussed in this unit, or were the sections slightly different? How does the way a report is divided into sections help the reader?

Try to remember the different activities you included in the schedule in Task 2.2. Think about why each activity is important and how it contributes to the final report.

Student notes for Unit 1

Unit 2 The *Materials and Methods* section

At the end of this unit you will know:
- **what to include in the *Materials and Methods* section of your report;**
- **how and why to write in the passive voice.**

Task 1 What do I include?

The first section of your report is *Materials and Methods*. In this section you answer the questions: What did I do? Where? When? How?

You should describe how you did the experiment, writing in sufficient detail for another scientist to repeat your experiment.

1.1 **In groups, brainstorm the following points. Choose a group secretary to write down the ideas you discuss.**

a) Examples of information that should be included in a good *Materials and Methods* section, e.g., temperature, volume.

b) Examples of information that does not need to be included in a *Materials and Methods* section. (Think about your reader: what does everyone in your subject area know about the everyday equipment and techniques that you use?)

Include | Do not include

1.2   Report back to the whole class.

1.3   Which two of the following statements do you agree with?

a) Even if well-known procedures or equipment have been used, it is necessary to describe it in detail.

b) All equipment used should be listed.

c) It is important to include clear references to published protocols and methods.

d) The method should be explained using numbered points, as in a set of instructions.

Task 2 How do I write a good *Materials and Methods* section?

You should include all appropriate information in your report. It is also important to use the most appropriate style.

> Weigh 10g air dried 2mm sieved soil into a 50ml centrifuge tube. Using an automatic dispenser add 25ml ultra pure water. Cap the tube and place on the shaker for 15 minutes

> **pH determination**
>
> Ten g of soil was placed in a 50ml centrifuge tube. Twenty-five ml of ultra pure water was added and the tube placed on a shaker for 1 hour. The pH was then measured using a calibrated pH meter.

2.1   Complete the paragraph below, using an appropriate word from the list that follows. There are more words than blanks, so you will not need to use them all.

> paragraphs   sentences   passive   active
> imperative   past   present   future

Laboratory schedules are usually written in the _____ as a list of instructions. However, when you write your report, you must summarize what you did in full _____ and well-developed _____ . You will usually write in the _____ tense and use the _____ voice.

2.2   Discuss these questions about the advice in 2.1 as a class.

a) Why is there a difference in grammar between laboratory schedules and reports?

b) Why is information divided up into paragraphs in a report?

c) Why is the passive voice so common in the *Materials and Methods* section of a report?

2.3   As indicated above, the *Materials and Methods* section of your report is usually written in the passive voice. The passive is used because the procedure is more important than the person who carried it out. Look at the following sentence.

I removed the skins from the onions and homogenized them in the blender.

In a scientific report this should be written:

The onions were skinned and homogenized.

In the second sentence there is no mention of the blender. Which of the following is the most likely reason?

a) It has been mentioned in a previous part of the text.

b) Only non-standard equipment should be mentioned.

c) The next sentence will state: This was carried out in a blender.

Task 3 Using the passive

The following two sentences describe the same event.

Active:

John conducted **the analysis.**   (**the analysis** is the object)

Passive:

The analysis was conducted by **John**.   (*the analysis* is the subject)

The analysis (or the methods, materials, and procedures) is more important information for the reader than who conducted the analysis (John). The analysis is therefore usually made the grammatical subject of the sentence.

3.1   Complete the following rule.

The object in the active sentence, *the analysis*, becomes the _____ in the passive sentence. The subject in the active sentence, *John*, changes position in the passive sentence as it comes _____ the main verb and is introduced with _____ .

3.2   Some verbs, such as *give*, have two objects.

Active:

We gave the caterpillars **one dose** *every three hours.*

We can therefore choose which object we want to make the subject. We choose the one we think is most important.

Passive:

a) *The caterpillars* were given **one dose** *every three hours.*

or

b) **One dose** *was given to* *the caterpillars* *every three hours.*

In the active sentence above, the two objects are _____ and _____ . One or the other can become the subject in the _____ sentence.

Other common verbs that can have two objects are: *bring, send, offer, ask, pay, lend, sell*. However, you are less likely to use these in scientific reports.

3.3   **Read the explanation about the use of tenses. Then complete the following sentences in the past simple.**

You write the *Materials and Methods* section of a scientific report in the **past** tense. This can be the *past simple*, the *past perfect* or the *past continuous*. Each tense works the same way in the passive. It is only the verb *to be* that changes, according to the tense chosen.

Past simple

The plant was taken.   The plants _____ taken.

A pot _____ made.   The pots were made.

The image was shown.   The images _____ _____ .

Past perfect

The solution had been shaken.   The solutions had been _____ .

The animal _____ been fed.   The animals _____ been fed.

The mixture had been kept.   The mixtures _____ _____ _____ .

Past continuous

A record was being made.   Records were _____ .

An attachment was being fitted.   Attachments _____ being fitted.

The result was being analyzed.   The results _____ _____ .

Note: In all passive sentences, *to be* is singular if the subject is singular, and plural if the subject is plural.

The box **was** being built.   The boxes **were** being built.

3.4 Look at the following draft of a student's *Materials and Methods* section and the professor's comments on it. In small groups, discuss what changes the student should make in response to the professor's comments. Make a note of the points you discuss in your group.

I started my field work recordings on February 12, 2007, and ended them on March 12, 2007. My partner used digital camera to record the animals found on the beach, and I marked the animals with quick-drying non-toxic paint. We were making recordings of environmental conditions, including the temperature, the salinity, and the substrate, at the same time. I began the laboratory experiments at the same time as the field work. Each day I collected 10 animals from beach and placed them in the controlled conditions in the laboratory until experiments began.

We set up the apparatus as shown in Figure 1, and I placed 1 crab in each specimen tube. By the time an experiment started, we had aclimatised the crabs for at least 2 days. I had fed crabs daily. I had prepared their food in advance. My partner used a digital camera at the end of each experiment to record the appearance of the animals. We had printed the photographs taken at the beach for comparison. We were analyzing results continuously. We analyzed our results using statistical tests.

Overall, a clear description of your methods. You could improve your writing by:
· focusing the reader's attention on the method, rather than who used the methods
· paragraphing more accurately
· checking your articles (the, a, an)

3.5 Write the final version of the section, using the professor's comments and the notes you made to help you.

Reflect

Look back over the unit and think about the conventions for writing scientific reports that you feel are the most important. Reflect on the reasons for your choice. For example, do you think it is important to use the passive voice, and if so, why?

Think about the kinds of mistakes and omissions you might have made in the past or you feel you are still likely to make. Reflect on how these mistakes might affect the way that other people regard your work.

Student notes for Unit 2

Unit 3

The *Results* section

At the end of this unit you will know:
- **what to include in the *Results* section;**
- **how to present and describe tables and figures;**
- **how to write about your results.**

Task 1 What to include

The *Results* section of your report enables you to present your data (findings or results) to show what you found and whether it matched your expectations.

This section needs to include a short paragraph or two describing and analyzing trends and results, as well as any relevant tables or figures that support your findings. It may be the shortest section of your report, but it is also the most important.

1.1 Match each of the diagrams below to the correct name in the box.

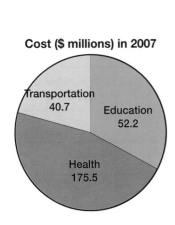

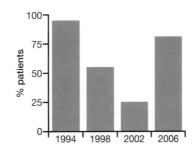

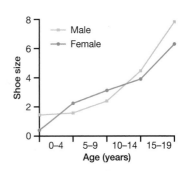

Study group	N	Mean age (years)	Mean height (m)
A	17	43.2	1.77
B	24	44.9	1.69
C	22	56.2	1.64

> table   histogram   pie chart   line graph

1.2 Discuss the following questions with another student.

a) What is the difference between a table and a figure in a scientific report?

b) Should the *Results* section always include tables or figures, or can the results be expressed by text alone?

c) Should the title of the figure or table be above or below it?

d) What do you think make tables and figures easier to interpret?

Task 2 Preparing tables and graphs

If you have a large quantity of data to present, or are comparing several different things, a table can show it more clearly than a graph. Graphs and other figures, on the other hand, are a good way of illustrating and emphasizing trends, particularly if they are dramatic.

2.1 **Tables 1 and 2 below present the same information but in different formats. Discuss with another student:**

a) the differences between Tables 1 and 2;

b) which of the tables is better organized and easier to read, and makes it easier to compare results;

c) whether it is appropriate to show this information in a graph.

2.2 **Work in groups and decide what features make a good table.**

Think about how to:

a) show your data to make it easy to compare significant information;

b) give units, arrange numbers, use abbreviations;

c) give table and figure numbers, and titles.

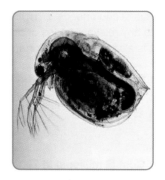

Table 1. Characteristics of three populations of Daphnia species collected at Rye Meads Pond on June 3, 2009

Species	Average length (mm)	Average number of eggs	Average number of animals per L
Daphnia magna	5.01	15.3	112.5
D. obtusa	2.33	8.2	68.7
D. longispina	2.77	6.8	40.4

Table 2. Characteristics of three populations of Daphnia species collected at Rye Meads Pond

Species	Daphnia magna	D. obtusa	D. longispina
Av. length	5.01	2.33	2.77
Aver. no. of eggs	15.3	8.2	6.8
Av. no. of animals	112.5	68.7	40.4

2.3 The results below are taken from a student's laboratory notebook and are followed by a graph that the student made based on the data to include in a written report.

Discuss the strengths and weaknesses of the graph.

Temperature °F	Rate of reaction, mg. products per hr
32	0
42	0.3
52	0.5
62	0.9
72	1.4
82	2.0
92	2.7
102	3.3
112	3.6
122	3.6
132	2.3
142	0.9
152	0

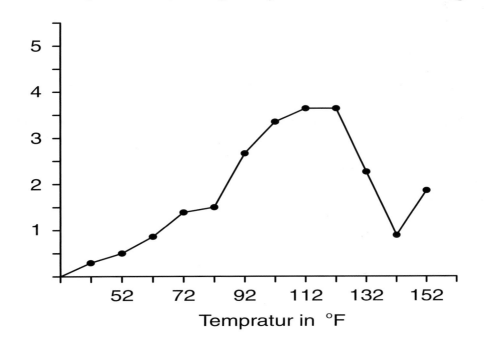

2.4   **Draw an improved version of the graph on the graph paper below.**

As you prepare your graph, you should consider the following questions.

a) Which is the independent variable (the one the investigator can control or manipulate)?

b) Which is the dependent variable (the one that changes in response to the independent variable)?

c) Are the axes organized correctly? (Note: The convention is that the independent variable is usually plotted on the horizontal or x- axis, and the dependent variable is plotted on the vertical or y- axis.)

d) Are the scales appropriate?

e) Are the axes labeled correctly, with units?

f) Are the data plotted accurately?

g) Are the abbreviations correct?

h) Does the graph have a figure number and a title that enables the reader to understand what the graph represents?

Note: You will usually produce graphs using a computer package (See TASK Module 7: Introduction to IT Skills).

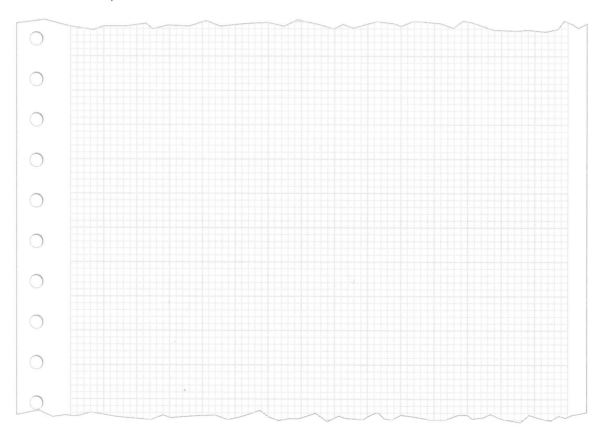

Task 3 Writing the text of the *Results* section

After you have presented your results graphically, you must describe your findings in the rest of your *Results* section. As you are now describing what the results were, rather than what you did, you will usually use the past tense in the active voice.

Start with a sentence that states each important finding and that refers to the table or figure that supports this finding. Next, write about the specific details of the data shown in the figure.

The following example is a paragraph taken from a *Results* section of a report.

> Oxygen production varied depending on the pH of the solution (Figure 1). At pH 2, oxygen production was 3ml, whereas at pH 7 it increased to a maximum of 6ml. At pH values above 7, oxygen production decreased and was at a minimum of 1ml at pH 10.

3.1 **Discuss with another student what points you would include in a description of the results presented in the graph you drew in Task 2. Then work individually and write a paragraph to describe the data.**

3.2 **When you and your partner have completed your paragraphs, evaluate each other's work.**

a) Work in a group of 3–5. Discuss what you feel are the main features of a good description of results.

b) Write a checklist giving advice for writing the *Results* section.

The Results section

-
-
-
-
-
-

Reflect

Reflect on what you have learned in this unit about using tables, figures, and text in the *Results* section. What do you think are the key things to remember?

Think about an experiment you have conducted or are going to conduct. Did you use tables, graphs, pie charts, or only text to present your results? If you wrote your results again, could you present them differently? Would the use of different kinds of figures or tables be more or less effective?

Student notes for Unit 3

Unit 4 Writing numbers and abbreviations

At the end of this unit you will be more familiar with:
- **when to use numerals and when to spell numbers in scientific reports;**
- **how to use very large and very small numbers;**
- **the conventions for using abbreviations.**

It is essential to use numbers correctly when writing a scientific report to ensure the reader is provided with an accurate account of what happened. Even if the numbers shown in a report are correct, it is easy for the reader to be confused or overwhelmed if they are not used in a clear and conventional way.

Task 1 Writing numbers

The guidelines on page 288 for writing numbers are according to the *Modern Scientific Number Style* recommended by the Council of Science Editors (updated 2000).

1.1   Read the guidelines on page 288 and find an example of the following.

a numeral   _____

an ordinal   _____

a fraction   _____

a decimal form   _____

1.2   Match the five words from the guidelines with their meaning.

a) adjacent   **i)** exact

b) non-quantitative   **ii)** worthy of attention

c) fraction   **iii)** next to each other

d) precise   **iv)** not a whole number

e) significant   **v)** not describing a specific amount

a) **Numerals are used to express quantities and mathematical relationships. This makes them stand out in the text.**

For example:
2 theories   7 mm
22 amino acids   0.5 nm
3 replicates   400 × magnification
378 specimens   100-fold

b) **Situations in which numbers should be spelled out include the following.**

When a number is at the beginning of a sentence.

For example: Fifteen g of peas were placed in the tube.

When two numbers are adjacent, use a numeral for the one that goes with a unit of measurement, spell out the other number.

For example: three 25 ml samples

When a number has a non-quantitative meaning.

For example: one of the specimens
was one of the most significant
the zero value

When writing ordinal numbers (numbers that convey order or rank) less than 10.

For example: the seventh sample
a second time

When a fraction is part of the running text.

For example: a third of the plants

Note: When a precise value is required, the decimal form is used.

For example: 0.5 ml

1.3   **Complete these sentences by choosing and underlining the correct option from each pair or group of words in italics.**

Example:

a) Experiments lasting *one / **1*** day indicated that temperature was ***one*** / *1* of the most important factors, whereas *seven / **7*** -day toxicity tests suggested that salinity was crucial.

b) *5 / Five* gammarus were placed in *fifty / 50* ml of *0% / zero percent*, *50% / fifty percent* and *100% / one hundred percent* sea water solutions.

c) The animals were collected at Swansea Bay and *one half / ¹/₂ / 0.5* were divided between *3 / three* *50 / fifty* ml pots.

d) After washing *2 times / twice* in buffer, the tissue was immersed in *2% / two percent* osmium tetroxide in *0.25 / .25* M phosphate buffer, for *one / 1 hr*.

Task 2 Common scientific abbreviations

Abbreviations are frequently used in scientific reports. Some abbreviations are used for technical or scientific words that occur three or more times in the text. In this case, you should define the abbreviation when you use it for the first time and put it in parentheses, e.g., Ampicillin resistant (AmpR). Other standard abbreviations can also be used, e.g., ml., min., and do not need to be defined.

2.1   Write the full form of the standard abbreviations below.

a) s   **g)** O

b) min   **h)** MW

c) h / hr   **i)** U

d) g   **j)** bp

e) mg   **k)** DNA

f) μm   **l)** UV

Task 3 Using numbers and abbreviations in the *Results* section

3.1   Look at the table, then read the extract from the *Results* section below. Discuss the following questions with another student.

a)   Are there any mistakes in the use or layout of numbers in the table?

b)   How effective are the abbreviations?

c)   Could anything else be added or changed to make the results clearer?

Ratios of M.L.D.s at a ratio of synergist; active ingredient of 10:1

	Flies		Bugs	
	pyrethrins	allethrin	allethrin	pyrethrins
Pip. butoxide	4.00	3.25	2.75	1.75
IN 930	$1^3/_4$	2	.75	1.5

Table 3 shows the ratios of the Median Lethal Doses at a 10.1 ratio of synergist; active ingredient. Piperonyl butoxide is shown to be more effective as a synergist with pyrethrins against houseflies, but more effective with allethrin against bedbugs. IN 930 is almost equally effective with both active ingredients against both insects.

Reflect

Look through a variety of experiments in journals and try to notice the way numerals, conventions, and abbreviations are dealt with. The more you notice, the easier it will become.

Student notes for Unit 4

At the end of this unit you will know:

- **what to include in the *Discussion* section of your report;**
- **how to cite references and write a *Bibliography*;**
- **how to write an appropriate *Title* and *Introduction*.**

The *Discussion* section is an important part of the report that follows on from the explanation of your methods and presentation of your results. After you have written the *Discussion* it will be easier to organize your *Bibliography, Introduction,* and *Title*.

Task 1 What to include in the *Discussion*

You now have an opportunity to interpret your results and explain their significance in the *Discussion* section.

1.1 Look at the table below. It shows results for an experiment that compared the distribution of beetles in two different woodlands. Think of some questions that you might ask about the results of the experiment.

Example:
Were there any significant differences between the two habitats?

Table 1: Mean number of beetles per quadrat for two woodlands

Scientific name	Common name	Mean number per quadrat	
		Pound Wood	West Wood
Aphodius nemoralis	A dung beetle	9.1	11.3
Curculio glandium	Acorn weevil	8.4	6.9
Coccinella septempunctata	7-spot ladybird	7.8	6.7
Adalia bipunctata	2-spot ladybird	6.3	5.9
Agonum assimilie	A ground beetle	5.1	4.9
Rhopalomesites tardyi	Holly weevil	3.9	4.2
Ampedus sanguinolentus	A click beetle	2.4	3.1
Byrrhus fasciatus	Banded pill beetle	3.1	2.5
Pogonocherus hispidulus	A longhorn beetle	2.6	1.3
Clytus arietus	Wasp beetle	3.0	3.0
Ampedus rufipennis*	A click beetle	0.8	0
Carabus intricatus*	A ground beetle	3.5	0
Dryphthorus corticalis*	A weevil	2.7	0
Gnorimus nobilis*	The noble chafer	1.7	0
Lucanus cervus*	Greater stag beetle	1.8	0

*Species of conservation importance

1.2   The paragraph below summarizes what to include in the *Discussion*. Complete the blanks with words from the box.

| hypothesis | suggestions | implications | conclusions | deviations |

The *Discussion* section of the report will generally move from the specific (the results of your experiment) to the general (how your results fit in with other scientific findings). Normally, the discussion should do the following.

- Explain whether your results support your original _____ .
- Consider any surprising data or _____ from what you expected.
- Relate your findings to previous results in the same area and derive _____ about the process you are studying.
- Look at the practical and theoretical _____ of your findings.
- Make _____ for extensions of your study.

1.3   Look at the discussion of the results in Table 1. on page 291.

a)   Identify which different elements from Task 1.2 have been included.

b)   Identify which of the following language structures and forms are used in the *Discussion*.

- the passive voice
- the past tense
- comparative structures

- modal verbs
- the imperative
- relative clauses

Discussion

The results show that populations of common beetle species were similar in both woodlands and were comparable to numbers found in previous studies. These common beetles are found in most woodland habitats and can be described as generalists. As expected, it was also found that the diversity of beetle species was higher in Pound Wood than in West Wood. Pound Wood was found to contain a surprisingly high number of beetle species that are rare in the region and that can be described as specialists.

The results show that for beetles, Pound Wood is of more conservation interest than West Wood. It is a suitable habitat for some beetle species that are rare in the region and are the subject of species recovery plans that aim to increase their numbers in local habitats. Pound Wood, therefore, should take priority in management and investment for beetle conservation purposes over West Wood. However, this data says nothing of the overall biodiversity of either of the woodlands. There may be other species of conservation importance present in West Wood that have not been recorded in this study. Therefore, further work should be carried out to assess the overall biodiversity of both of these woodlands before any decisions regarding management or investment are made for either.

Task 2 Citing references and writing a bibliography

In the *Discussion* section, you may compare your results with other studies. This will require you to cite references to other reports and published material.

You will also need to list all the references that you have referred to in your report in a bibliography at the end of your report. (See TASK Module 10, *Research and Referencing,* for more detailed information on citing sources and writing bibliographies). It is important to use a standard layout for this, such as the APA System.

2.1   Read the citation below and make a note of the order in which the author, publisher, date, and place of publication are written.

Southwood, T.R.E. (1984). *Ecological Methods with Particular Reference to the Study of Insect Populations, 2nd ed.* New York: Chapman and Hall.

2.2   In scientific writing, many bibliography references will be to articles in scientific journals. Look at the two citations below and answer the following questions.

a)   What do the numbers 13,2025-2036 in the second citation refer to?

b)   What abbreviations are used in the second citation?

c)   What is the main difference between the two citations?

Wallace, M.J., Newton, P.M., Oyasu, M., McMahon, T., Chou, W.H., Connolly, J., and Messing, R.O. (2006). *Acute Functional Tolerance to Ethanol Mediated by Protein Kinase C Varepsilon.* Neuropsychopharmacology, Published online.

Yamada, K., Fukaya, M., Shimizu, H., Sakimura, K., and Watanabe, M. (2001). *NMDA receptor subunits Glurepsilon 1, GluRepsilon 3 and GluRzeta 1 are encircled at the mossy fibre-granule cell synapse in the adult mouse cerebellum.* Eur. J. Neurosci. *13, 2025-2036*.

2.3   Compare your answers with another student and discuss the bibliography conventions.

It is advisable to start your bibliography with full details and in the correct format as soon as you start reading references. Then you can add references to your list as you go along. In this way you will find that you avoid omissions and errors, and will save yourself time.

To help you do this, always keep a detailed record of your references; for example, make notes when reading in the library without a computer.

When you have finished the report, give your bibliography a final check, making sure it is complete and presented in the correct format.

Task 3 What to include in the *Introduction*

Now that you have written the *Materials and Methods, Results,* and *Discussion* sections, you are in a position to write an *Introduction* to your report.

3.1 Look at the questions and decide which ones might be addressed in the *Introduction*. Discuss your ideas in groups.

    a) When did you do your experiment?

    b) What was the background of your experiment?

    c) What was the aim of your experiment?

    d) Were there any unexpected results?

3.2 Look at the following example of an *Introduction* and put the sentences in the correct order.

Beetles in Woodland Habitats

Introduction

a) Many of these species are the subject of species recovery plans designed to manage suitable habitat and increase their numbers. Organizations with responsibilities for areas of woodlands are often lacking in sufficient resources to protect the entire woodland habitat under their jurisdiction.

b) Woodland habitats have been in decline throughout the region for centuries. This decline has been most notable since the Industrial Revolution and the mechanization of farming practices.

c) Therefore, they have to prioritize woodlands that are in need of immediate protection.

d) The organisms under most threat are the plants and the insects. These organisms tend to have low dispersal rates and are slow to colonize new habitats. Many species of plants and invertebrates are now threatened with extinction due to a loss of habitat.

e) With the decline in woodland, many organisms are under threat from a loss of habitat.

f) This study assesses the importance of two woodland habitats to beetle conservation.

Task 4 What makes a good *Title*?

The *Title* gives the reader a concise and informative description of the focus of your report. It summarizes the information contained in the *Introduction* and *Results* sections. You may use a "working title" during the writing stages, but you should revise it when your report is complete.

The title should give the reader a complete description of the study and include important keywords and phrases.

4.1   Look at the following titles. Work in groups and decide which one is better and why.

   Title 1: *Determination of metabolic rate*

   Title 2: *The effect of temperature on oxygen consumption in mice*

4.2   Discuss your findings as a class.

4.3   Work with another student and compare the following two pairs of titles. Think about the different information each pair gives the reader. Come to a clear conclusion about the importance of an appropriate title.

   Title 1: *Species composition of summer phytoplankton in Lake Ontario, Canada*
   Title 2: *Sampling plankton in a lake*

   Title 1: *Effects of pollutants on Daphnia*
   Title 2: *Morphological and ultrastructural effects of sublethal cadmium poisoning on Daphnia species*

Reflect

You have now done work on all aspects of a piece of scientific writing. Think about what you have learned in Units 1 to 5 and how the information in each unit ties in with the others.

Student notes for Unit 5

Unit 6 Editing and revising your report

At the end of this unit you will:
- **be more aware of how to check your work for grammatical and vocabulary mistakes;**
- **be more aware of how to edit your work to ensure that you use full sentences that are clear and concise.**

Task 1 What do I check for?

After you have written your report, it is important to check for mistakes and errors. You will get into the habit of editing more efficiently if you are aware of the key areas in which you tend to make mistakes.

> Sp.
> "The high temperature effected the results."

1.1 **Working in groups, look at the questions below and discuss which problem areas you feel are the most important.**

- Is the use of vocabulary appropriate?
- Is the general vocabulary correctly spelled?
- How about the specialist vocabulary? Do you need to look any of it up?
- Does the numbering follow the correct conventions?
- Is your punctuation accurate?
- Is writing clear and concise?
- Can you find any errors in grammar?

1.2 **Compile a checklist of problem areas you should look for to revise and edit a report.**

1
2
3
4
5
6
7
8

Task 2 Use of tenses

In this module, you have looked at the academic conventions for use of different tenses and aspects in scientific reports. It is important to remember to use these correctly and consistently in your work.

2.1 The table below shows sections and topics that might be included in a scientific report. For each one, choose whether the past or present tense should be used in the example sentence.

Section of report	Example sentence
a) *The Materials and Methods* section	The apparatus **is /was** set up as shown.
b) Referring to a table or graph	Table 1 **presents / presented** the results from sites 3 and 4.
c) Stating (quoting) the findings of published work	Cadmium **is / was** a highly toxic metal to freshwater fish (Ball, 1999).
d) The *Results* section	Oxygen production **varies / varied** depending on the pH of the solution.
e) Referring to someone else's work	Smith (2002) **finds / found** that …
f) To make a general statement	Respiration **is / was** a complex series of chemical reactions that **results / resulted** in the release of energy from food.

2.2 Identify any sentence(s) that use the passive voice. Then discuss why you think it should be used.

Task 3 Common mistakes with vocabulary

The following exercise identifies some words that are commonly confused with each other in scientific writing.

3.1 Look at the following pairs of sentences. Choose the correct word to complete each one.

a) affect / effect

1) Temperature strongly _____ the rate of reaction.

2) The study investigated the _____ of temperature on rate of reaction.

b) continual / continuous

1) The tank was provided with a _____ supply of nitrogen.

2) Impurities can be eliminated by _____ heating, cooling, and reheating.

c) site / cite

1) Smith's study _____ several previous incidents.

2) The _____ chosen for the experiment was a nearby pond.

d) their / there

1) _____ is more than one way to do this.

2) The crabs were fed daily and _____ food supply was adjusted gradually.

3.2 Now write sentences of your own for each of the pairs of words below. Use a standard dictionary to check the meaning and spelling of terms.

a) fewer / less

_____

_____

b) breath / breathe

_____

_____

c) rise / raise

_____

_____

d) consecutive / concurrent

_____

_____

3.3 Compare your ideas with another student.

Task 4 Plurals

Scientific words often have irregular plurals, particularly if they come from Greek or Latin terms. You will need to notice and remember common patterns, such as those on the next page.

You should also make sure you are consistent in your use of plural nouns and that plural subjects agree with the verb that follows them.

4.1 Complete the following table of singulars and plurals of common scientific terms.

Singular	Plural
analysis	
	bacteria
	criteria
datum	
formula	
hypothesis	
medium	
ratio	
	phenomena

4.2 Complete the following sentences.

a) Greek- or Latin-based singular nouns that end in ~*um* generally form the plural by changing

....

b) Greek- or Latin-based singular nouns that end in ~*is* generally form the plural by

....

4.3 Decide whether the subjects and verbs agree in the sentences below. Correct them if necessary. (Note: Two sentences are correct, and two need to be changed.)

a) This data is supported by evidence from other studies.

b) Ten drops of hydrochloric acid were added to each sample.

c) The period of immersion for crabs at different times of the tidal cycle are presented in Table 1.

d) One source of error in these experiments are the inaccuracy in recording light intensities.

Task 5 Be clear and concise

When writing reports, it is important to consider your audience. Unless you take great care to write clearly, it is easy to confuse the reader, particularly if you are describing a complex experiment or set of results.

One way to ensure clarity is to make sure that you do not use more words than necessary.

5.1 **Work with another student or in small groups. Discuss how you would revise the following sentences to eliminate unnecessary words.**

Example:
In the experiment, the test animals were subject to analysis for investigation of their gut contents.

The gut contents of the test animals were analyzed.

a) One of the environmental conditions to which the zooplankton were shown to be affected by was pH.

b) The experiments alone are insufficient to tell what the optimum conditions are.

c) Ten test tubes were labeled with the following concentrations of sodium chloride and 50 ml of those solutions were then prepared and placed in the test tubes: 0%. 5%, 10%, 15%, 20%, 25%, 30%, 35%, 40%, 45%.

Task 6 Write in complete sentences

Another reason why reports are sometimes difficult to read is that they are not written using complete, well-formed sentences.

6.1 **With another student, revise a, b, and c to make complete well-formed sentences. When you have written your paragraphs, compare them with other pairs in the group.**

Example:

In accordance with the Law of Limiting Factors, the rate of photosynthesis is affected by light intensity, temperature, and carbon dioxide concentration. Resulting in maximum rates in optimum conditions.

In accordance with the Law of Limiting Factors, rate of photosynthesis is affected by light intensity, temperature, and carbon dioxide concentration, and maximum rates occur in optimum conditions.

a) In the third set of experiments, citric acid concentration was doubled and at each temperature three sets of readings.

b) Enzymes are denatured at high temperatures. Because molecular conformation is altered.

c) The reaction occurred at its maximum; copper was absent.

Student notes for Unit 6

Module 9

Web work

Website 1 Using the passive voice

http://www.geocities.com/CollegePark/Classroom/8012/quizzes/Grammar_Goblins/GGvpassive.html

Review

This site provides 45 exercises in using the passive voice. You can check your answers and get instant feedback.

Task

Complete exercises listed on the site.

Website 2 Interpreting graphs

http://www.oup.com/pdf/elt/catalogue/0-19-431517-7-b.pdf

Review

This site presents five exercises in "Interpreting Graphs." You can test your knowledge of the use of verbs and prepositions in describing line graphs. The final exercise tests your skill in interpreting and describing information in a pie chart.

Task

Complete the exercises on the site.

Extension activities

Activity 1

Before writing your first report, it is helpful to study a few short papers in a major scientific journal, such as *Ecology, Developmental Biology*, or *Genetics*. Choose papers in journals from your own field. You don't need to read for content, but look at the way in which the paper is crafted.

Answer the following questions.

a) What is included in the *Introduction*?

b) How much detail is given in the *Materials and Methods* section?

c) How are the results presented in the *Results* section? If graphs are presented, how are axes labeled?

d) How are titles written for tables and figures?

e) What is included in the *Discussion*?

f) How are references cited?

When you have written the first draft of a scientific report, use the following checklist to edit and revise your report.

Editing checklist

- Is the *Title* descriptive and concise?
- Does the *Introduction* include background information, supported by references from the literature?
- Does the *Introduction* include the aim of the study?
- Is the *Materials and Methods* section written in the past tense?
- Is the *Materials and Methods* section written in the passive voice where appropriate?
- Does the *Materials and Methods* section contain all the information required to repeat the experiment?
- Does the *Results* section contain tables and figures, with titles that inform and can be understood without reference to the text?
- Does the *Results* section contain text describing results with reference to each table and figure?
- Does the *Discussion* explain what the results mean?
- Does the *Discussion* compare results with those from other studies and cite references?
- Does the *Discussion* assess errors and unexpected results and suggest extensions?
- Is the *Bibliography* presented correctly?
- Are *References* cited in the text?
- Is writing clear and concise?
- Are numbers, abbreviations, punctuation, and spelling correct?

Module 9

Glossary

Analyze (v) To break an issue down into parts in order to study, identify, and discuss their meaning and/or relevance.

Bibliography (n) A list of *references* to sources cited in the text of a piece of academic writing or a book. A bibliography should consist of an alphabetical list of books, papers, journal articles, and websites and is usually found at the end of the work. It may also include texts suggested by the author for further reading.

Checklist (n) A list of tasks to do or aspects to consider when planning and preparing for an event such as an academic assignment, journey, or party.

Cite (v) To acknowledge sources of ideas in your work. This may be done through an in-text reference to an author, a reference in a *bibliography* or footnote, or a verbal reference in a talk or lecture.

Concise (adj) Used to describe something that is expressed clearly in a few well-chosen words.

Conclusion (n) In academic terms, the final part of an essay or presentation, usually involving a summary of your results or argument, and a judgment.

Criteria (n) Qualities, rules, or standards on which decisions or judgments are based.

Deadline (n) The date or time by which something needs to be completed. In academic situations, deadlines are normally given for handing in essays and assignments.

Decimal (n) (adj) 1 A fraction expressed using numbers to the right of a decimal point. For example, one-quarter expressed as a decimal is 0.25. 2 Used to describe any numbering based on tens.

Dependent variable (n) In an *experiment* or study, a variable that changes in response to the independent variable or control. For example, if the response of insects to a particular chemical is being measured, the *independent variable* is the amount of chemical that is administered and the dependent variable is the degree to which the insects respond.

Deviation (n) A variation or movement away from a standard or expected result.

Discussion section (n) The section of a scientific paper that analyzes the findings or results of an experiment.

Draft (n) (v) 1 (n) An early version of a piece of academic writing that is used as the starting point for further work. 2 (v) To create an early version of an essay, knowing that you will go back afterwards to develop and *edit* your language and ideas.

Edit (v) To select, rearrange, and improve material to make it more suitable for its final purpose. Editing material involves reorganizing it, correcting errors, improving the wording or content, and changing its length by adding sections or taking them out.

Evaluate (v) To assess information in terms of quality, relevance, objectivity, and accuracy.

Experiment (n) A test under controlled conditions to examine whether or not a *hypothesis* is true.

Field work (n) Research or information collected away from the classroom, office, or laboratory where you usually do your work.

Figure (n) A diagram, graph, or picture that illustrates information in a text.

Formula (n) An equation, fact, or rule expressed in symbols and sometimes numbers, for example, $\pi r2$ (pi r squared) is the formula for the area of a circle.

Fraction (n) The expression of a number as part of a whole. It is shown as a quotient, where one number (the numerator) is divided by another (the denominator), such as ¼, ½, and ⅜.

Histogram (n) A form of graph that uses horizontal or vertical bars. The width (when horizontal) or height (when vertical) of the bars are in proportion to the values of the data items they represent.

Hypothesis (n) An idea about, or explanation of, an observation, phenomenon, or scientific problem. Hypotheses are tested by experimentation or analysis.

Implication (n) Something that can be interpreted or inferred but is not directly stated.

Independent variable (n) The variable in an *experiment* or study that the investigator can control or manipulate. For example, if the response of insects to a particular chemical is being measured, the independent variable is the amount of chemical that is administered and the *dependent variable* is the degree to which the insects respond.

Interpret (v) Give the meaning or explain the significance of something as you understand it.

Keyword (n) An important word in a text. Keywords are often used as a reference point to search for other words or information

Laboratory schedule (n) A list of procedures or instructions for conducting an *experiment* or operation in the laboratory.

Layout (n) The way that things are positioned within a space; for example, the way text, pictures, and diagrams are arranged on a page or computer screen.

Line graph (n) A graph that highlights trends by showing connecting lines between data points.

Materials and Methods section (n) The section of a scientific report that gives an account of the procedure that was followed in an *experiment*. It also details the materials and equipment that were used.

Numeral (n) A symbol used to represent a number: 1, 2, 3, 4, etc., are numerals.

Ordinal (n) Symbols that show the position of a numbered item in a series. For example, 1st, 2nd, 3rd, and 4th.

Peer review (n) The process of getting colleagues or other students to check your work. The idea is that peers can identify each other's errors quickly and effectively.

Pie chart (n) A graphic representation of amounts or percentages that are shown as segments of a circle (like a pie that has been divided up). It can be used instead of a table in the Results section of a scientific writing report.

Plot (v) To mark points on a graph or chart.

Protocol (n) Standard procedures and principles that are followed, for example when writing a report or conducting an *experiment*.

Quotation (n) A part of a text written or spoken by one author and reproduced in a text, piece of academic writing, or talk by another author. When you quote someone's words or ideas, you do not change the wording at all and should put them in quotation marks to signal that it is a quotation.

Ratio (n) The relation between two quantities expressed as the quotient of one divided by the other. For example, the ratio of 9 to 4 is 9:4 or 9/4.

Reference (n) (v) 1 (n) Acknowledgment of the sources of ideas and information that you use in written work and oral presentations. 2 (v) To acknowledge or mention sources of information.

Research (v) (n) 1 (v) To gather information from a variety of sources and *analyze* and compare it. 2 (n) Information collected from a variety of sources about a specific topic.

Scale (n) A sequence of marks at fixed intervals used to show measurements on, for example, a ruler, graph, or map.

Source (n) Something (usually a book, article, or other text) that supplies you with information. In an academic context, sources used in essays and reports must be acknowledged.

Theoretical background (n) Academic ideas and information that must be studied and understood before conducting an *experiment*, and that should be considered and referred to in the discussion stage of a scientific report.

Trend (n) The general direction in which something moves, or a sudden change in direction.

Module 10: Research and Referencing

Introduction

In higher education, you need to be able to research other people's ideas and gather resources in order to support arguments, both in seminars and in written assignments. Many students find it difficult to understand how they can quote the words and ideas of other writers without being accused of copying other people's work, i.e., plagiarism. It is of crucial importance that students understand what plagiarism is and how to avoid it in essays, exams, and dissertations. A misunderstanding of this issue can result in students failing.

This module will help you familiarize yourself with conventions for acknowledging your use of outside sources and clarify what you can and cannot do when quoting the words of authors and academics.

Unit 1 highlights the need to refer to other sources of information in order to strengthen ideas in your essays. It also looks at some of the difficulties students have in doing this in English-language universities. Unit 2 will familiarize you with a range of information sources and help you to evaluate them. Unit 3 underlines the importance of a bibliography and teaches you the basics of how to write one. You will learn how to differentiate between citing and quoting in Unit 4 and how to identify plagiarism and avoid it in your work in Unit 5. Finally, in Unit 6, you will put the skills you have learned into practice: you will select information from different sources and write some paragraphs that include quotes and citations. You will also write an appropriate bibliography to accompany your work.

After completing the module, you will feel more confident about researching and referencing essays in your classes. You will be able to strengthen your own ideas by including quotes and citations appropriately in your work and be able to write a more structured and effective bibliography.

Skills Map

Why research?

Understand the need to use other sources of information to strengthen your essays.

The research process

Familiarize yourself with the range of sources of information and consider their strengths and weaknesses.

Writing a bibliography

Understand the use and importance of a bibliography and learn the basics of writing one in the APA system

Referring to other sources in your essay

Understand the uses of quotations and citations and familiarize yourself with the APA system of referencing.

Plagiarism

Understand what plagiarism is and how to recognize it in a piece of writing so that you can use other sources in your writing in an acceptable way.

Using supporting arguments

Identify relevant information in your research notes and understand how to use it in your essay to support arguments in an acceptable way.

Destination: Research and Referencing

Why research?

At the end of this unit you will:
- understand the need to refer to other sources;
- be aware of different conventions and attitudes to research in different cultures.

Task 1 Why research?

1.1 Imagine you are going to write an essay on homelessness. In groups of 3–5, spend 10 minutes discussing homelessness.

   a) What is homelessness?

   b) How big of a problem do you think it is?

   c) What causes homelessness?

   d) What impact does it have on individuals and society?

   e) What can be done to address the problem?

1.2 Now discuss the following questions with your whole class.

   a) How much did you know about homelessness before your discussion?

   b) What have you learned from the discussion?

   c) What extra information or ideas would you need to know to write an essay on homelessness?

   d) What sources of information could help you write this essay?

Task 2 Supporting evidence and arguments

2.1 Read the essay on the next page and underline the answers to these questions.

   a) How big is the problem of homelessness?

   b) What are its main causes?

   c) What are its effects?

   d) Can homelessness be alleviated?

What are the causes and impacts of homelessness?
by Andrew Student

Andrew Student

One of the world's most pressing problems is that of homelessness. In recent years, there has been a dramatic rise in the number of people who have found themselves living on the streets.

Homelessness can be defined as the condition of people who lack regular access to adequate housing. This problem can affect a wide range of people, including children, the elderly, and, in some cases, whole families.

People become homeless for many reasons, including poverty, a lack of employment, a shortage of affordable housing, domestic violence, mental illness, and drug addiction.

Homelessness has a profound effect on those who experience it. It is likely to have a negative impact on physical and mental health, sense of identity, and social integration. In the case of homeless children, academic performance may be impaired as well.

Homelessness is clearly becoming an urgent problem, given the increasing number of people who are affected and the severity of its impact on individuals and society. To address the problem, its root causes need to be targeted, rather than just its symptoms. Otherwise, the problem of homelessness will simply be perpetuated.

2.2   In your groups, discuss the following questions and write notes.

   a) What new information have you learned about homelessness?

   b) Has the writer shown a good knowledge of the topic?

   c) Do you agree with the definition of homelessness?

   d) How convincing is the argument in this essay?

2.3   Work individually. Underline the parts of the essay where you could add supporting points and evidence to strengthen the essay. Then compare with a partner.

Task 3 Academic cultures

3.1 The following comments were made by four international students at American universities. Read about their experiences and discuss the questions below with your partner.

a) Have you had similar experiences?

b) What are the main differences between university writing in the US and in these students' countries?

c) How do the international students feel about these differences?

d) What advice would you give them?

Kris:

In my country, we don't do much writing at the undergraduate level. We go to lectures, take notes, and learn the information. At the end of the year we have an exam, but it's oral. In the US, you have to do so many essays. At first I found it strange, but now I like it because the essays make me think about the topics we are studying, and I can use the essays to help me review for exams.

Bo:

I am a science student, and the way we write our reports is so different to how people do it here in the US. One thing is the length. In the US, writers add a lot of stuff that is totally irrelevant and boring. The beginnings and the ends of the reports are full of quotations from other people's research. In my country, we talk about the problem, the methodology, and the solution. There is no point in talking about other people's work. It's in the library and a good student knows it already. It is boring to mention it again.

Edward:

I didn't write a bibliography (a list of sources) until I was writing a long essay in my final year. Before that, my professors didn't require one. After I had finished writing the essay, I just put all the books I had used in a big pile on my desk and wrote out their details in a list. My only problem when I'm writing in English is that I have to keep stopping to add a reference and make sure the book is in my bibliography, too. Sometimes, it makes me forget my ideas.

Phan:

In my country, we are taught not to steal other people's ideas or writing. So when we do university writing, we write a list of all the books we have used in a bibliography. We don't give a reference in the text of our essay. It's enough to mention the books in our bibliographies. Also, if the idea is well known or if it comes from a lecture, we don't mention it in a bibliography because the professors and students know where the idea is from. At first, I kept forgetting this type of thing in my bibliographies, but now I am beginning to change.

Reflect

In this unit you have learned about the importance of researching sources to support your arguments. This will clearly lead to extra work, particularly as you need to make reference to sources. It is important that you work out your attitude to this right from the beginning.

First of all, think about how important it is to refer to other sources in the academic culture of your country. If what you are used to is very different, you will need to find good reasons to change. The most basic reason is that you have to accept the change, rather than fight it, to ensure that you get a good diploma or degree at the end of your studies.

But a more positive way of looking at this issue is that higher educational study is an opportunity to broaden your learning. The more you have to put into your studies, the more you will get out of them. Once you get used to research and referencing, you will probably find that the benefits outweigh the drawbacks.

Reflect carefully on these issues and decide where you stand and where you feel your best interests lie.

Student notes for Unit 1

2 The research process

At the end of this unit you will:
- be aware of a range of sources of information;
- be able to identify the strengths and weaknesses of different sources;
- be able to note down bibliographical details for books and websites.

Task 1 Research options

1.1 Work in groups of 3–5. Look at the list of sources of information below and discuss which ones you have already used. Add to the list any other sources of information that you are familiar with.

a) books

b) websites

c) journals

d) ....

e) ....

f) ....

g) ....

1.2 In your group, discuss the strengths and weaknesses of the different sources of information in your list above. Refer to your own experience of using these various sources. Make notes in the table on the following page.

You should consider:

a) authority

b) ease of access

c) reliability

d) amount of information

e) relevance

f) time

What else might you consider?

Source	Strengths	Weaknesses
books		
websites		
journals		

Task 2 Preparing research questions

Now you are going to write a list of sources (a bibliography) that could be used to strengthen Andrew Student's essay on homelessness.

2.1   Look back at your notes for Task 2.2 in Unit 1. Identify what information would be useful.

For example:

Definitions of homelessness, size of the problem

2.2   Turn these notes into three research questions and write them below. Leave space after each question to add notes and sources later on.

For example:

How has homelessness been defined by other writers? What information indicates the size of the problem?

Research question 1:

Notes:

Reference sources:

Research question 2:

Notes:

Reference sources:

Research question 3:

Notes:

Reference sources:

Task 3 Information for a bibliography

You are going to find some sources to answer your research questions and write a bibliography. This is a complete list of sources that have been used to prepare an essay, and it usually appears at the end of an essay. It is important to keep a note of the bibliographical information. Without this information, you cannot use the source in your essay.

3.1   To find the necessary bibliographical information for a book, look on the title page and the copyright page (usually on the first few pages of a book). Below are examples of these.

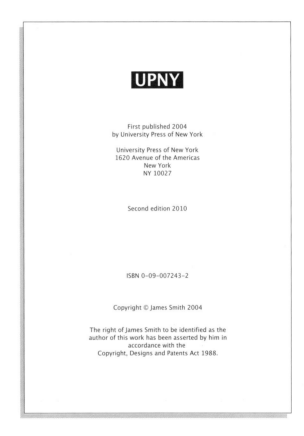

Find the following bibliographical information and then compare your answers with a partner.

a) Author's full name

b) Date of publication

c) Title

d) Edition

e) Place of publication

f) Publisher

3.2 A bibliography also includes any websites you used to research your essay.

Find the following bibliographical information and then compare your answers with a partner.

a) Author's full name _____

b) Date the information was last updated _____

c) Title _____

d) Web address: http:// _____

3.3 You might need to look carefully to find when a website was last updated. Type the following into a search engine and see how each one is organized: homeless+last updated.

3.4 Ask your instructor or a librarian for help with the bibliographical details you need to have for other types of information source. Alternatively, the Internet is a good source of information on writing bibliographies.

Task 4 Researching

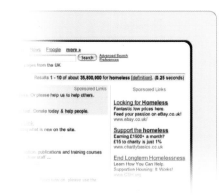

4.1 Use a library to find two books and two websites that help answer the research questions you wrote in Task 2.2. During this task, think about the reliability and authority of your sources.

Look back at the research questions you wrote in 2.2 and add brief notes after each one. Keep a record of the bibliographical details of your source on the same page as your notes.

4.2 From your notes, write down the bibliographical details for your sources in the table on the next page.

Tips

a) Most libraries now make use of electronic search engines. If you are not familiar with them, ask a librarian for help.

b) You can use a search engine such as Google or Yahoo to find relevant sites.

http://google.com
http://yahoo.com

c) You can also use web directories.

http://www.lycos.com
http://dir.yahoo.com/

d) Academic search engines are also a good source of information. The one provided by Bielefeld University is a good example.

http://www.base-search.net

e) You can also make use of commercial search engines, such as Highbeam, which are usually free for a trial period:

http://www.highbeam.com

Or by the US government at:

http://www.ich.gov
http://www.hhs.gov/homeless/index.html
http://www.hud.gov/homeless/index.cfm

Books

Author's family name and initial	Date of publication	Title	Edition	Place of publication	Publisher

Websites

Author's family name and initial	When last updated	Title	Date you accessed the site	Web address
				http://
				http://

Reflect

There are a variety of reasons for referring to sources in your writing. For example, you might use them when:

- giving factual information;
- providing examples;
- referring to relevant theories;
- presenting an argument or counterargument;
- supporting your own argument or counterargument.

Think about the research you carried out into homelessness. Which types of information did you tend to look for? Did you look for any other information types?

Now consider your future studies. Do you think you will tend to use the same information types, or more of a variety?

Student notes for Unit 2

Unit 3 Writing a bibliography

At the end of this unit you will:
- understand the purpose of a bibliography;
- be able to produce a bibliography using the APA System.

Task 1 Why include a bibliography?

1.1 In groups of 3–5, spend 10 minutes discussing bibliographies.

a) How much experience have you had of writing bibliographies in the past?

b) Why is a bibliography useful for the reader?

c) Why is writing a bibliography useful for you, the writer?

1.2 Now think about when you found sources to strengthen Andrew Student's essay on homelessness. Discuss the following questions with your class.

a) How did you use the bibliographies you found in the sources for the homelessness essay?

b) Why is it important for a bibliography to be complete and accurate?

Task 2 Bibliographies and the APA System

2.1 There are many different systems of citation, and they often differ from one academic field to another. In this exercise you will practice one of the most widely used ones—the APA System. The example below shows this system.

Bibliography

Baumohl, J. (1996). *Homelessness in America.* Phoenix: Oryx Press

Blau, J. (1993). *The visible poor: Homelessness in the United States.* Oxford: Oxford University Press.

Daly, G. P. (1996). *Homelessness: policies, strategies, and lives on the street.* Kentucky: Routledge

Salerno, D., Hopper, K. & Baxter, E. (1984). *Hardship in the heartland: homelessness in eight U.S. cities.* University of Michigan: Community Service Society of New York, Institute for Social Welfare Research.

Use the bibliography to answer the following questions:

a) What is the name of the book that was written by Joel Blau?

b) When was *Homelessness in America* published?

c) Who published *The visible poor: Homelessness in the United States*?

d) Where was *Homelessness: policies, strategies, and lives on the street* published?

e) What did Dan Salerno, Kim Hopper, and Ellen Baxter write?

f) If a book has three authors, how is the entry written?

g) In which order should entries be placed?

2.2 Look at the examples in the bibliography on page 319. What are the rules for writing a bibliographical entry for a book? Consider the order of information and punctuation.

2.3 Take the book sources you found in Unit 2, Task 4.2. Using the rules you have discovered, write bibliographical entries for your sources.

Task 3 Bibliographies and electronic sources

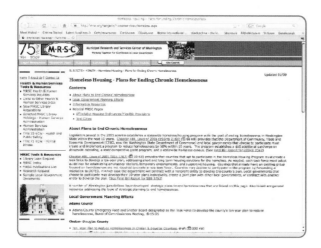

There is an increasing amount of information available on the Internet. This kind of information can be a valuable source, but it is important to use it correctly.

Before you use an electronic source in your essay, you need to decide if it is reliable. The publishing of a book is a much more careful process than the publishing of a website. You should use reliable sites, for example the official sites of universities or well-known companies.

As the three examples below show, the bibliographical rules for electronic sources differ slightly from books. It is important to give the address of the page, not just the address of the website. You can copy this from the browser window.

> Grassian, E. (2000). *Thinking critically about World Wide Web resources.*
> Retrieved October 24, 2006, from http://www.library.ucla.edu/libraries/college/11605_12337.cfm

> National Coalition for the Homeless. Factsheets. *Summary of 2009 Public Policy Recommendations*
> Retrieved August 12, 2009 from http://www.nationalhomeless.org/factsheets/#basic

> Homeless Youth in the United States: Recent research findings and intervention approaches. 2008.
> http://aspe.hhs.gov/hsp/homelessness/symposium07/toro/index.htm

3.1   Use the bibliography above to answer the following questions.

a) When was *Thinking critically about World Wide Web resources* written?

b) When did the writer of the bibliography visit the site *Thinking critically about World Wide Web resources*?

c) Why does *Summary of 2009 Public Policy Recommendations* not have a family name and initial as an author?

d) What information suggests that *Thinking critically about World Wide Web resources* is a reliable source?

3.2   Look at the examples of Internet source entries in the bibliography on page 321. What are the rules for writing a bibliographical entry for a website page?

3.3   Take the Internet sources you found in Unit 2, Task 4.2, and put them into the format shown above.

3.4   Work in groups of 3–5. Discuss the following questions and write notes.

a) Why do you include the date you accessed a website in a bibliography?

b) How reliable are the websites you chose to use for the homelessness essay?

Reflect

Think of how much use you made of bibliographies before starting your higher education studies. Compare that with the use you are beginning to make of them now.

Reflect on how useful you have found bibliographies since beginning your studies. Have you used them for follow-up research? Have you checked the dates of sources cited? Have you checked to see what else the authors have written?

Try to imagine your future studies. Do you think there will be a significant increase in your use of bibliographies?

Student notes for Unit 3

Unit 4 Referring to other sources in your essay

At the end of this unit you will:
- understand how to decide between citing and quoting;
- be able to acknowledge your sources in the body of your essay.

Citing and quoting are two methods of referring to other sources in your essays.

Task 1 Citing

> According to Frankish (2005), one reason for the difficulty in getting a clear idea of the scope of homelessness in Canada is the lack of a consistent definition of homelessness.

Frankish, C James
Canadian Journal of Public Health
March 1, 2005

The challenges associated with obtaining a clear picture of the scope of homelessness in Canada include the lack of a consistent definition of homelessness, …

Citing is reporting ideas or information from another source using your own words. This differs from copying verbatim (exactly word for word) and without acknowledgement, for two reasons. First, you can select and summarize important points from the source. Secondly, you make it clear from whom and where you got your ideas.

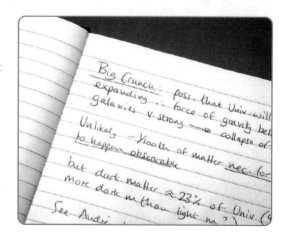

To avoid copying another writer's words directly into your essay by mistake, good note-taking technique is important. Using keywords, symbols, and paraphrasing at the note-taking stage all make it less likely to copy by mistake. It is also vital to write down the bibliographical details of the source accurately.

Look at this example.

Bibliographical entry for the source:

Grassian, E. (2000). *Thinking critically about World Wide Web resources.*
http://www.library.ucla.edu/libraries/college/11605_12337.cfm

Exact sentence from the source:

"The World Wide Web has a lot to offer, but not all sources are equally valuable or reliable."

Citing the source in an essay

According to Grassian (2000), Internet sources vary in accuracy and usefulness.

Or

In her evaluation of websites, Grassian (2000) argues that Internet sources vary in accuracy and usefulness.

1.1   **Discuss these questions with your partner.**

   a) How original is Grassian's idea?

   b) Why has the essay writer used Grassian's idea in the essay?

   c) How has the essay writer shown whose idea is given?

   d) Why doesn't the essay writer include Grassian's initial (E.)?

   e) How has the essay writer shown the reader where to find Grassian's idea?

   f) What changes did the essay writer make in order to avoid copying Grassian's text word for word?

1.2   **In groups of three to five, discuss the following questions.**

   a) Why is the APA style widely used?

   b) Have you used a similar system before?

   c) Why is it better to add the author and date information to your essay at the same time as you write your essay, rather than after you have finished writing it?

Task 2 Quoting

Quoting is another method of reporting the ideas from another source. Unlike citing, you may use the exact words of the source's writer. Similar to citing, however, you make sure your reader understands who the words belong to and in which source they appear.

As a rule, quotations are used less often than citations. One reason for quoting is when you feel the author expresses an idea or opinion in such a way that it is particularly succinct, memorable or interesting. For example:

Quoting the source in an essay

A number of studies (Anderson & Thompson, 2005; Fitzpatrick, 2000) have found that young homeless people's definitions of homelessness differ from the definition used by the government, which is discussed above. One interviewee says, "I think I was homeless, not because I was living in the street, basically because we, me and my sister, were living at a different house every week and basically living out of a bag in that house" (Anderson & Thompson 2005, p. 21).

2.1 Discuss with your partner.

    a) Why did the essay writer decide to quote, rather than paraphrase, Anderson and Thompson's text?

    b) Which words are from Anderson and Thompson's text?

    c) Which words are the essay writer's words?

    d) How do you know which words are from Anderson and Thompson's text?

    e) Why has the essay writer included 2005 in parentheses?

    f) What does p. 21 mean and why has the essay writer included this information?

2.2 A second reason for quoting is to strengthen your own argument by referring to an authority. Look at the references below to sources on homelessness in the UK. Then discuss the questions with a partner.

> **Bibliographical entry for the source**
> Fitzpatrick, S., Kemp, P., & Klinker, S. (2000). *Single homelessness: An overview of research in Britain.* Bristol: The Policy Press and Joseph Rowntree Foundation*
>
> **Quoting the source in an essay**
> Fitzpatrick et al. (2000, p. 121) define homelessness as a "lack of right to or access to … secure and minimally adequate housing space."
>
> *The Joseph Rowntree Foundation is one of the largest social policy research and development charities in the UK.

    a) Why might the authors of *Single homelessness: An overview of research in Britain* be authorities on the subject of homelessness?

    b) What does *et al.* mean and when is it used?

    c) In the middle of the quotation there are three dots (…). What does this punctuation mean?

2.3 The layout of a long quotation is different from the examples of short quotations above. A long quotation is usually considered to be three or more lines of text. Look at the example below about a UK housing and homeless charity. Then discuss the questions on the next page.

Adam Sampson, director of Shelter, made the following comment in response to the homelessness statistics issued by the government:

Although the number of people being accepted as homeless has fallen, the fact remains there are still record numbers of people trapped in temporary accommodation and hundreds of thousands more in overcrowded or unfit housing. (Sampson, 2005).

From this, it can be seen that Sampson is aware that the new statistics may be used to give the misleading impression that homelessness is no longer a pressing problem.

a) How are the layout and punctuation of a long quotation different from those of a short quotation?

b) What is the maximum length of a quotation?

c) It is usual for a quotation to be followed by a page number in the in-text reference, but in this example there isn't one. When is it possible not to give a page number?

2.4 In groups of 3–5, discuss the following questions.

a) What is the difference between the following uses of the same source?

According to Weller (1949, p. 87), "East, west, home is best …"

Weller (1949) believes that it doesn't matter where one travels to, in the end most people prefer their homes.

b) Why is citing usually preferable to quoting?

c) What is your professor's view likely to be if you link together long but accurately acknowledged quotations with a few words of your own in your essay?

d) What is your professor likely to think if you don't represent a source writer's ideas or opinions accurately in your writing?

e) What may happen if you don't acknowledge that an idea or a quotation belongs to another writer?

Task 3 Citing and quoting practice

3.1 Work individually. Look at your sources about homelessness. Underline two important points and copy them verbatim (word for word) into the box below. Make notes in the box too. Use keywords and symbols and change the language of the source text as much as possible.

Using your notes, write two citations. Try to use both book and Internet sources.

Citation:
The words in the source:
Your notes:

Citation 1

Citation:
The words in the source:
Your notes:

Citation 2:

Citation:
The words in the source:
Your notes:

3.2 **Work with your partner. Discuss the following questions.**

a) Do your partner's citations change the meaning of the source?

b) Has your partner clearly changed the language of the source?

c) Has your partner given an accurate in-text reference?

3.3 **Work individually. Find two examples in your sources that you could quote in an essay on homelessness. Write them in the boxes below as they would appear in your essay. Try to use both book and Internet sources.**

Quotation:

Quotation:

3.4 Work with your partner. Discuss the following questions.

    a) Why has your partner decided to quote, rather than paraphrase, these parts of the source text?

    b) Has your partner acknowledged the source accurately?

Task 4 Referencing practice

4.1 Working in groups of 3–5, read the passage below and underline the sections that have not been properly referenced. Then compare your work.

In a recent article on homelessness in Chicago, an expert analyzed the reasons behind the growing numbers of homeless people in the city and concluded that drug abuse was the primary cause of homelessness amongst young people. This claim is, however, questioned by another academic on the website www.homeless.org. According to the second author, the first author's statement that drug abuse is common amongst homeless people under the age of 20 is not supported by the statistical evidence provided by the National Statistics Bureau.

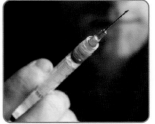

Reflect

When citing from a source, you need to make sure you use your own words. Think about the way you paraphrase from sources at the moment.

Can you think of any steps you could take to improve the way you do this and ensure that you do not steal the source writer's language or ideas by mistake? Think about note-taking, the use of vocabulary, different ways of constructing sentences, and any other ideas that might help.

Student notes for Unit 4

Unit 5 Plagiarism

At the end of this unit you will:
- understand what plagiarism is;
- understand how to use sources in your writing;
- be able to recognize plagiarism in a piece of writing.

Task 1 What is plagiarism?

1.1 In groups of 3–5, discuss your answers to the following questions.

a) Why is it necessary to refer to other sources when writing an essay or report?

b) What do you understand by the term *plagiarism*?

The origin of the word *plagiarism* is a Latin word meaning *a thief*. Plagiarism is a type of academic theft, in which ideas and/or language are stolen from someone else. In its most obvious form, plagiarism involves the word-for-word copying of large sections of another person's material with no indication of the original source. Because of the lack of in-text reference, the plagiarist is claiming the ideas and language as his or her own.

In a less extreme form, the plagiarist copies shorter phrases from a source and links these together with his or her own words. This is also plagiarism if there is no in-text reference to show that the ideas come from another source or if there are no quotation marks around shorter quotations to show that the words belong to someone else. In scientific subjects, plagiarism could also be copying another person's results, calculations, or program code, perhaps with minor changes in accuracy, explanation, layout, or identifiers.

 Plagiarism is a form of cheating and is liable to punishment.

1.2 Read the text above. In groups of 3–5, discuss your answers to the following questions.

a) What is the difference between plagiarism and acceptable reference to other sources?

b) Why do professors take plagiarism so seriously?

c) Has the Internet made plagiarism easier?

d) Is plagiarism a problem just for non-native speaker students?

e) What might the penalty be if you plagiarize a piece of assessed work?

Task 2 Plagiarism and other misuses of sources

2.1 Look at how four writers have used a source text in a paragraph in their essays. Discuss your answers to the questions below in your group.

a) How has each writer used the language of the source?

b) How has each writer used the ideas from the source?

c) Which paragraphs show the writer has understood the ideas in the source?

d) Which of the four paragraphs is not plagiarized?

Source text

Forrester, G. (2006). *Push factors in youth homelessness.* 3rd ed. Reading: Garnet.

A paragraph taken from p. 22

Push factors account for a high proportion of youth homelessness, possibly as much as 80% (Centrepoint, 2005). Push factors tend to make young people leave home without much pre-planning, leaving them vulnerable. These factors may be interpersonal, for example disputes with family members, family breakups, and various forms of violence. Push factors may also be related to lack of resources in the shape of poverty or lack of space in the family home. Young people affected by push factors tend to leave home before the age of 16 and consequently often lack the skills and resources to set up their own home. A recent survey found that over 40% of the young homeless interviewees had no formal qualifications and 24% had no source of income (Centrepoint, 2005).

Paragraphs

(a) *Push factors account for a high proportion of youth homelessness. Possibly as many as 8 out of 10 young homeless people leave home because of push factors, which include disputes with family members, violence, and poverty (Centrepoint, 2005). Push factors tend to make young people leave home without much pre-planning, leaving them vulnerable. Young people affected by push factors tend to leave home before the age of 16 and consequently often lack the skills and resources to set up their own home.*

(b) *Push factors in youth homelessness may be divided into two categories: "interpersonal" factors and factors relating to a shortage of resources (Forrester, 2006, p. 22). In the UK, these factors play a significant role in young people becoming homeless. According to a survey carried out by the London-based charity Centrepoint, approximately 80% of cases of youth homelessness are the result of push factors (Centrepoint, 2005, cited in Forrester, 2006).*

(c) *Push factors cause a large proportion of homelessness, approximately 80% (Centrepoint, 2005). Push factors are inclined to make juveniles leave home without much pre-planning, leaving them weak. These factors might be interpersonal, for instance disputes with relatives, relations breakups, and a mixture of forms of violence. Push factors may also be interconnected to lack of wealth in the nature of lack or not having enough space in the family home. Young people exaggerated by push factors tend to leave home before the age of 16 and so often lack the skills and resources to set up their own abode. A recent survey found that over 40% of the young destitute interviewees had no strict qualifications and 24% had no cause of income (Centrepoint, 2005).*

(d) *Forester (2005) states that push factors can be categorized in two groups: interpersonal factors, such as arguments with other members of the family and violence within the home on the one hand, and resource-related factors, such as lack of money or sufficient living space on the other. She adds that these push factors often cause young people to leave the family home before they are 16, with the result that these young people are particularly at risk because they may have no recognized qualifications.*

Notes

Reflect

Think about the various reasons that students plagiarize. Some possible reasons are given below:

- Lack of confidence
- Laziness
- Trying to impress
- Other students do it
- It's not really wrong
- Professors encourage it

Which ones do you think are valid? Which are more common? What other reasons can you think of?

When you have come up with a clear list, carry out the following procedure. Imagine that you are an instructor discussing the issue with a group of students. The group of students gives reasons for plagiarizing from your list. Find ways of countering their arguments.

Student notes for Unit 5

Unit 6 Using supporting arguments

At the end of this unit you will:
- **be able to select relevant information from your research notes;**
- **be able to support your arguments;**
- **be able to acknowledge your sources acceptably.**

Task 1 Using supporting statements

This final unit asks you to strengthen Andrew Student's essay (Unit 1, Task 2.1). To do this, you will select relevant information from your research notes and add this support to the argument.

1.1 Below is the essay on homelessness written by Andrew Student. Andrew has some good ideas, but he has not given enough data, examples, and supporting points. To get a good grade, he will have to support his argument with statements and ideas from other sources.

Using your notes from Unit 1, Task 2.3, put an arrow and a number where the argument needs support.

Andrew Student

```
What are the causes and impacts of homelessness?
by Andrew Student

One of the world's most pressing problems is that of
homelessness. In recent years, there has been a
dramatic rise in the number of people who have found
themselves living on the streets.

Homelessness can be defined as the condition of
people who lack regular access to adequate housing.
This problem can affect a wide range of people,
including children, the elderly, and, in some cases,
whole families.

People become homeless for many reasons, including poverty, a lack of
employment, a shortage of affordable housing, domestic violence, mental
illness, and drug addiction.

Homelessness has a profound effect on those who experience it. It is
likely to have a negative impact on physical and mental health, sense of
identity, and social integration. In the case of homeless children,
academic performance may be impaired as well.

Homelessness is clearly becoming an urgent problem, given the increasing
number of people who are affected and the severity of its impact on
individuals and society. To address the problem, its root causes need to
be targeted, rather than just its symptoms. Otherwise, the problem of
homelessness will simply be perpetuated.
```

1.2 Look at the notes you made from your sources to answer your research questions (Unit 2, Task 4.1). Choose the most relevant information to support Andrew Student's argument. This will probably include examples, statistical data, and more specific points that support his argument.

1.3 Decide which information needs quoting and which needs citing.

1.4 Write each citation and quotation in the appropriate box below the excerpt. Number each one to match the arrows and numbers you have added to the essay. Make sure that all the citations and quotations are correctly referenced.

1.5 Write a bibliography for the sources you have used in APA style.

What are the causes and impacts of homelessness?—by Andrew Student

One of the world's most pressing problems is that of homelessness. In recent years, there has been a dramatic rise in the number of people who have found themselves living on the streets.

Homelessness can be defined as the condition of people who lack regular access to adequate housing. This problem can affect a wide range of people, including children, the elderly, and, in some cases, whole families.

People become homeless for many reasons, including poverty, a lack of employment, a shortage of affordable housing, domestic violence, mental illness, and drug addiction.

Homelessness has a profound effect on those who experience it. It is likely to have a negative impact on physical and mental health, sense of identity, and social integration. In the case of homeless children, academic performance may be impaired as well.

Homelessness is clearly becoming an urgent problem, given the increasing numbers of people who are affected and the severity of its impact on individuals and society. In order to address the problem, its root causes need to be targeted, rather than its symptoms. Otherwise, the problem of homelessness will simply be perpetuated.

Bibliography

Task 2 Thinking about the argument

2.1 In groups of 3–4, present your additions to Andrew Student's essay. Take turns explaining what was weak in the essay and how each of your additions strengthens the essay.

2.2 In the same groups, discuss your work in detail.

a) Do you agree about which points need strengthening?

b) Which pieces of information are most persuasive?

c) Is the source of each piece of information shown clearly?

Task 3 Thinking about the research process

3.1 In the same group, discuss the process of researching and referencing the essay. Consider the following questions.

a) When is the best point to find sources in the essay-writing process?

b) What should you do if you cannot find appropriate sources?

c) Which part of the process did you enjoy most?

d) Which part did you find most difficult?

e) What is the most important thing you have learned?

What advice would you give to another student who is starting this module?

Reflect

Reflect on how the essay on homelessness has been improved by the addition of your research. Then think about how the skills you have used in this research could be used in subjects such as science, maths, engineering, etc.

Student notes for Unit 6

Module 10

Web work

Website 1 Keyword searching

http://www.sussex.ac.uk/library/infosuss/planning_a_search/index.shtml

Review
A guide to planning a search.

Task
Access the site and complete the tutorial and quiz.

Website 2 Evaluating sources

http://www.sussex.ac.uk/library/infosuss/evaluating_information/practical.shtml

Review
A guide to evaluating sources.

Task
Access the site and complete the tutorial and quiz.

Website 3 Avoiding plagiarism

http://www.princeton.edu/pr/pub/integrity/08/intro/index.htm, then click on *Examples of plagiarism*.

Review
A good guide that shows varying grades of plagiarism.

Task
Access the site and complete the online activities.

Extension activities

Quoting and citing

Look at the following essay extracts and consider the differences. Which one(s) incorporate another person's ideas correctly, and which would be unacceptable? Which version(s) do you prefer?

a)

> In the words of the song, 'There's no place like home'. Nevertheless, for a large proportion of the world's population, staying at home has become impossible. Wars, famines, and religious persecution have caused many to leave their homes.

b)

> According to the old adage: "There's no place like home." (Payne, 1822). However, for a large proportion of the world's population, staying at home has become unfeasible. Conflicts, famines, and religious persecution, to name but a few, have caused many to desert their homes.

c)

> Payne (1822) believed that there is no place like home. This may be true for many people, but for others in economically deprived areas of the world, home has had to be abandoned.

Choosing appropriate reporting verbs

Match these reporting verbs (a)–(e) to their effects (1)–(5)

a) claims

b) proves

c) suggests

d) illustrates

e) outlines

1. has strong evidence

2. gives examples

3. is an opinion that not everyone agrees with

4. gives the main points only

5. has weak evidence

What effect do the following reporting verbs have?

argues   asserts   believes   persuades us   points out   questions   reminds us

Module 10

Glossary

Academic culture (n) The values and beliefs that exist in academic institutions, particularly those that inform and influence academic *conventions*.

Academic field (n) Subject area or branch of knowledge that someone may choose to study or specialize in.

Access (a site) (v) To go to a website.

APA System (n) One of a number of "citation styles" that set out how to *reference* sources in a *bibliography* or in the body of the text.

Assignment (n) A piece of work, generally written, that is set as part of an academic course and is normally completed out of class and submitted by a set date to be assessed.

Author (n) The person who writes a book, article, or other printed text, electronic article, or system such as a website.

Bibliography (n) A list of *references* to *sources* cited in the text of a piece of academic writing or a book. A bibliography should consist of an alphabetical list of books, papers, journal articles, and websites and is usually found at the end of the work. It may also include texts suggested by the author for further reading.

Cite (v) To acknowledge sources of ideas in your work. This may consist of an in-text reference to an author, a reference in a *bibliography* or footnote, or a verbal reference in a talk or lecture.

Conventions (n) Widely used and accepted practices that are agreed upon. Academic conventions for research include: dividing essays and reports into sections, referencing all *sources*, and writing a *bibliography* according to certain styles, such as the APA System.

Corporate author (adj) A term used to describe authorship of a text that does not have a named author (or authors), such as a report or an article produced by a government department or other organization.

Counterargument (n) An argument that opposes or makes the case against another argument.

Dissertation (n) A long essay, which may involve original research, and that is often a key component of a degree or diploma program.

Edition (n) All the copies of a version of a published text produced at one time are known as an edition. Later editions of a text may include changes, corrections, and additions so, if known, it is necessary to state which edition of a text you cite in a *bibliography*.

Electronic source (n) Any text that has been accessed on the Internet or from a CD, audiocassette, or video rather than from a printed source.

Essay (n) An analytical piece of academic writing that is usually quite short in length. Students are required to write essays as assignments and in exams so that their learning can be assessed.

Evaluate (v) To assess information in terms of quality, relevance, objectivity, and accuracy.

Higher education (n) Tertiary education that is beyond the level of secondary education and usually offers first and higher degrees. A university is an institution of higher education.

In-text reference (n) A *reference* that is in the body of the text. It is normally put in parentheses and is shorter than the reference in the *bibliography*. It should include the author's name and the year of publication as a minimum.

Journal (n) A publication that is issued at regular and stated intervals (such as every month or quarter), and that contains articles and essays by different authors. Journals include magazines and newspapers as well as academic periodicals that contain more scholarly articles on specialized topics.

Paraphrase (v) To alter a piece of text so that you restate it (concisely) in different words without changing its meaning. It is useful to paraphrase when writing a summary of someone's ideas; if the *source* is acknowledged, it is not *plagiarism*. It is also possible to paraphrase your own ideas in an essay or presentation; that is, to state them again, often in a clearer, expanded way.

Plagiarism (n) The act of presenting someone else's work, i.e., written text, data, images, recording, as your own. This includes:

- copying or paraphrasing material from any *source* without an acknowledgment;
- presenting other people's ideas without acknowledging them;
- working with others and then presenting the work as if it was completed independently.

Plagiarism is not always deliberate, and it is important to adopt the academic *conventions* of always indicating ideas and work that are not your own, and referencing all your sources correctly.

Quotation (n) A part of a text written or spoken by one author and reproduced in a text, piece of academic writing, or talk by another author. When you quote someone's words or ideas, you do not change the wording at all and should put it in quotation marks ("~") to signal that it is a quotation.

Reference (n) (v) 1 (n) Acknowledgment of the *sources* of ideas and information that you use in written work and oral presentations. 2 (v) To acknowledge or mention the *sources* of information.

Research (v) (n) 1 (v) To gather information from a variety of *sources* and analyze and compare it. 2 (n) Information collected from a variety of *sources* about a specific topic.

Research question (n) A statement or question that helps you to start gathering together ideas, notes, and information in a focused way in preparation for writing an essay, report, presentation, or dissertation.

Search engine (n) A website comprising a large database of other websites. A search engine's crawler collects Web pages and the search engine then allows visitors to do a keyword search to find useful pages.

Seminar (n) A small group discussion led by a professor or guest speaker. Students are expected to take an active part in the seminar.

Source (n) Something (usually a book, article, or other text) that supplies you with information. In an academic context, sources used in essays and reports must be acknowledged.

Supporting argument (n) It is necessary to provide supporting evidence, arguments, and statements to strengthen your ideas and opinions in an academic essay. This support may include reference to other *sources*, quotations, and data.

Module 11: Presentations

Introduction

This module will familiarize you with each of the steps involved in preparing and delivering an oral presentation. Being able to give an effective oral presentation is an essential skill in both academic and professional life, and prospective employers often look for experience and proficiency in speaking to large groups. In higher or continuing education, you may be asked to give presentations (alone or in groups) for a variety of reasons: you might be given a topic to speak on by your professor, you might be required to give a summary of your essay research, or you might be asked to inform a class of your laboratory research methods and results. Such talks may be formally assessed, or they may function as a more informal information-sharing experience. By following the activities and exercises in this module, you will learn how to optimize your communication skills in this area and develop confidence through a series of micro-tasks.

Unit 1 focuses on what makes a good presentation and how presentations may be assessed. Unit 2 looks at the particular skills and strategies involved in giving a group presentation. In Unit 3, you will learn how to plan the topic, focus, and content of a talk, and in Unit 4 you will analyze and practice the required language and communication skills. In Unit 5, you will study how to choose and use visual aids appropriately. Finally, in Unit 6, you will learn how to use slideshow software to create presentation slides and notes.

By putting the micro-tasks together, you will be prepared to deliver a short presentation on any topic of an academic nature. The extension activities at the end of the module will suggest different types of presentations for you to prepare and deliver.

Skills Map

Unit 1 — About presentations
Familiarize yourself with the process of preparing to give a presentation.

Unit 2 — Group presentations
Learn the specific skills needed for giving a group presentation.

Unit 3 — Content
Plan the topic, focus, and content of a presentation

Unit 4 — Communication
Learn the language and delivery skills needed for a competent and confident performance.

Unit 5 — Visual aids
Explore the use of visual aids to appropriately support and enhance main points.

Unit 6 — Slideshow tutorial
Familiarize yourself with presentation software in order to prepare a series of slides.

Destination: Presentations

About presentations

At the end of this unit you will be able to:
- recognize what makes a good presentation;
- understand the process of preparing a presentation.

Task 1 What makes a good presentation?

A presentation is essentially a talk given to share information with other people. You have probably had many experiences of different kinds of presentations (both academic and non-academic) in your life.

1.1 Think about the presentations you have given or listened to in the past.

Consider as many different aspects of a presentation as possible, e.g., the speaker, the topic, the material, the language, and discuss the following questions in groups of three to five.

a) What makes a good presentation?

b) What makes a bad presentation?

1.2 Presentations benefit from good preparation. Now work in pairs and think about the process of preparing a presentation. In your notebook, write a list of the steps you will need to go through from the beginning of the process to the finished product (the final presentation).

Task 2 Planning checklist

Compare your answers to Task 1.2 with the following checklist. Check the tasks that you thought of.

Planning checklist

Choose your topic In some cases, the topic will be given to you by your instructor. If not, make sure that it is appropriate by asking your instructor before the next step.	
Make sure you understand the grading criteria Make sure you know what is expected of you.	
Conduct research Research will help you know enough about your topic for the presentation. Think about where you can find the information you need (the library, the Internet). References to the sources you have used should be included in a bibliography. This can appear as a final slide in a slideshow, or as a handout.	

Decide on a specific focus It is advisable to avoid a general speech, such as, "All we know about ...." Remember what you are trying to show or prove. Focus the topic to a manageable number of main points.	
Plan what you are going to say Write notes to help you remember the main points of your talk. You should not, however, just read from a script.	
Choose and prepare visual aids Which visual aids will help you communicate your message best?	

Task 3 Grading criteria

If your presentation is going to be assessed, you should find out in advance what assessment criteria will be used. This will help you to plan and give a more effective presentation.

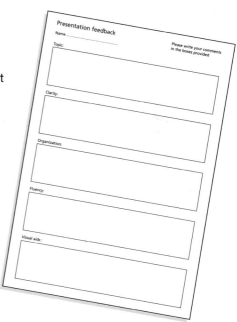

3.1 Make a list below of the major criteria you think could be used to assess a presentation. You could use the Planning checklist from Task 2 as a guide.

· Organization: The presentation is well planned and has a clear and logical structure.

Reflect

Look at the criteria for a good presentation again, and think about how these apply to you. Reflect on the following three areas:

- What are your strengths when speaking in front of a group?
- What aspects of presentation-giving could you realistically improve in the short term?
- What aspects of presentation-giving should you allow a longer time to improve?

Student notes for Unit 1

Group presentations

At the end of this unit you will:
- **understand how to organize the preparation process;**
- **have a clear idea about individual roles and responsibilities.**

You will sometimes be expected to give a presentation as a member of a group. In this unit, you will explore the dynamics of group presentations and then work with some other students to prepare a presentation on an academic topic. Your instuctor will help you decide on this topic. Then, for the rest of this module, you will use the tasks in each unit to help you plan and present your talk together. If you would like more information on teamwork, you can refer to the TASK *Teamworking* module.

Task 1 Advantages and disadvantages

Work in groups of three to five. Discuss the following questions and make notes.

    a) What are the advantages of giving a group presentation?

    b) What are the disadvantages of giving a group presentation?

Task 2 Working together

Remember that a group presentation involves team effort. It is always clear to the instructor when students do not work with their group, as their pieces of the presentation do not fit together with the other group members' pieces on the day of delivery.

2.1   **Work in your presentation group. Look back at the Planning checklist from Unit 1, Task 2, and discuss which of the tasks you should work on as a team and which ones could be done individually. Write your answers in the table on page 348. (You may also decide that some tasks should be tackled individually first and then discussed in a group.)**

Team tasks	Individual tasks

2.2 Would the following activities be team tasks or individual tasks? Add them to the table.

- Plan who will do or say what
- Set deadlines
- Select a team coordinator
- Organize a series of meetings for team members
- Rehearse the presentation

Task 3 Group work

Use your Planning checklist to get organized and prepare your talk. Remember that you should share the work equally. Arrange to meet the other members of your group at least three times outside of class time to plan and practice your presentation before the final delivery.

It is important to keep a record of the planning for your presentation. If your group presentation is going to be assessed, these records will contribute towards the grade you are awarded.

3.1 Your first step is to arrange a meeting with your group to agree how you are to proceed. Organize your meeting times using Table 3.1.

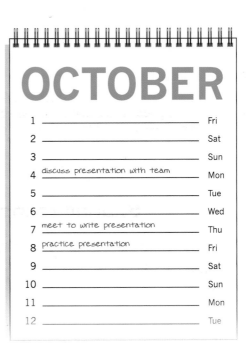

OCTOBER

1		Fri
2		Sat
3		Sun
4	discuss presentation with team	Mon
5		Tue
6		Wed
7	meet to write presentation	Thu
8	practice presentation	Fri
9		Sat
10		Sun
11		Mon
12		Tue

Table 3.1: Meeting information

	Place	Time	Purpose
Meeting 1			
Meeting 2			
Meeting 3			
Meeting 4			

3.2   You should also keep a record of attendance at the meetings.

Table 3.2: Attendance record

Team member's name	E-mail	Phone number	Meeting attendance			
			M1	M2	M3	M4

It will also aid your organization if you keep a record in note form of what was discussed and what was agreed at your meetings. The individual members of your group could take turns taking these notes and then distribute them to the other members.

Task 4 Sharing responsibilities

It is important that every member of the group take responsibility for the preparation of your presentation.

Record who is responsible for each task in the grid on page 350. This will ensure that the work is shared equally and that nothing is forgotten.

Table 4.1: Actions and responsibilities

Name	Responsibility	Action

Reflect

Think about why it is essential for members of a group to rehearse their presentation together.

Do you feel that you played an appropriate role in planning the presentation?

Could you have done anything differently?

Student notes for Unit 2

Content

At the end of this unit you will:
• understand how to prepare and organize a presentation.

Task 1 A short presentation

1.1 Imagine you are giving a talk on "How to deliver an effective presentation." In groups, discuss what you would include in your presentation.

1.2 Write the characteristics of a good presentation as a series of bullet points.

Characteristics of a good presentation

• Interesting topic

•

•

•

•

•

•

•

1.3 Compare your answers with another student. Were your bullet points similar or different? Add any ideas that you agree with to your list.

1.4 Work in groups. Use your bullet point notes as the basis of a brief presentation to your group. Try to speak spontaneously on the basis of each point you have on the list.

1.5 Discuss the structure of the presentations you have just given as a class. How did you feel about the structure and organization? Did you feel that there was a clear beginning, middle, and end?

Task 2 Introduction to planning

Each presentation group should have agreed on a topic and completed the necessary research. It is now time to plan what you are going to say by preparing the content in a clear and logical way. This will enable your audience to both engage with your presentation and recall what you have said.

2.1   Study the diagram and be ready to explain the structure of a presentation to the rest of the class.

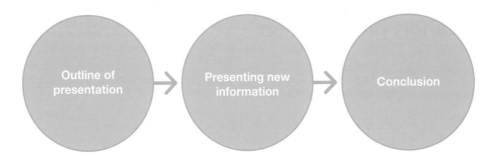

Outline of presentation → Presenting new information → Conclusion

2.2   In your presentation groups, give a brief overview to the rest of the class of the following:

- the topic of your presentation;
- the main points of your presentation.

Task 3 Planning your presentation

3.1   Continue in your presentation group and plan your introduction. Answer the three questions below together to create an introduction that you feel will get the attention of your audience. Make sure that one of the members in your group keeps a clear record of the points you make.

Introduce yourself and your topic:

How will you address the audience and what will you tell them about yourself?

What is your topic and why have you chosen it?

Thesis:

What research question are you going to answer in this presentation?

3.2   Continue in your presentation group. Think about the main points that you would like to make. These should be closely related to your thesis. For each main point, give some support; this could be detail, explanation, or evidence. If contrasting opinions exist, make sure you consider both sides of the argument.

Make sure that one member of the group keeps a record under the following headings:

First main point:

  Support:

Second main point:

  Support:

Third main point:

  Support:

Fourth main point:

  Support:

3.3 **The conclusion should describe clearly what your presentation has shown.**

As your conclusion is the final thing your audience will hear, it is particularly important that it make an impact. For example, when you go over points you have already made in the main body, make sure you do this clearly and concisely without simply repeating what you have said before.

Work on your conclusions in your presentation group. Then present your conclusions to the class.

3.4 **It is useful to prepare a bibliography to hand out to the audience after your presentation. Make a list of the sources (books, websites, journal articles, etc.) you used to support your points/arguments.**

Task 4 Preparing notes

Giving a presentation is not the same as reading an essay out loud. This is why it is useful to write your presentation in note form rather than continuous prose. You should already know what you want to say; the notes just provide a framework so you can keep to the structure you have planned.

4.1 **Discuss in groups the presentation you did in Task 1. How did you like using the bullet point notes?**

4.2 **In your presentation groups, use the information from Task 3 to write your own set of notes. Take account of anything you have learned from the discussion in Task 4.1.**

Reflect

Think about the outline plan you made for your presentation.

What helped you to organize your ideas?

How are the preparation stages for a presentation similar to or different from those of planning an essay?

Student notes for Unit 3

Unit 4 Communication

At the end of this unit you will be:
- more familiar with the language of presentations;
- able to use appropriate body language.

Once you have researched and prepared the content of a talk, it is essential to focus on its delivery.

Task 1 The language of presentations

The language you use can help indicate the structure of your presentation and guide the audience.

1.1 Match the functions a–e below with the appropriate groups of phrases 1–5 underneath. These phrases are known as signposts because they help to clarify where your presentation is going. The first one has been done for you as an example.

a) _2_ Introducing your presentation

b) _____ Outlining what you are going to say

c) _____ Making your first point

d) _____ Adding more points

e) _____ Closing

1
- Finally, I would like to turn to …
- My final point is with regard to …

2
- My presentation today concerns …
- I would like to talk to you today about …

3
- To begin with …
- Turning then to the first point …

5
- My next point concerns …
- That brings me to …
- I want to turn now to … / I'd like to turn now to …

4
- I will be looking at the following areas:
- I have divided my talk into the following areas:

1.2 Similar phrases can be used to signal when you are doing other things within each stage of your presentation. Match the functions f–j to the phrases 6–10 below.

f) .... Giving emphasis (for example, in your conclusion)

g) .... Adding more information

h) .... Making a generalization

i) .... Balancing an argument, stating opposing views

j) .... Giving an example

6
- It must be remembered that …
- It should be emphasized that …
- I would like to underline the point that …

7
- To illustrate this point, …
- For instance, …
- A good example of this is …

8
- In addition, …
- Furthermore, …
- Not only … but also …
- I should add that …

9
- On the whole, …
- Generally speaking, …

10
- On the one hand … but on the other hand …

Task 2 Delivering a presentation

In addition to your command of English, your body language will also affect how your presentation is received. Some of the things that speakers often do during a presentation are listed below.

2.1 **With a partner, discuss what impression each one may give the audience. Can you add anything to the list?**

- smile at the audience
- sit down
- walk around
- look only at notes
- use hand gestures
- play with hair/change in pocket/earring, etc.

- lean against a wall
- point at the audience
-
-
-
-

2.2 **Body language is not universal. If your body language and gestures are misinterpreted, it can result in confusion. Discuss the following questions in groups of three to five.**

a) What sort of differences have you noticed in the way that people from other cultures use gestures and body language?

b) Have you ever experienced a communication breakdown due to a misunderstanding about the meaning of a gesture?

Reflect

Think about occasions in the past when you have had to speak in front of an audience or speak in a stressful situation, for example at an interview. Try to remember the kind of language you used and what your body language communicated about yourself.

Now think about the changes in your language and body language that you feel will be useful for you in future formal speaking situations. Refer back to some of the ideas in this unit.

Student notes for Unit 4

Unit 5 Visual aids

At the end of this unit you will be:
- more familiar with a range of appropriate visual aids;
- able to use visual aids effectively.

Visual aids can greatly enhance an oral presentation by highlighting key points or information and helping the audience to understand the information.

Task 1 Choosing and using visual aids

There are many kinds of visual aids available. Think about presentations and lectures you have attended in the past and consider the visual aids that were used.

1.1 Discuss with another student which of the following you have either seen or used. What do you think are the advantages and disadvantages of each of them, for the audience and/or for the speaker?

Visual aid	Advantages	Disadvantages
Posters		
Overhead transparencies		
Videos		
Whiteboard		
Printed handouts		
PowerPoint slides		

1.2 Visual aids are useful to help get your message across to your audience. Nevertheless, even with good visual aids, things can go wrong if they are not used appropriately. Look at the list of "don'ts" below and discuss why each point is a problem.

DON'T:

- crowd too much information into one visual
- put unimportant details in the visual
- forget to talk about information in a visual
- use 12-point font or less
- put visuals in a different order to that of information in the presentation

Task 2 Preparation of visual aids

Once you have chosen (or been assigned) a particular visual aid for your presentation, it is important to be clear on the preparation that will be involved.

The following example indicates seven questions you should ask yourself in order to prepare any visual aid. If you can answer each question with confidence, then you know what you have to do.

In the example, the questions have been applied to giving a poster presentation, as this is a popular visual aid and it is quite likely you will present or view posters while you are a student.

Question	Answer
a) What visual aid am I going to use?	Poster presentation
b) What is it?	A poster is a large document (usually mounted on a card backing) that can be used to communicate your research at a presentation or meeting. A poster usually contains both text and pictures/graphs. The presenter generally stands next to his/her poster ready to answer questions as people pass by and read what it says.
c) Are there any special requirements or constraints?	Make sure you know the size of the poster you are expected to produce, as this is usually set in advance.
d) What materials/ equipment do I need?	• backing card or poster board cut to the required size • 8.5 x 11-inch paper • glue and scissors
e) How will the content be organized?	A poster presentation is one large document that is generally subdivided into some or all of the following sections: • Title • Introduction • Methods • Results • Discussion • Conclusion • References
f) What is the best layout?	A poster has to be legible from a distance, so the most important advice here is to have limited text and interesting graphics. Techniques are: • use short sentences and bullets • use large font size • use pictures, charts, and graphs to illustrate information • use color carefully to add interest
g) How do I put it all together?	The easiest way is to print out each section of your poster on 8.5 x 11-inch paper and place these smaller elements of the poster into position on the backing. This method allows more flexibility in design, as you can move sections around until you are happy with the results. Here is one possible layout: | Title		| |---|---|---| | Introduction | Graphs/ pictures | Conclusion |

2.1　Work with a partner and choose another type of visual aid from the table in Task 1.1. Apply the same seven questions to the visual aid and fill in the table below.

Question	Answer
a) What visual aid am I going to use?	
b) What is it?	
c) Are there any special requirements or constraints?	
d) What materials/equipment do I need?	
e) How will the content be organized?	
f) What is the best layout?	
g) How do I put it all together?	

2.2 Work with another pair who chose a different type of visual aid. Swap information about the visual aids you chose to think about. Fill in the table below with your new partners' information.

Question	Answer
a) What visual aid am I going to use?	
b) What is it?	
c) Are there any special requirements or constraints?	
d) What materials/equipment do I need?	
e) How will the content be organized?	
f) What is the best layout?	
g) How do I put it all together?	

Reflect

Choose one or two situations where visual aids have been used for your benefit, whether at school or at other kinds of presentations. Try to remember how you felt about the use of the visual aids and whether they were beneficial to the overall learning experience.

Apply anything you have gained from your reflections to your own presentation. For example, what problems might you have with the type of visual aid you have chosen?

Think about how you could prepare a backup plan if things go wrong with the visual element of your presentation.

Student notes for Unit 5

Unit 6 Slideshow tutorial

At the end of this unit you will be able to:
- **make a slideshow;**
- **understand how a slideshow can help you to get your message across.**

Use of ICT (Information and Communication Technology) for the purpose of presentations is now commonplace, both in the classroom and in the world of work. An understanding of how to make use of slideshow software can greatly enhance the delivery of a presentation. Use the following 10-step guide to familiarize yourself with the process of creating presentation slides.

Step 1:   Opening a new slide show

First, open your slideshow software package by clicking on its icon on your desktop or selecting the program from the *Start* menu. It's a good idea to make it a habit to save your presentation often by selecting *Save* from the *File* menu at the top of your document.

Step 2:   Creating your slides

When you first open your software, a blank page may appear. If this is what happens, go straight to Step 3.

Alternatively, you may be asked to select a page from an *Auto Layout* screen. This enables you to choose the structure of your slide(s) from a range of options. If you are asked to choose from the *Auto Layout* screen, choose the slide in the top left-hand corner. You will be able to experiment with alternatives after completing this tutorial.

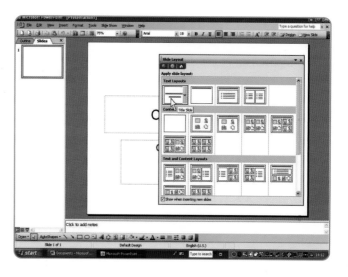

Step 3: Adding text

On the main screen, follow the
instructions *Click to add title* and
Click to add subtitle. These guide
you through the process of creating
a basic text slide.

Step 4: Adding design features

To create a more advanced slide
with more sophisticated design
features, click on the *Design* button
at the top of your screen or select
Slide Design from the *Format* menu.

A variety of design options will be
displayed on the right of your
screen. You will then be able to
choose a style template with
different colors and images from
a series of predesigned templates.
This will help you to personalize
your presentation.

Step 5: Adding additional slides

To create additional slides, click on
the *New Slide* button on your toolbar,
or select *New Slide* from the *Insert*
menu. This will create an additional
slide. You may also be asked to
choose the layout of your new slide
using the *Auto Layout* menu, as
indicated in Step 2 above.

Step 6:   Reordering your slides

If necessary, you can change the order of your slides by clicking and dragging the smaller versions of the slides that appear on the left-hand side of your screen.

Step 7:   Adding pictures

In addition to the use of text, your software also allows you to insert pictures to improve the appearance of your slides. There are two main methods of finding and inserting images.

Method 1: Internet images

Copying and pasting images from the Internet can be an effective way to increase the impact of your slides. First, find a web page with a suitable image. Next, place your mouse pointer over the image and click the right-hand button on the mouse. Then select *Copy*. Finally, go back to your slideshow software and select *Paste* from the *Edit* toolbar. The image should then appear in your presentation slides. Don't forget to acknowledge the source of the image. Cut and paste the web address of the image under the image on your slide.

Method 2: Clip art

In addition to the images that are available on the Internet, your software will also contain a series of images stored in an area called *Clip Art*. You can access *Clip Art* by clicking on the *Insert* menu on the toolbar at the top of your screen. You will then be able to search for relevant pictures using key words. If a suitable picture is available, you can then click on the image and it will appear in your presentation.

Step 8:   Using animation

To control the way in which text and images first appear on your slides, a variety of animation effects can be used.

Select *Animation Schemes* from the *Slide Show* menu in the toolbar at the top of your screen. You will then be presented with a range of different animation choices. You can experiment with these by clicking on the different text and image elements of your presentation and choosing a suitable animation for that element. You can test the animation to see what it looks like by clicking on the *Play* button.

Step 9:   Viewing your presentation

To see what your finished presentation will look like when it is shown to your audience, you will need to select the *View Show* option from the *Slide Show* menu. *View Show* displays your slides to their best advantage, using the full screen.

Step 10: Printing your presentation

To print copies of your slides onto paper or onto overhead projector transparencies, choose *Print ...* from the *File* menu of the toolbar at the top of your screen. You will then be able to choose whether to print full slides or smaller versions of your slides for use as handouts or notes.

Reflect

Ask your instructor for more information about the presentations that you will have to give during your current program of study. Plan ahead and start to think about how the available software could help to enhance your delivery.

If you decide to use computer technology, think about the preparation you will need to make, for example: make sure that the room in which you will give your presentation has the appropriate facilities and that you know how to use the facilities before the day of your presentation.

Student notes for Unit 6

Module 11

Web work

Website 1 — Presentation planner

http://elc.polyu.edu.hk/cill/tools/presplan.htm

Review

This website is designed to help you plan, organize, and write your presentation by following a series of prompts. It will also provide note cards and a script of your finished product, and a record of what your presentation will sound like.

Task

Once you have a finished presentation, use this presentation planner to do a test run of your talk. If you are pleased with the finished result, take advantage of the option of printing out note cards.

Website 2 — PowerPoint in the classroom

http://www.actden.com/pp/

Review

The tutorial takes you through all the steps in creating and editing PowerPoint slides.

Task

If you still feel that you need more help with PowerPoint, try the tutorial offered here.

Extension activities

Activity 1 — PowerPoint practice

Practice your PowerPoint skills by making slides to illustrate the key steps of the Planning checklist in Unit 1.

Look back at the Planning checklist in Unit 1 and make PowerPoint slides to give a short presentation of this information. What information would you include on the slide, and what would you say to illustrate the main point?

Compare your work with another student. Have you handled the checklist in similar ways?

Some presentations require you to conduct your own research and then present the results to your class. In this activity, you will give a presentation detailing the results of a short questionnaire on student attitudes to a particular aspect of university life, e.g., exams, seminars, oral presentations, and note-taking.

There are several parts to the activity:

1 Design a short questionnaire to find out information about students' attitudes to the aspect of university life that you have chosen.

You could include questions on:

- Extent of experience with …

- Views on advantages and disadvantages of …

- Self-rating of skill at …

- Opinion of usefulness of … skills beyond university

2 Obtain responses from at least 10 other students.

3 Compile your results and share them with the rest of your class in a presentation with visual aids.

Glossary

Animation (n) Moving picture images such as cartoons, video, or moving diagrams. Animation can be used in *presentations*.

Balance an argument (v) To make sure that both sides of an argument have been considered and explained.

Bibliography (n) A list of *references* to *sources* cited in the text of a piece of academic writing or a book. A bibliography should consist of an alphabetical list of books, papers, journal articles, and websites and is usually found at the end of the work. It may also include texts suggested by the author for further reading.

Body language (n) Non-verbal communication of feelings and ideas through movements of the body. For example, certain body movements such as fidgeting and yawning may indicate boredom.

Checklist (n) A list of tasks to do or aspects to consider when planning and preparing for an event such as an academic assignment, trip, or party.

Communication breakdown (n) A situation in which individuals or groups are unable to understand each other at all due to differences in language, culture, or belief.

Constraint (n) Something that places a limit or restriction on what you want to do. For example, if you are doing a *presentation*, there may be time constraints.

Coordinator (n) Someone who is responsible for arranging how a group or workforce shares out duties and for ensuring that the final product or results are brought together effectively.

Deadline (n) The date or time by which something needs to be completed. In academic situations, deadlines are normally given for handing in essays and assignments.

Dynamics (n) The way that things work together to produce energy and results. For example, it is important that group dynamics are effective so that everyone works well together.

Emphasize (v) To highlight or draw attention to something that is important.

Evidence (n) Information and data that establish whether something is true or not.

Framework (n) A basic *structure* that is an *outline* of something more detailed.

Gesture (n) (v) 1 (n) An action meant to communicate an idea non-verbally or to *emphasize* a thought or meaning. 2 (v) To make such an action. For example, putting one's hand over one's heart indicates sincerity.

Grading criteria (n) The basis on which something will be assessed. It is important to know what the grading criteria consist of when writing an academic assignment. For example, a piece of work may be assessed on grammatical accuracy and/or how well it is presented, or it may be evaluated on its content alone.

Handout (n) Paper-based information that is given out by the professor in a lecture or seminar. It usually gives a summary, *bibliography,* or extra information connected with the lecture topic. It may also be a worksheet.

ICT (also IT) (n) Information and communication technology. Technology, such as computers, *presentation* software, DVD, and other media, that helps people to manage information electronically.

Layout (n) The way that things are positioned within a space, for example, the way text, pictures, and diagrams are arranged on a page or computer screen.

Outline (n) (v) 1 (n) A rough sketch of the main ideas in a text or *presentation*. 2 (v) To give or make a rough sketch of the main ideas or events in a text or *presentation*.

Overhead transparency (OHT) (n) Clear, plastic film on which text and visuals can be reproduced, enlarged, and projected onto a wall or screen using a computer or overhead projector (OHP). This type of *visual aid* is often used during lectures and *presentations*.

Poster presentation (n) A *presentation* that involves displaying posters with information and pictures or diagrams. The audience generally reads the posters while the presenter stands next to them and explains information where necessary.

PowerPoint (n) The brand name for a type of software known as a presentation program. The software enables users to write and design slideshows for *presentations*. The slides may be viewed on computer, projected onto a screen, and/or printed out.

Presentation (n) A short lecture, talk, or demonstration (usually formal) given in front of an audience. The speaker prepares and *structures* his or her presentation in advance and will often use *visual aids* or realia to illustrate it.

Reference (n) (v) 1 (n) Acknowledgment of the *sources* of ideas and information that you use in written work and oral *presentations*. 2 (v) To acknowledge or mention *sources* of information.

Rehearse (v) To practice a speech, dialogue, play, or *presentation* that is going to be performed in front of an audience.

Research question (n) A statement or question that helps you to start gathering ideas, notes, and information in a focused way in preparation for writing an essay, report, *presentation,* or dissertation.

Role (n) The part someone plays in a group (or any situation that involves interacting with other people). In some situations, these roles may be flexible or unspoken, in others they are well-defined, such as the leader of a team.

Signposts (n) Words, phrases or other organizational features such as headings and opening sentences in a text that help the audience or reader identify a section. For example, a professor may signpost the conclusion of a talk by prefacing it with "to sum up...."

Source (n) Something (usually a book, article, or other text) that supplies you with information. In an academic context, sources used in essays and reports must be acknowledged.

Spontaneous (adj) Describes an action that is taken without preplanning, that is, without prior discussion and rehearsal.

Structure (n) (v) 1 (n) A *framework* or arrangement of several parts, put together in a particular way. 2 (v) In academic terms, to put together ideas or arguments in a logical way for an essay or *presentation*.

Support (n) (v) 1 (n) *Evidence* and ideas that back up an argument. 2 (v) To back up an argument with evidence.

Thesis (n) The controlling idea, main argument, or question in a piece of academic writing or a *presentation*. It is stated in the introduction and *supported* by *evidence*.

Visual aid (n) An object or image that is used in a lecture, *presentation,* or class to help clarify information visually. For example, diagrams, pictures, posters, models, and video are commonly used visual aids.

Module 12: Exam Technique

Introduction

Preparing for exams can be difficult and confusing. Despite years of experience, many students can still find it difficult to prepare themselves effectively for timed assessments. As a result, they may struggle to organize the way they review and to make the most of the information available to them.

This module presents a tool to help you prepare for exams in any academic discipline. It will help you develop study and memorization techniques and also familiarize you with different exam question types and tasks.

In Unit 1, you will be guided through the review planning stage, building on what you already know about exams and how to prepare for them. Memory styles and the importance of active learning are examined in Unit 2, so that you can assess which memorization techniques are best for you. Unit 3 deals with ways to review and prepare for exams and suggests strategies that can be used. Units 4 and 5 look at different exam question types, instructions, and tasks, along with some of the more common pitfalls and problems. Steps to avoid exam-related stress are then discussed in Unit 6.

After completing the module, you will have developed a more structured and tailored exam technique for your individual study purposes. You will also be more aware of what the exam questions are asking you to do and what to include in your answers.

Skills Map

 Unit 1

Planning for exams

Prepare your review schedule by planning and building on your existing knowledge.

 Unit 2

Memory styles and active learning

Find out how you understand, learn, and remember best.

 Unit 3

Review strategies

Familiarize yourself with a range of study aids and review techniques.

 Unit 4

Understanding the exam paper

Learn to maximize your exam performance by following question paper instructions.

 Unit 5

Understanding exam tasks

Learn to recognize what the exam task requires of you.

 Unit 6

Managing exam stress

Discover some techniques to manage exam nerves.

Destination: Exam Technique

Planning for exams

At the end of this unit you will have:
- a good understanding of your exam's requirements;
- a review plan.

Task 1 The purpose of exams

Exams are an important part of most students' life at university as they are such a common method of assessment.

1.1   **Work with a partner. Discuss the following questions.**

    a) Have you taken a written exam before?

    b) If so, how did you prepare for the exam?

    c) How did you feel a month before the exam?

    d) How did you feel on the day of the exam?

1.2   **Work in groups of three to five. Share your ideas about the following questions.**

    a) What is the purpose of exams?

    b) What are the advantages of exams?

Task 2 Exam requirements

Although you are not likely to know the exact content of your exams in advance, there are several ways in which you can prepare and plan for the exam experience.

2.1   **Work with a partner. Discuss all the possible sources of information about exam requirements and complete the list below.**

> a) student handbook
>
> b)
>
> c)
>
> d)

2.2 Work individually. Consider each module/subject for which you will have an exam and complete a table similar to the one below. This will help you to identify what you already know about your exams. Write down information about the topics you will be examined on and the location/timing and structure/organization of each exam.

Module/Subject title: ....

Exam location and timing	Exam structure and organization	Topics

2.3 Compare your table with another student who is taking an exam in the same subject/module.

Task 3 Exam planner

When you have completed Task 2, ask your professors to help you complete the sections in the exam planner below. This will help you to get organized in advance of the big day.

Exam Planner	
Module/subject	
Date of exam	
Location of exam (Campus, building, room)	
Items required, e.g., a form of identification	
Materials permitted for use in exam	
Contribution of exam to final grade	
Date of review classes	
Number of papers in exam	
Recommended time allocation for each section of exam	
Types of question in each of the different question papers	
Subject areas covered in exam	
Recommended books and further reading	

Task 4 Review schedule

Using the information from the Exam Planner you completed in Task 3, complete this Study Planner. Plan to start reviewing at least four weeks before the day of your first exam.

Study Planner	Monday	Tuesday	Wednesday
Week 1	Subject:........................ Time:........................ (Hours completed:..........)	Subject:........................ Time:........................ (Hours completed:..........)	Subject:........................ Time:........................ (Hours completed:..........
Week 2	Subject:........................ Time:........................ (Hours completed:..........)	Subject:........................ Time:........................ (Hours completed:..........)	Subject:........................ Time:........................ (Hours completed:..........
Week 3	Subject:........................ Time:........................ (Hours completed:..........)	Subject:........................ Time:........................ (Hours completed:..........)	Subject:........................ Time:........................ (Hours completed:..........
Week 4	Subject:........................ Time:........................ (Hours completed:..........)	Subject:........................ Time:........................ (Hours completed:..........)	Subject:........................ Time:........................ (Hours completed:..........
Week 5	Subject:........................ Time:........................ (Hours completed:..........)	Subject:........................ Time:........................ (Hours completed:..........)	Subject:........................ Time:........................ (Hours completed:..........
Week 6	Subject:........................ Time:........................ (Hours completed:..........)	Subject:........................ Time:........................ (Hours completed:..........)	Subject:........................ Time:........................ (Hours completed:..........

Date and time of exam:

Thursday	Friday	Saturday	Sunday
ubject:.....................	Subject:.....................	Subject:.....................	Subject:.....................
ime:.....................	Time:.....................	Time:.....................	Time:.....................
Hours completed:..........)	(Hours completed:..........)	(Hours completed:..........)	(Hours completed:..........)
ubject:.....................	Subject:.....................	Subject:.....................	Subject:.....................
ime:.....................	Time:.....................	Time:.....................	Time:.....................
Hours completed:..........)	(Hours completed:..........)	(Hours completed:..........)	(Hours completed:..........)
ubject:.....................	Subject:.....................	Subject:.....................	Subject:.....................
ime:.....................	Time:.....................	Time:.....................	Time:.....................
Hours completed:..........)	(Hours completed:..........)	(Hours completed:..........)	(Hours completed:..........)
ubject:.....................	Subject:.....................	Subject:.....................	Subject:.....................
ime:.....................	Time:.....................	Time:.....................	Time:.....................
Hours completed:..........)	(Hours completed:..........)	(Hours completed:..........)	(Hours completed:..........)
ubject:.....................	Subject:.....................	Subject:.....................	Subject:.....................
ime:.....................	Time:.....................	Time:.....................	Time:.....................
Hours completed:..........)	(Hours completed:..........)	(Hours completed:..........)	(Hours completed:..........)
ubject:.....................	Subject:.....................	Subject:.....................	Subject:.....................
ime:.....................	Time:.....................	Time:.....................	Time:.....................
Hours completed:..........)	(Hours completed:..........)	(Hours completed:..........)	(Hours completed:..........)

Task 5 Review schedule

5.1 It is important to spend some time relaxing during your reviewing period. Too much reviewing without incentives or free-time activities can lead to boredom and lack of concentration.

Take another look at your study plan and add at least two fun activities for each week. Focusing on your studies may be easier if you have a few enjoyable activities to look forward to in the near future.

Reflect

Now that you have finished your study plan, reflect on what you have done. Are you sure you have the right balance? For example, think about what time you are most focused. At what time of day do you find it easiest to study?

Spend time reflecting on all the relevant issues before making any changes to your study plan.

Student notes for Unit 1

Unit 2 Memory styles and active learning

At the end of this unit you will:
- understand your personal memory styles better;
- know strategies to help you memorize.

Task 1 Your memory style

1.1   Work individually. Answer the questions below. When you have finished each question, write down what you did to help you remember.

   a)   What color are your best friend's eyes?

   _____

   b)   What is your (cell) phone number?

   _____

   c)   How does your favorite song start?

   _____

   d)   What was your favorite food when you were a child?

   _____

   e)   What is your computer login?

   _____

   f)   How do you get to the closest bus stop?

   _____

   g)   On what date did you start this course?

   _____

1.2   Work with a partner and compare how you remembered the information.

1.3   Work individually. Look at the word list on the next page. Use a highlighter to color four words. Draw an appropriate picture around or next to four words. Underline four words. Draw circles around four other words and link the four circles together. Do this as quickly as possible. Now spend 90 seconds memorizing the words. After this time, close the book and write down all the words you can remember on a separate piece of paper.

Word list

love	law	ORANGE	book	argues
lounge	little	square	China	journal
CHICAGO	low	cat	cause	twenty
concludes	thirteen	Egypt	shouts	green
however	purple	exam	WEBSITE	chips
circle	oblong	SMALL	claims	dog
Peru	ten	tiny	red	tape

1.4 **Now compare your word list with your partner's and discuss the following questions.**

a) Did you remember the same words?

b) Which method of identifying words helped most, e.g., underlining, highlighting, etc.?

c) Did you remember the words in capitals?

d) Did you tend to remember words that belong in a group, e.g., colors: *orange*, *purple*, *green*, and *red*?

e) Did you remember words that start with the same sound, e.g., *love*, *law*, *lounge,* and *little*?

f) Did you remember the words you looked at first or last?

g) Did you tend to remember words from one part of the chart, e.g., top left-hand corner?

How people memorize information is affected by their learning styles.

The three main learning styles are:

* visual (eye memory)

* auditory (ear memory)

* kinesthetic (body movement memory)

People generally use a mixture of these styles. However, one style will probably be dominant.

1.5 Read the descriptions of the different learning styles and then match them with the most appropriate strategies.

Visual learners

Visual learners prefer information to be written down. They tend to like notes, pictures, and diagrams. In a lecture, these students need to take notes even when the professor provides a detailed lecture outline. They make up roughly 60% of the population.

Auditory learners

Auditory learners like information to be spoken. Often, a lecture outline is of little help before a lecture as this type of student understands through listening. During a lecture, auditory learners often prefer not to take notes. They tend to do this afterwards. These students represent about 30% of people.

Kinesthetic learners

Kinesthetic learners learn best through movement and imitation. They tend to learn by doing. Moving their bodies is a useful way to help them learn and remember. Only about 5% of people fall into this category.

Useful memorizing strategies

a) recite information

b) sing information to a tune

c) link information with an image

d) turn information into diagrams

e) read information out loud

f) move around the room while memorizing

g) write down first-letter phrases, e.g., *Every Good Boy Does Fine* = in music, the notes on the lines of the treble clef

h) teach the information to someone else

i) use a highlighter to mark important information

1.6 Work with a partner. Think back to Tasks 1.1 and 1.3 and discuss the following questions.

a) Which learning style do you think is strongest for you?

b) In the past, have you tended to use the strategies indicated for your style?

Task 2 A deeper understanding

Understanding information and ideas is important to both learning and remembering. To do this, it is useful to link ideas together into a framework or map. This map of ideas helps us to understand smaller pieces of information. It also helps us to remember them by linking them together into a meaningful whole. For example, it is easier to remember irregular verbs when we group them together. All academic subjects have core concepts. These are what help us make the framework or map.

2.1 **Look at the following parts of a bicycle. Put them together to make a two-dimensional view of the whole object.**

To make the object, you identified the different parts and organized them to make an understandable whole. This is also true of concepts.

2.2 **Read the following definition of "society." Break it down into its smaller parts by filling in the table.**

Society can be defined as a group of people who live in a particular place and tend to share a distinctive culture and set of institutions.

Concept	Parts
Society	

Task 3 Organizing information into groups

3.1 Read through the list of words below once and then close your book and write down as many as possible.

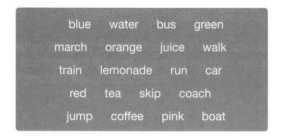

blue   water   bus   green

march   orange   juice   walk

train   lemonade   run   car

red   tea   skip   coach

jump   coffee   pink   boat

3.2 Now try to write the words again. This time, try to remember the words by using four categories: colors, drinks, ways of moving, and transport.

3.3 Discuss with your partner.

a) Did you remember more words the second time?

b) If so, why?

Task 4 Reorganizing information into diagrams

4.1 Read the following descriptions of different types of diagram and match each description to a type.

Mind map
Although this is less structured than a concept map, it also focuses on links between ideas. The key concept is in the center of the map. Thick lines are connected to this center and the thinner lines branch off these. Next to each line is a keyword.

Flow chart
This is a diagram that is often used to show a process. It usually includes a starting point, an end point, and a set of questions that require a decision.

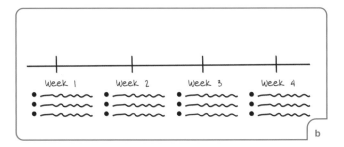

Time line
This type of diagram is used to put information in time order.

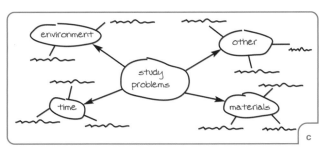

4.2 Choose a set of notes that you have taken on your subject area. Working individually, you should choose the most appropriate type of diagram to use to rewrite part of your notes. When you have finished, explain your diagram to your partner.

Task 5 Reorganizing information into summary notes

5.1 Choose a different part of your notes. Read through the section carefully and divide up the information into three levels: thesis statement or most general claim; more specific claims; and supporting points or evidence. Rewrite the notes as a summary, using a different color pen for each level of information.

5.2 Teach the information in your notes to your partner.

Reflect

What do you remember from each of the memory tasks? Take time to reflect on each of the tasks and see how easy it is to remember if you work with your memory in an appropriate way.

Try explaining what you have learned in this unit to a student who is not participating in this class. Notice that if you try to convey your interest in the topic rather than just remembering what you have studied, you will recall the information much more easily.

Reflect on the understanding you have gained about your learning style. How do you think you can adapt the techniques in this unit to maximize your own learning?

Student notes for Unit 2

Review strategies

At the end of this unit you will:
- be aware of the benefits of active reviewing;
- have a personal review strategies tool kit.

Task 1 Pass or fail

1.1   In the space below, make a list of reasons why a student might pass or fail an exam. Which factors do you think could affect performance? Then work in groups of three to five to compare your answers.

Pass

Fail

1.2   Think about an exam on which you did well. What helped you to do well? Discuss your answers with a partner.

Task 2 Identifying exam skills

2.1　Consider the different types of questions you might need to answer in an exam. What do you need to be able to do in an exam? Make a list in the "Type of question" column of the table below.

2.2　Next, complete the table by identifying which skills you will need to be able to answer each question properly.

Type of question	Skills practice required
Answering questions based on a text	• understanding questions fully • skimming and scanning
Essay writing	• essay planning • title analysis

Task 3 Active and passive review

The best reviewing advice is to review actively. Active reviewing helps you develop a bigger picture of the subject area. You should aim to develop your understanding and link any new ideas to what you already confidently understand.

3.1 **Read the comments in the letter below, which were sent to an advice column in a student newspaper. What advice would you give this student to help improve her active reviewing? Make rough notes as you read.**

Dear Study Doc

I really need some help with my reviewing. In preparartion for my end-of-year exams, I went to the library everyday. I just don't know why I didn't get the grades I was expecting.

Nearly every day I arranged to sit with Zahra, one of the really brainy girls from my economics class. She seemed to follow a really strict study schedule. I watched her studying, and she wrote the most detailed notes. She was really focused on what she was doing. I could even see which subject she was studying by the color of her folder!

I remember that the view from my desk overlooked the playing fields, and I could see a different sport every day, both in the morning and in the afternoon.

That really helped me to relax. On average I was in that library for about seven hours every day. I work better in the mornings, so I tried to make myself study for at least three hours without a break. Then, in the afternoons, I gave myself a short break every 15 minutes.

I really don't know how Zahra managed to study so hard and take such great care of her appearance. She wore a different outfit every day. I used to try and guess what she would be wearing before she arrived.

Although I spent more than ten consecutive days in the library before my exams, I didn't find the exam easy at all. The day before my economics exam, I spent a whole day trying to understand our textbook, but even though I read the same passages over and over again, the ideas never really stuck in my head. I read and reread the same pages, but I seemed to get more and more confused.

What do you think I'm doing wrong? I'd appreciate your advice.

Olena Gavin

Olena Govorovska (Undergraduate: business and economics)

3.2 **Work in groups of three to five. Discuss your advice and make a note of any points that you hadn't thought of.**

3.3 Now write your reply below.

Dear Olena

Task 4 Reading past papers

It is possible that your professor will be able to provide you with past exams that have been used for assessment in previous years. Alternatively, they may be available in the university library or on the home page for your university department.

4.1 Why do you think it might be useful to look at past exams? Discuss your ideas with another student.

4.2 Once you have a copy of a past exam, use the four stages below to help you to learn from it.

Stage 1

Choose a question from one section in your exam and calculate the amount of time that is realistically available to answer the question. Base your answer on the overall exam time and the recommended time allocation for each part of the exam.

Stage 2

Build into your time limit some time to read the question thoroughly and plan your answer. In your plan, you will need to consider the following elements:

- key points to include
- how the question relates to the syllabus
- how the answer could be structured
- examples and evidence

Stage 3

Having decided on the amount of time you need to plan and answer the question, write your answer within that time.

Stage 4

After completing your answer, compare it with your notes and check for accuracy. Monitor the time you have used and ensure that your schedule is realistic.

Task 5 Review tool kit

5.1   Students rely on a range of different review tools according to their academic discipline and their learning style. Think back to what you learned in Unit 2. Then look at the list of review strategies below and select at least five that you feel could realistically assist you in your reviewing. Check the boxes for those strategies that you think you could use in your personal tool kit.

- Check your understanding by comparing your notes with published material. ☐
- Make sure that your notes are complete. Refer to lecture outlines and any recommended reading. ☐
- Summarize your notes by identifying key theories and information. ☐
- Make summaries of your notes in diagrammatic form. ☐
- Produce index cards with key facts and data in an easy-to-remember format. ☐
- Think and make a note of connections between different topics to see how subjects interrelate. You can draw mind maps for this. ☐
- Adapt a series of data for use in a table or graph. ☐
- Familiarize yourself with past papers and question formats. ☐
- Practice identifying key elements in the question rubric. ☐
- Consider different ways of answering a question and evaluate them. ☐
- Meet with other students to discuss and compare your understanding of different topics and to identify gaps in your knowledge. ☐
- Schedule meetings with your professor to monitor your reviewing progress. ☐
- Use over-learning: Rewrite information from notes and read it often. Do this for a short amount of time, but over several days. ☐

- _____
- _____
- _____
- _____

5.2 Add any missing strategies to the list above.

Student notes for Unit 3

4 Understanding the exam paper

At the end of this unit you will:
- have a better understanding of how the exam is organized;
- be able to follow instructions on question papers more accurately.

Task 1 The question paper cover

Look at the cover of the question paper below, and identify the key information and important points to remember.

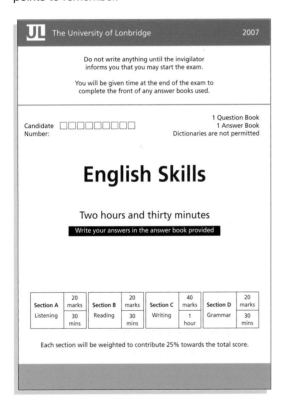

The University of Lonbridge   2007

Do not write anything until the invigilator informs you that you may start the exam.

You will be given time at the end of the exam to complete the front of any answer books used.

Candidate
Number: □□□□□□□□

1 Question Book
1 Answer Book
Dictionaries are not permitted

English Skills

Two hours and thirty minutes

Write your answers in the answer book provided

Section A	20 marks	Section B	20 marks	Section C	40 marks	Section D	20 marks
Listening	30 mins	Reading	30 mins	Writing	1 hour	Grammar	30 mins

Each section will be weighted to contribute 25% towards the total score.

Task 2 The rubric

2.1   Read the following examples of rubrics from question papers.

  a) What are the most important items of information?

  b) What types of mistakes do you think students are likely to make?

Answer a total of three questions: two questions from Section A and one question from Section B.

Answer any ten of the following questions:

Students should answer five complete questions only.

Answer all of Part A, two questions from Part B, and one question from Part C.

Task 3 Following instructions

3.1 Complete the tasks given in the following paper as you would under exam conditions—this means you cannot speak. Try to do the tasks as fast as possible. Raise your hand when you have finished.

Please follow the instructions below carefully.

Read through all the instructions before starting the tasks.

Use your answer sheet where necessary.

1 Write your name in the top left-hand corner of the answer sheet.

2 Underneath write your birthday, favorite color, and favorite food.

3 Draw a box around this information and pass the answer sheet to the person on your right.

4 On the new answer sheet you have received, write your name in the middle of the sheet and the date of your birthday, eye color, and shoe size underneath. Draw a box around this information and pass the answer sheet to your right.

5 At the bottom of the new answer sheet, write a sentence comparing the information about the two people.

6 Pass the answer sheet to the right again. Read the sentence and underline the most interesting information.

7 Add another sentence, explaining why you believe the part you underlined is the most interesting information.

8 Pass the answer paper to the right. Read the sentences on your new answer paper. Decide whether you agree with the opinion or not and write a sentence explaining your opinion.

9 Return the answer paper to the person whose name is in the top left-hand corner.

10 Ignore instructions 1 to 9. Close your books.

3.2   Look at the instructions given in the question paper and the completed answer sheet below. What mistakes has the student made? Work individually and then compare answers with your partner.

The student should answer one question from Section A and all questions from Sections B and C. Answers should be transferred onto the answer sheet before the end of the exam.

Section A Questions 1 to 3

Circle the correct answer.

(1)   Which one of the following descriptions best explains the term "membrane"?
    A   the liquid in an animal cell
    B   what gives plant cells their shape
    C   the liquid-filled space in a plant cell
    D   the thin outer layer of an animal cell

(2)   Which organ in the picture is the kidney?

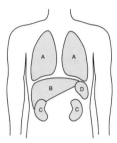

(3)   Which two of the following statements are true?
    A   When cells divide, two identical cells are formed.
    B   Cell division is necessary for growth.
    C   A cell must have a nucleus in order to divide.
    D   A cell must have a wall in order to grow.

Section B Questions 4 to 6

Complete the following description of respiration. Write no more than one word for each answer.

Respiration may be defined as the process of (4) _____ energy from food. The analogy of burning fuel is often used to describe the process. Here the fuel is (5) _____. For this, (6) _____ is the key molecule. In plants, this is produced through photosynthesis.

Section C Questions 7 to 10

Complete the following equation for respiration, using chemical symbols.

    (7) _____ + O_2 = (8) _____ + (9) _____ + energy

(10)   What is the full name of the special energy-rich molecule in which the energy is stored?

Answer sheet

1   the thin outer layer of an animal cell
2   B, C
3   A
4   releasing some
5   glucose
6
7   Glucose
8   Carbon dioxide
9   Water
10 ATP

Student notes for Unit 4

5 Understanding exam tasks

At the end of this unit you will:
- have a better understanding of how to answer essay questions;
- be able to maximize your performance on multiple-choice questions.

Task 1 Instruction words

1.1 **Work individually. Match the instruction words with their explanation.**

| analyze   comment on   compare   contrast   define |

_____ Identify the main issues and give an informed opinion.

_____ Show how two things are different. Explain the consequences of dissimilarities.

_____ Examine in detail by dividing up. Identify the main points.

_____ Give the precise meaning of a term. This may include explaining what is problematic about defining the term.

_____ Show how two things are similar. Explain the consequences of the similarities.

| describe   discuss   evaluate   examine   explain |

_____ Look at the most important aspects of something in a balanced way, i.e., advantages and disadvantages, for and against.

_____ Give the main features, characteristics or events.

_____ Assess how important or useful something is. It is likely to include both positive and negative points.

_____ Provide reasons for why something happens, or why something is in a particular state.

_____ Take a detailed look at something.

illustrate	interpret	justify	outline	make a case

_____ Put forward an argument either for or against a claim.

_____ Give the meaning or significance of something.

_____ Give the main ideas or information, without any details.

_____ Show what something is like, using examples and/or evidence.

_____ Support a claim with evidence, but taking into account opposing views.

relate	state	summarize	to what extent	trace

_____ Put the steps and stages of a process or event into order.

_____ Give the main points only, using fewer words than the original.

_____ Give the connections between things.

_____ Say how much something is or isn't true.

_____ Give just the main points, very clearly.

1.2 **Compare your work with a partner and discuss any differences of opinion.**

1.3 **Now look at the following instructions. How does the change in instruction word change the task?**

a) Trace the events that led to the French Revolution.

b) Interpret the significance of the French Revolution for contemporary France.

c) Analyze the impact of the French Revolution on nineteenth-century Europe.

1.4 **Working with a partner, discuss which instruction words are most common in your academic area.**

Task 2 Question styles

If possible, work with another student who is in a class with you. Answer the following questions to discover what you already know about the exams you are going to take.

- Will you need to answer essay questions? If so, how many?
- Which different types of essay might you expect to have?
- Will you have multiple-choice questions?
- Which other question types are you likely to have?
- Do any of your subjects require "calculations" to be shown? Why is it important to show this if it is required?

Task 3 Exam essay planning and title analysis

3.1 Read the essay title below, which was given to a group of students studying in a language and study skills program.

"Studying the English language in an English-speaking country is the best way to learn the language. It is not possible to learn the language properly without spending time living in an Anglophone environment." Discuss.

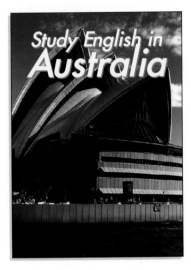

3.2 When you have read the title, break it down into smaller parts by asking yourself questions relating to the different sections. For example:

a) How many parts is the essay title made up of?

b) Which issues need to be discussed in Part 1?

c) Which issues need to be discussed in Part 2?

d) What is the overall task you are expected to do?

   i Put a process in order.

   ii Show what an English-speaking country is like, giving examples.

   iii Look at the question in a balanced way.

   iv Give a one-word answer.

3.3 Now write a short plan for the essay. Make sure that you address every part of the essay title.

On page 409, you will find a model of how Task 3.3 *could* be completed.
Do not look at this model until you have completed this activity.

Task 4 Planning and analysis in practice

Next, choose one of the essays below and repeat the steps suggested in Task 3 above. Try to spend no more than five to ten minutes on this activity, as you won't have a lot of time during the exam.

Essay titles

a) "High schools should redesign the curriculum in order to concentrate solely on teaching children the academic disciplines that are required for employment. It is a waste of time to devote school time to subjects such as art and general studies." Discuss.

b) "Exams are the only way to judge students' abilities. Institutions insist that without exams, it is difficult to judge a student's proficiency in any field." Do you agree or disagree? Give reasons to support your answer.

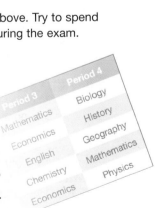

Task 5 Timed essay writing

Now practice writing one of the essays above, using the plan that you have already completed. Remember to be strict with the time available. Use the same amount of time as you will have in the real exam. Don't forget to deduct the time you have already spent on your plan. For further guidance on academic writing, consult the *Essay Writing* and *Scientific Writing* modules from this book.

Task 6 Answering multiple-choice questions

Many students find it difficult to answer multiple-choice questions if they do not know the answer immediately. This situation becomes worse when there are many similar answers to choose from. Nevertheless, there are some techniques to help you choose the correct answer more easily. You will be able to practice one such technique in the task below.

Select a series of multiple-choice questions from a past exam and follow the four steps indicated below.

Step 1
Read all the questions for the first time and write a * next to those questions that you think you are able to answer easily. Write ? next to those questions that you are not sure about. Lastly, write ! alongside any questions that you really do not know the answer to.

Step 2
Answer all the questions that you have marked with an asterisk. This should be the quickest section to complete, as you are fairly certain that you know the answers.

Step 3
Now that you have had some time to think about the questions in front of you and you have completed the most straightforward items, answer the questions that have been marked with a question mark. These are the questions that you need to think more carefully about. This section will probably take a little longer than the questions in Step 2.

Step 4
The remaining questions, which have been marked with an exclamation point, are the questions that you find the most difficult. In some multiple-choice exams, you will lose grades if you give a wrong answer. This is called negative grading. If this system of grading is being used in your exam, you should avoid giving an answer that you are not sure of. But if negative grading is not used, you should always attempt to give an answer even if you are not sure that it is correct. However, don't spend a great deal of time on the questions that you don't know the answer to. You can return to these questions at the end of the exam if there is any time remaining.

Reflect

Reconsider the strategies that have been suggested in this unit and think carefully about your own exams in the subjects you are studying. Your instructors are the best people to ask for specific advice, as they have all had success in exams just like the ones you are taking. Take advantage of their knowledge and ask them to give advice on reviewing from their own past experience.

Student notes for Unit 5

 Unit 6 Managing exam stress

At the end of this unit you will:
- understand how to manage anxiety while you are reviewing;
- have a plan for managing your stress on the day of the exam.

Task 1 Begin to take control

One important aspect of coping with exam stress is staying in control. People often feel stressed if they are unable to manage or control a situation. Obviously you can't control the content of your exams, but you can take control of the exam situation in other ways.

Discuss with another student ways in which you could take control of your reviewing and the preparation for your exams based on what you have covered so far in this module.

Task 2 Taking a positive attitude

2.1   Read through the following advice. Then work with another student to add two more pieces of advice.

a) Make time in your reviewing schedule to relax. Find the best time of day and the best way to do this: take an exercise class, sing in the shower, listen to music, etc.

b) Try to picture yourself arriving for the exam feeling happy and confident. Imagine this in as much detail as possible. This can help you replace any negative thoughts with more positive ones.

c) Avoid last-minute panic. Try not to review up until the minute before the exam starts.

d) _____

e) _____

2.2   Discuss with your partner which ideas would work best for you.

Task 3 Managing your anxiety

3.1 **Read through some ways of managing your anxiety during the exam. Match the headings a)–e) with the techniques 1)–5).**

Headings:

a) Paying attention to detail

b) Ouch!

c) Think positively

d) Stop!

e) A calming presence

Techniques:

1) Think of a person or a place you have positive associations with. Bring or wear an object to the exam that reminds you of this person or place. Touch it when you need to calm down.

2) Replace negative thoughts such as "I'm totally useless at this" and "I just can't do this" with more positive ones: "I am feeling stressed but this exam won't kill me" and "This isn't as bad as I thought it might be."

3) To stop yourself having negative thoughts, listen to yourself shout "STOP!" in your head, or imagine a STOP road sign.

4) Distract yourself from negative thoughts by listening hard for a few moments. Pay attention to all the sounds you can hear.

5) When the body feels pain, the mind pays attention to this pain rather than to thoughts. Try pinching yourself. This can help you block out negative thoughts.

3.2 **Think back to the work you did on learning styles. Which techniques would be most suitable for the different learning styles: visual, auditory, and kinesthetic? Work individually and then compare your ideas with your partner.**

Task 4 Action points

The following recommendations have been identified as key to the management of exam stress. Read the bullet points and consider how you might put each recommendation into action.

For example:

• Get in control

  I would make sure that I have allowed enough time for sufficient study.

• Ensure you are both mentally and physically prepared.

  I would _____

- Make sure you have the necessary equipment.

  I would _____

- Make sure that you know what the format of the exam will be and what the grading system is.

  I would _____

- Tackle your weak areas of understanding well in advance.

  I would _____

- Think positively.

  I would _____

- Discuss your concerns.

  I would _____

Reflect

Think about stressful times you have experienced. Has the stress always been negative, or has it sometimes added something to your life? You will probably find on looking back that there has been a positive aspect.

Reflect on the positive aspects of stress and think about how you can harness this for exam preparation.

Student notes for Unit 6

_____

_____

_____

_____

_____

_____

_____

_____

Module 12

Web work

Website 1   **Learner styles**

http://www.learning-styles-online.com/inventory/

Review
This website provides a free online learning styles quiz. It represents your results graphically.

Task
Go online and take the test. Read about different learner styles in more detail and then use the information to plan your review strategies.

Website 2   **Identifying exam stress**

http://www.adelaide.edu.au/counselling_centre/Test.html

Review
This website has a test that you can use to decide if your exam stress is motivating or paralyzing.

Task
Take Alpert and Haber's Achievement Anxiety Test to find out if your stress is likely to have a positive or negative impact on your exam results. If you think your stress will cause you problems, talk to your instructor.

Website 3   **Managing exam stress**

http://www.open.ac.uk/skillsforstudy/managing-stress.php

Review
This website provides a guide for coping with exam stress.

Task
Print out the guide and use a highlighter to mark the advice that you feel you could realistically apply.

Extension activities

Activity 1

Prepare a "To Do" list for each of your exams and summarize the key areas that you will need to review before your exam. As your studying progresses, you will be able to check off the subjects that you have already covered and be able to see at a glance the areas that remain.

When you have compiled your "To Do" list, have it checked by your instructor to make sure you haven't left anything out.

Activity 2

Complete a mock exam under timed exam conditions. This will give you experience of writing within a limited time frame. Ask a friend to time you to make sure that you keep to the time limit. Practice any question types that you find difficult to complete under pressure.

Glossary

Analyze (v) To break an issue down into parts in order to study, identify, and discuss their meaning and/or relevance.

Auditory learner (n) Student who responds to sound when learning or recalling information. For example, an auditory learner may find it useful to memorize language through rhythmic repetition, like to receive information aurally, and remember sounds, tunes, and rhythms.

Claim (n) (v) 1 (n) Something that is stated as true by a person or group but is not universally accepted as a fact. 2 (v) To make a statement that you may believe to be true but that is not universally accepted as such.

Concept (n) The characteristics or ideas associated with a class or group of objects. For example, the concept *city* brings to mind traits common to all places classed as *cities*. *Paris* is not a concept as it refers to a single, specific place.

Concept map (n) A way of organizing ideas that is similar to a *mind map* but is more structured. It links a key general *concept* to more specific ideas with arrows.

Contrast (v) (n) 1 (v) To compare two or more things and identify differences between them and any consequences of their dissimilarities. 2 (n) The differences that are evident between two things.

Data (n) A collection of raw facts such as statistics and figures. These need to be studied and *interpreted* in order to reach conclusions.

Define (v) To give the precise meaning of a term or idea.

Evaluate (v) To assess information in terms of quality, relevance, objectivity, and accuracy.

Evidence (n) Information and *data* that establish whether something is true or not.

Flow chart (n) A diagram that shows a process. Steps or ideas are shown in a structured way (for example, from left to right or from top to bottom) and linked by arrows.

Format (n) (v) 1 (n) The material presentation of information. Information to be reviewed can be put into several different formats, for example, in note form, as keywords and sentences on index cards, or visually, as a *concept map*. 2 (v) To apply a consistent style of presentation to information or *data*.

Grade (n) (v) 1 (n) A result for an essay, an exam, or overall performance in class. Grades often correspond to a number, letter, or word, such as *70%*; or *Pass/Fail*. 2 (v) To assess an essay, an exam, or overall performance and assign a *grade*.

Interpret (v) Give the meaning or explain the significance of something as you understand it.

Justify (v) Put forward a case for or against a knowledge *claim* or idea.

Kinesthetic learner (n) A student who responds to movement and imitation when learning or recalling information. For example, a kinesthetic learner may find it useful to memorize language by copying it out, and often takes extensive notes, draws pictures (doodles), or moves his/her hands and feet (fidgets) when memorizing new information.

Learning style (n) A style of thinking about, processing, and remembering information that you have to learn. Different styles can be classified in a variety of ways. For example, you may have an *auditory* or *kinesthetic* learning style.

Memorization (n) The process of learning "by heart" or committing to memory.

Mind map (n) A visual representation of ideas that are connected to each other. A key idea is written in the center of the page and *related* ideas are written around it and connected by arrows (without too much deliberation). Mind mapping can be done in a group or individually to stimulate memory and/or organize thoughts.

Multiple choice (adj) Describes a question or task where students are given a set of several possible answers, normally only one of which is correct. They are required to choose the correct answer.

Negative grading (n) An evaluation system (usually in an exam) where *grades* are deducted for incorrect answers.

Outline (n) (v) 1 (n) A rough sketch of the main ideas in a text or presentation. 2 (v) To give or make a rough sketch of the main ideas or events in a text or presentation.

Over-learning (n) The process of going over information several times, even when you think you have learned it. It may include rewriting of notes, rereading of texts, etc.

Past exams (n) An exam that has been given in the past. These are often released for students to practice answering exam questions. They may be used in class or obtained for self-study.

Relate (v) To show the connections between two or more things.

Rubric (n) Written instructions for procedures and tasks on a test or exams, or in a course book or handout.

Scan (v) To look through a text quickly and pick out specific information.

Schedule (n) (v) 1 (n) A plan that specifies the steps to take to complete a project and gives a clear time frame and/or deadlines for each part. 2 (v) To make a plan for how and when to complete a project.

Skim (v) Read quickly through a text in order to get the gist or main idea.

Strategy (n) A plan of action that you follow when you want to achieve a particular goal. For example, it is possible to have a clear strategy for passing an exam.

Study aid (n) A device, system, or support mechanism that makes study easier or helps you organize your study. For example, electronic organizer, study handbook, highlighter, etc.

Summarize (v) To write or give a brief account of the main points of a text, lecture, or idea.

Supporting evidence (n) Information from academic sources that should be included in a piece of academic writing. This *evidence* illustrates and backs up your ideas and adds credibility to your work.

Syllabus (n) A statement, *outline* or list of all the topics, skills, and/or structures that will be covered in a program of study.

Technique (n) A method or way of doing something that involves skill and/or efficiency. For example, it is possible to learn useful techniques for answering exam questions.

Thesis statement (n) A statement that explains the controlling idea or main argument in a piece of academic writing. It is stated in the introduction and supported by reasons in the body of the essay.

Time allocation (n) The time permitted or set aside to do something. For example, in an exam, some time may be allocated to read through the exam questions.

Timeline (n) A visual representation of a set of events in a specified period that are shown on a line in the order that they happened.

Title analysis (n) To break down an essay title into parts so that you can decide what type of essay it is, what to include in it, and how to order your ideas.

Tool kit (n) In academic life, this is a collection of resources, *techniques,* or aids that help you to do something, for example, prepare for an exam.

Trace (v) Put the steps and stages of a process or event into the correct order.

Visual learner (n) A student who responds to things they can see when learning or recalling information. For example, a visual learner often makes notes that are well laid-out, may highlight information using color, and likes to have handouts, slides, and clear diagrams in a lecture.

Unit 5: Task 3.3 Example

"Studying the English language in an English-speaking country is the best way to learn the language. It is not possible to learn the language properly without spending time living in an Anglophone environment." Discuss.

Part 1

- Is studying the English language in an English-speaking country the best way to learn the language?

- Are there any other ways of learning a language effectively?

Part 2

- Is it true that it is not possible to learn the English language without spending time living in an Anglophone environment?

Essay plan

- Introduction, including definition of key terms, and a thesis statement. (Use James and Miller quote.)

- Explain the advantages of studying in the home culture in order to learn basic grammar. (Use cautious language, e.g., *One advantage may be* …)

- (Signposting, e.g., *On the other hand*) Describe the advantages of studying in an Anglophone environment in order to practice listening and speaking. (Use cautious language.)

- (Signposting, e.g., *To conclude*) Conclude that learning the basic grammar may be more effective in the home culture and that developing listening and speaking skills is often more successful in an English-speaking country.